A History of Heaven

OTHER BOOKS BY JEFFREY BURTON RUSSELL

✥

Dissent and Reform in the Early Middle Ages (1965)
Medieval Civilization (1968)
A History of Medieval Christianty: Prophecy and Order (1968)
Religious Dissent in the Middle Ages (1971)
Witchcraft in the Middle Ages (1972)
The Devil: Perceptions of Evil from Antiquity to Primitive Christianity (1977)
A History of Witchcraft: Sorcerers, Heretics, Pagans (1980)
Medieval Heresies: A Bibliography 1960–1979, with C. Berkhout (1981)
Satan: The Early Christian Tradition (1981)
Lucifer: The Devil in the Middle Ages (1984)
Mephistopheles: The Devil in the Modern World (1986)
The Prince of Darkness: Evil and the Power of Good in History (1988)
Inventing the Flat Earth: Columbus and the Historians (1991)
Dissent and Order in the Middle Ages: The Search for Legitimate Authority (1992)
Lives of the Jura Fathers, with K. and T. Vivian (1997)

A History of Heaven

THE SINGING
SILENCE

JEFFREY BURTON RUSSELL

PRINCETON
UNIVERSITY
PRESS

Library of Congress Cataloging-in-Publication Data
Russell, Jeffrey Burton.
A history of heaven : the singing silence /
Jeffrey Burton Russell.
p.   cm.
Includes bibliographical references and index.
ISBN 0-691-01161-3 (cloth : alk. paper)
1. Heaven—History of doctrines.   I. Title.
BT846.2.R87   1997
236′.24′09—dc20   96-41002

FOR DAVID JEFFREY RUSSELL,

ANNA RUSSELL, AND

ROXANA FARMER

✛

Ad audiendum silentium narrationis eius, et
videndum invisibilem formam eius.

(To hear the silence of his speech and to see
his invisible nature.)

—*Augustine*

Oh ineffabile allegrezza!

(O joy beyond words.)

—*Dante*

✜ *Contents* ✜

CONTENTS

✥ *Illustrations* ✥

Following page 90

✤ *Preface* ✤

To the modern mind heaven often seems bland or boring, an eternal sermon or a perpetual hymn. Evil and the Devil seem to get the best lines. Dante knew better: nothing could possibly be as exciting as heaven itself. The human idea of heaven is a complex tapestry shot with flashes of glory.

The central theme of this book is the fulfillment of the human longing for unity, body and soul, in ourselves, with one another, and with the cosmos. The book is aimed at deepening understanding of a blessed otherworld by engaging the Christian tradition of heaven. It focuses on the Christian concept of heaven for a variety of reasons. A survey of the radically diverse notions of afterlife around the world that might be forced to fit under the word "heaven" could not be a historically coherent subject. Only the three Western religions (Judaism, Christianity, and Islam) have ideas of heaven that are historically and theologically connected with one another. The honor, love, and deepening identification I feel for Judaism makes me increasingly aware that I know too little to venture far in that tradition. Both the reader and I must be content here with only passing reference to the wealth of materials on heaven within Judaism and also within Islam. Unfolding the concept of heaven through the time of Dante's *Paradiso* allows for a coherent, diachronic historical treatment of the most powerful and enduring Christian ideas of heaven in their richness and complexity.

The book investigates the concept of heaven from its origins about 200 B.C.E. to the completion of Dante's *Divine Comedy* in 1321 and the publication of the papal decree *Benedictus Dei* in 1336, which theologically defined the vision of God enjoyed by the blessed in heaven. It ends with Dante because the *Paradiso* is the highest expression of the tradition: Dante took what had been said before him, both theologically and poetically, and restated it with unparalleled conviction.

I approach the subject as an inquiry into the concept of heaven by the intellect, though intellect is ultimately surpassed by love. The best history must be written both without bias and with personal commitment. This book is a personal as well as a historical statement. I believe in the Christian concept of heaven, not in the sense that this concept can fully or exclusively represent a reality that is beyond all human imagination and understanding, but in the sense that it, like other traditions, opens toward that reality. Heaven is not either/or; it is both/and. To understand heaven is not to narrow down and define but rather to open up to beauty. Heaven is the song that God sings to the world out of his silence.

Heaven, a concept that has shaped so much of Christian thought and so much of the Christian attitude toward life, has been strangely neglected by modern historians. Jean Delumeau's *Histoire du paradis* (1992) deals, not with heaven, but only with the earthly paradise; *Heaven: A History* by Colleen McDannell and Bernhard Lang (1988) offered sociological insights but little grasp of the interiority of the subject compared with Alan Bernstein's masterful study of hell, whose first volume, *The Formation of Hell*, appeared in 1993. The most valuable parallel study to the history of heaven is Bernard McGinn's *The Presence of God*, whose first two volumes appeared in 1991 and 1994.

This book is intended to open the variety and richness of the Christian tradition to believers and nonbelievers alike. Because the topic is vast, I only glance at related subjects such as apocalypticism, angels, predestination, free will, and physical cosmology. The book does not dwell on the use of the term "heaven" as a metonymy for God himself, or upon its use to denote the physical sky. In Hebrew, Greek, and the Germanic and Romance languages, the same word denotes the divine heaven and the physical sky; in distinguishing between "heaven" and "sky," English is atypical. Many languages make no clear distinction between the celestial paradise (the abode of the elect) and the earthly paradise (the Garden at the beginning of the world), but I treat the earthly paradise only in its relationship to the celestial one.

Because I hope that this present book will be a prolegomenon to a detailed, multivolume study of heaven, and because of the enormous number of sources and modern works consulted, I have limited footnotes almost entirely to direct quotations. A full bibliography appears at the end of the volume.

I owe much to others, especially Giuseppe Laterza and Brigitta van Rheinberg. The National Endowment for the Humanities and the University of California have been generous. I am particularly grateful to Professor Alan Bernstein of the University of Arizona for his thorough and learned suggestions. Warm thanks are also due to Joseph Amato, Mark Boyd, Don Brodale, Caroline Walker Bynum, Marcia Colish, Jan Emerson, Mark Emerson, Dag Oistein Endsjo, Sharon Farmer, Hugh Feiss, Frank Gardiner, Mark Gardner, Richard Hecht, Edith Huey, Rachel Howes, Rachel Jacoff, Barbara Kline, Edgar Laird, Robert Laures, Maria Lichtmann, N. C. Luebben, Gary Macy, Elwood Mather, Christine McCann, Kathryn McClymond, Bernard McGinn, Sharan Newman, Nancy Partner, Mark Russell, Brenda Schildgen, Laurence Shields, Susan Snyder, Daniel Terkla, Zacharias Thundy, Catherine and Michael Tkacz, Tim and Miriam Vivian, Victoria Wilson-Schwartz, and Roy Zyla. Christine McCann is a research assistant of almost angelic powers.

Santa Barbara, California
1996

A History of Heaven

✛ 1 ✛

Understanding Heaven

A NORMAL human being longs for three things that cannot be attained in this life: understanding of self, understanding of others, and understanding of the cosmos. We cannot be sufficient unto ourselves. We are created for the connection with others, for the connection with the cosmos, for the dynamic connection among ourselves and with God. When we ask for connection, we are often met by silence. But if we listen, the silence sings to us.

This book recounts the search for the fulfillment of this existential longing. A corollary theme is the eternal unity of the human being, body and soul. Other themes are tensions within the concept of heaven: between salvation of body and salvation of soul; between salvation through the intellect (knowledge) and salvation through the will (love); between salvation of individuals and salvation of community; between the theological need for an abstract heaven and the artistic and everyday need for physical images. Another motif is the tension inherent in human language when it attempts to relate the ineffable, see the invisible, understand the incomprehensible.

Heaven itself cannot be described, but the human concept of heaven can be. Heaven is not dull; it is not static; it is not monochrome. It is an endless dynamic of joy in which one is ever more oneself as one was meant to be, in which one increasingly realizes one's potential in understanding as well as love and is filled

more and more with wisdom. It is the discovery, sometimes unexpected, of one's deepest self. Heaven is reality itself; what is
not heaven is less real. Hell is the contradiction of heaven; it is
the absence of reality. Satan is exiled and imprisoned; the citizens of heaven enjoy their true home, free from death, pain,
hatred. Humans are at their most real in heaven, resting dynamically in endless and increasing light and brilliance, joy and
glory. The opposite of glory is worldly, unredeemed, alienated
incompleteness, but glory is the living light of love that pulses in
God and in every seeking creature. The glow of glory lights
heaven and unites creator and creatures in a circuit of love.
Heaven is a festival combining utmost intensity with perfect
peace. It is the home of paradox, where one flies open and free
while one is hugged fast in the arms of the First Lover, Dante's
primo Amante. Heaven is the singing silence, the stillness of God
that he sings to the world. And it is a mystery. When Paul tells
the Corinthians (1 Cor 15) that he will tell them a "mystery," he
means something unfathomable that he attempts, with inevitable human inadequacy, to express. "Eye has not seen, nor ear
heard," he says, "the things that God has prepared for those
who love him" (1 Cor 2.9). The mystery of the concept of
heaven has raised a number of perennial questions. Estimates as
to what proportion of the human race number among the blest
have ranged from very few to all, but one may hope that all are
in heaven who open themselves even a little to love.

Opinions have also varied as to the gender, age, and appearance of the resurrected body. Some have held that humans share
heaven with angels, some that we share it with the whole cosmos. Underlying all is the question, What sort of language, what
sort of speech, can express, distill the silence?

For Christians, heaven is where Christ is. Going to heaven or,
better, being in heaven is being in the presence of Christ,
whether one encounters him, sees him, merges with him, or in a
sense becomes him. One is in heaven insofar as one is "in"
Christ. *Theosis,* "divinization" of a human being in the sense
that the person's self or ego is replaced with Christ, is a hallmark

of spirituality, especially in Eastern Christianity. Integration with Christ is not a dissolution of the self but rather the fullest realization of self. Divinization is not something that we can claim as a merit due to our own work; it is a free gift: we are in God because God takes us in. Our choice is whether to obstruct him or to allow him to grow in us. The center of the relationship in heaven between humans and Christ is a love where the human rose and the divine fire are one, a love that gives all and accepts all, a love in which God loves us perfectly and we love him perfectly, to the degree that subject and object become one—love loves love—and eventually only the verb remains: "loves."

The most important aspects of the concept of heaven are the beatific vision and the mystical union. In the beatific vision of God, the person's "seeing" is his or her complete understanding and love of Christ. In this earthly life one can "see" this understanding and love only "through a glass darkly"; in heaven one sees "face to face" (1 Cor 13.12). On earth one may have a transitory intimation of the mystical union; in heaven the union is intense, permanent, complete. In the heavenly union complete love and complete knowledge are one and the same.

Ideas of the quality and degree of mystical union vary. The dissolution of the individual in God, a view common in Asian religions, finds little place in Judaism, Christianity, or Islam. Eastern Christianity has long distinguished between God's *ousia*, his essence, which we can never "see" or unite with, and his *energeia*, his expression of himself in the cosmos. Heaven is not an achieved and unchanging state but a process of transformation.

Heaven is the state of being in which all are united in love with one another and with God. It is an *agapē*, a love feast. Whenever less than the whole world is loved, with all the creatures in it, whenever anyone or anything is excluded from love, the result is isolation and retreat from heaven. Heaven is the community of those whom God loves and who love God. All retain their personal characters, but woven together in perfect charity, so that in God's generous embrace each person among the millions whom God loves loves each other person among the millions whom God loves. It is like a weaving in which each thread touches every other thread in a spark of loving light, so that the whole web shines like a field of stars. In heaven all see and observe their love and grace and peace spread out to everyone and through everyone, so that the love of each is realized perfectly and extended totally to each and to all. The union of humans with one another in Christ does not simply "take place" in heaven; it is heaven itself, heartwhole and fine.

Universalism, the belief that all are in heaven, may be too simple; it may be that all are woven into the web of love but some, turning in on themselves, become dead knots by choosing not to participate in the joy. Perhaps some never know the joy of heaven. If so, the saved are pained to see damned those they loved on earth and, now that their love is linked to every creature, they are pained at the fate of even Judas or Nero, Hitler or Stalin. The cosmos grieves for them. Yet this grief is compatible with love, even with joy, for grace takes up grief and transforms it into love. One can love even Judas as God intends him to be.

Heaven itself is ineffable, beyond words. The term *ineffabilis* was established in theology in the fifth century by Augustine (354–430), who said that it is easier to say what God is not than to say what he is. God is not only incomprehensible to humans but is himself beyond all categories; heaven is therefore also beyond categories. Yet we have no way of discussing heaven except in the only speech we know, human language. In the present age of materialism, the statement "heaven exists" may seem paradoxical, and perhaps "heaven subsists" might be preferable, for heaven does not exist in the way that a planet or star does but rather as a reality that underlies (subsists) physical existence.

Metaphors of heaven, expressing the reality of heaven, are written in the language of earthly delight: sound (melody, silence, conversation); sight (light, proportion); taste and smell (banquet, sweetness); touch (embracing the beloved). Heaven, like God, is special and peculiar in that "heaven" is itself true language, true meaning. God is a poet whose Word (*Logos*) speaks the universe. In heaven, lies, folly, vanity, and meaning-lessness are drained away, and God's language stands out clear and clean.)

Traditional Jewish and Christian use of language differs from general modern usage, and it is essential to grasp this difference in order to understand what the traditional language intends. Moderns are used to dichotomies between true and false, fact and fiction, they are put off by comparative terms such as "more real" or "more perfect," and they create a dichotomy between "literal" and "metaphorical." Moderns tend to consider state-ments as "literally true" if they are statements intended to assert scientific or historical "facts"; they regard statements employing metaphor as poetic or even fanciful. The modern assumption is that the so-called factual statement relates to "outside reality" and that the metaphorical statement is subjective and unrelated to "outside reality." This assumption is so deep and so common that we are likely to forget that it is not the only way of looking at things. It most definitely was not the way of Jewish and Chris-tian writers about heaven.

In order to understand what their way was, it is best to set aside the modern use of the term "literal meaning" for the sci-entific or historical meaning and instead to reserve the term "literal" for what the author of a text intended. Traditional Christian writers used the term in a variety of other ways. For example, the literal meaning of the Bible includes both what the writer of the text intended and what God intends. When in 401, for example, Augustine wrote his *On the Literal Interpre-tation of Genesis (De Genesi ad litteram)*, what he meant by "literal" was what God intends the Book of Genesis to mean. Because of the ambiguity of the term "literal," I seldom use it in this book. What is important is to distinguish the traditional mode of viewing reality from the modern mode. The traditional mode does not so much analyze, reduce, and narrow down to-ward definition as it uses metaphor to expand and open out meaning.

Avoiding the term "literal," then, I contrast the "overt sense" to the "symbolic sense." For example, the statement that God's throne is in heaven is rarely meant in an overt sense; usually it is intended as a metaphor of God's sovereignty, in which case the literal meaning is the metaphor. Exegetes believed that the Bible could be read in both overt and the symbolic senses. Some statements are best read in the overt sense, as when Jesus refers to his interlocutors as hypocrites (Mt 22.18), but they can be opened up beyond the overt: the interlocutors may stand, for example, for all who pretend honest motives to mask their own desires. Other statements are best read in the symbolic sense, as when Jesus warns those who have a log in their own eye not to condemn those with a speck in theirs (Mt 7.3–5). It has always been obvious that Jesus was not suggesting that people were walking around with logs sticking out of their eyes.

Traditional Jewish and Christian thinkers recognized that metaphor expresses a deeper reality than can be attained through the overt sense. This manner of thinking can be called "metaphorical ontology." Ontology is the study of "being" as such and in itself; it attempts to penetrate to the essence ("is-ness") of particular things and of the cosmos in general. Metaphor is the use of words overtly denoting one kind of object or idea in place of another to suggest an analogy between them or a deeper meaning beneath them. When the Psalmist says that the Lord will cover you with his feathers and that you shall trust "under his wings" (Ps 91.4), he was not suggesting that you will be a bluejay or an eaglet in the nest. When Jesus speaks of himself as a door, he does not mean that he is a construction of planks; when he calls himself the good shepherd, he does not mean that he intends to concentrate his time on animals. Nor did being both a door and a shepherd mean that Jesus was a wooden herdsman (Jn 10.1–18). "Metaphorical ontology" is the use of figures of speech to go beyond science, history, and poetry to indicate the deepest, divine, heavenly reality.

As the sign of greater or deeper truth, metaphor was close to sacrament. Because the vastness and richness of reality cannot be expressed by the overt sense of a statement alone, metaphorical ontology is necessary. It is also necessary because a sense of contemplation and wonder are at least as important for understanding the world as efforts to determine facts. Traditional writers might well have regarded the term "metaphorical ontology" as a pleonasm, because they understood ontological reality as being inherently metaphorical. God is a poet at least as much as a scientist or a historian. God is the great poet, the maker (Greek *poiētēs*), of the universe, and his meaning is eternally expansive. I use the phrase "metaphorical ontology" in this book to distinguish it from the materialist ontology that dominates modern Western thought. We think we can understand a poppy by grasping it and dissecting it; perhaps we understand more when we allow the poppy to grasp us.

For traditional writers, metaphor and allegory *are* ontology. The epistemology of traditional Judaism and Christianity opens up toward truth with metaphors that continually grow. Thus heaven is best understood by metaphor. And not only is language about heaven metaphor: heaven is itself the metaphor of metaphors, for a metaphor opens to more and more meaning, and heaven is an unbordered meadow of meaning. Heaven is where language collapses into perfect language and then further—into the truth beyond language. Heaven is what things really mean; it is where all the blurring and sliding amongst terms and concepts and words is caught, finally, by I AM WHO I AM (God's own name for himself as given to Moses: Ex 3.14).[1]

Human language is baffled by eternity, which is beyond human imagination and reason, except in metaphor. Eternity is commonly understood as an unending length of time; or as timelessness; or as a state that both includes and also transcends time. The intellect can conceive of these options, but the imagination balks—as it does in quantum physics. Originally, the

---

[1] I AM WHO AM is a better rendering of the Hebrew EHYEH ASHER EHYEH than the more frequently used I AM WHO I AM. Anything is what it is; I AM WHO AM has the additional (essential) sense that God is what is, that God is Being itself.

most common meaning of eternity in Judeo-Christian thought was "on and on," but it is as difficult to imagine an infinite succession of moments as it is to imagine a timeless moment; both images seem to go against the subjectively experienced finiteness of time. In this world, humans lack the imagination and vocabulary to define or describe heaven without using the metaphor of time.

Heaven could not subsist "before" the creation of the cosmos, for nothing other than God subsists "before" the creation. No thing existed before any thing existed. When God created, he created space and time; there was no time before the creation. God did not, as it were, sit around in time, waiting until he felt like creating the cosmos. God is eternal: he subsists outside time and space, creates time and space, and permeates them. God sees, understands, loves all points in spacetime as in one moment, *totum simul*, "all at once." Whatever meaning we assign to *totum simul*, it goes beyond human experience. Language breaks down in the overt sense, for we have no verb tense for an action that occurs in a dimensionless point outside time and space. Space, according to Aristotle (384–322 B.C.E.), is the measure of the relationship of bodies in respect to three dimensions; time is the measure of the motion of these bodies in respect to "before" and "after." Time, therefore, connotes nonidentity and nonsimultaneity.

If time connotes nonsimultaneity, and if language is a function of time, then language cannot express simultaneity. Augustine implied this in his *Confessions*, describing his divine vision at Ostia as a vision of simultaneity and his return from the vision as a sinking back into language and time, with their beginnings and endings. Boethius (d. 524–26) later observed that even if time is infinite, with no beginning or end, it is not eternal, for even infinite time has no moment that comprehends and embraces totum simul, and what is not "simul" is not eternal. Endless life is one thing, but God's ability to comprehend and embrace all time in one moment is another. Endlessness is perpetual, but only the existence of the entire space and time of the cosmos in one moment is eternal.

God is eternal, but even if heaven is also eternal, it is unclear whether it can be said to exist either perpetually or "after" the end of the cosmos. The earthly paradise that existed at the beginning of the world is not the same as the heavenly paradise at the end. It is meaningless to speak of the existence of anything after the end of the cosmos. There can be no space without objects, no time without the motion of objects. To speak of heaven as existing after the end of the cosmos—which is the end of time—is to speak of it as existing in some way outside of space and time. Perhaps, then, it exists in eternity. But the idea of eternity works for God much better than it does for heaven. We can conceive intellectually of (though we cannot imagine visually) an Absolute Being who perceives all time and space totum simul. But it is not conceivable that creatures such as human beings, with processes of sense, intellect, and emotion, could exist without space and time. If the blessed dwell in heaven eternally (hence timelessly) with God, time does not exist in heaven. But if there is no time, there can be no sequence. We cannot sing a psalm without beginning and continuing it. This tension between perpetuity and eternity, which puzzled philosophers, proved a creative force for poets and the language of metaphor.

Theological efforts to evade the problem of time by considering heaven the abode not of physical bodies but of spirits or of glorified bodies would have been doomed without metaphor. Even glorified bodies cannot function without time, for it takes time to sing a hymn or even to think a thought. It is difficult to conceive of human intellect and will, reason and affect, existing without a brain and therefore a body. "Body is flux and frustration, a locus of pain and process. If it becomes impassible and incorruptible, how is it still body?"[2]

---

[2] Caroline Walker Bynum, *The Resurrection of the Body in Western Christianity from 200 to 1336* (New York, 1995), 59.

Even if the independent existence of spirits without bodies is granted, even then their acts of praising, knowing, or loving occupy time. Mental experience is a process; we cannot, even as spirits, think, love, and live totum simul, as God can. Thought requires a moment of time spilling out beyond the micro-moment; further, thought structures the meaningless micro-moments into a meaningful pattern. A human life is a succession of "nows," which, when joined together, form a story through time.

Even God is affected by the existence of time, because our experience of time in heaven is a real experience, and God's total experience of the totum simul must embrace the reality of our experience of time. Because humans experience change, God's experience must encompass our experience of change.

If time in heaven is different from time defined as a measure of motion within the cosmos, then this noncosmic nontime is a metaphor of time that is ontologically real, a "heaventime" distinct from ordinary time. It does not help to say that heaven persists after the end of the cosmos, for the term "after" makes no sense once ordinary time is abolished. It may be better to say that the door to eternity can open from any moment in space-time, as a breakthrough of heaventime to us or—what amounts to the same thing—of us to heaventime.

Whether heaven is a space or place is an equally difficult question. If glorified bodies exist in heaven, it must be a place. Even if only spirits exist there, so long as they are capable of motion (even internal change), it must be a place. If a place, it should be a part of the cosmos, for "place" is meaningless except within space and as a part of space. If heaven is beyond space, it cannot be a place as place is normally defined. As with time, heaven is often seen as existing in a space other than the sort of space that we inhabit. The words "space" and "time" as applied to heaven are ontological metaphors referring to something beyond the limits of the human mind. Some writers speak of going up to heaven; others of heaven coming down to us. Most metaphorical language refers to heaven as "up," but it is equally "down," "out," "ahead," or "in."

The tension between the idea that heaven is somehow on earth (among us) and the idea that heaven is beyond earth is another perennial dilemma; if heaven is on earth, it is on an earth transformed and sanctified. The "space," like the "time," of heaven is the original earthly paradise, *and* the kingdom of God within us, *and* the paradise at the end of the world. Paradise is also equated with Christ, the Christian community (Greek *ekklēsia*, Latin *ecclesia*), and the soul. To ask which of these paradise "really" is, is to misunderstand, for it is all of these, because the more the metaphor opens up toward truth, the more inclusive it is, the more real it is.

Traditionally, heaven is a place, a sacred space. The sacredness of this space is expressed in metaphors of kingdom, garden, city, or celestial spheres. Jesus refers to it most often as a reign or kingdom, a metaphor of God's sovereignty over all that is. This is coupled with the imagery of God's throne in the center of heaven. Kingdom was the more common metaphor in the Eastern tradition, city in the Western.

The garden is the most common metaphor. Its origin is in the Hebrew Bible: the garden of the earthly paradise at the beginning of the world. It was linked through the "garden enclosed" of the Hebrew Bible to the Greco-Roman images of the *locus amoenus*, the "lovely place." In the overt sense, the *hortus conclusus* (enclosed garden) is the original dwelling of Adam and Eve. The imagery closest to that of Genesis is orchard or wood. This image can be opened out indefinitely; the Christian writer Ephraim the Syrian (306–73) wrote:

> If you wish to climb to the top of a tree, its branches range themselves under your feet and invite you to rest in the midst of its bosom, in the green room of its branches, whose floor is strewn with flowers. Who has ever seen the joy at the heart of a tree, with fruits of every taste within reach of your hand? You can wash yourself with its dew and dry yourself with its leaves. A cloud of

fruits is over your head and a carpet of flowers beneath your feet. You are anointed with the sap of the tree and inhale its perfume. (*Hymn of Paradise* 9.5–6)

Associated with the wood or trees are the mountain and the river, especially the waters flowing from a spring or fountain beneath the throne of God out to the world in four rivers. In the overt sense the rivers are the Tigris and Euphrates (and sometimes the Nile and Danube as well). In the symbolic sense, fountains and rivers are signs of the spurting forth of life and its renewal by grace. The image of paradise embraces both garden and pasture. The Hebrew Bible already contains pastoral images; later, Christ is portrayed both as pastor and sheep: he is both the Good Shepherd and the sacrificial Lamb of God, images rooted in Psalm 23 and Isaiah 40.11.

The image of the city is even more clearly human. The city is powerfully and persistently linked with the kingdom, for the ruler of the city is the *mashiach*, the Messiah, the Anointed One, the King of Israel. The image of the city also is rooted in the Hebrew Bible; Jewish thought has consistently identified heaven with the City of Jerusalem or Zion (by metonymy Mount Zion stands for Jerusalem). This means both the geographical city and also a glorified Jerusalem descending to earth, or raising earth up to it. The City of Jerusalem does not connote a modern sprawl of inhabitants but a sacred space or sanctuary ruled by the Messiah. The image was further enhanced by the Greek concept of the *polis* as a community of free citizens.

The new or heavenly Jerusalem goes as far back as Ezekiel (sixth century B.C.E.). Many rabbis combined the physical Jerusalem with the heavenly city, which preexists the earthly city; the earthly city is merely the representation of its great type. After the repression of Judaism with the destruction of the Temple in 70 C.E. and the crushing of the Bar-Kochba rebellion in 135 C.E., the desire to recapture the earthly Jerusalem mounted, and the rabbis moved away from the idea of the heavenly city. Heaven is the center of the cosmos, the holy city ruled by God.

In the very center is the Lord upon his throne, in his tabernacle (the Ark or tent of the Covenant), or in his Temple.

The image of heaven as the sky, the starry dome, is rooted in both Hebrew and Greek thought. Tent or canopy represents the firmament stretching above the holy place. The connection of heaven with the planetary and stellar spheres and hence with circles derives from Greek and Hellenistic thought, especially Neoplatonism; it appears in Jewish thought in the apocrypha (writings sometimes included in the Bible) and pseudepigrapha (writings widely believed to be inspired but never included in the Bible). Our true homeland is heaven, not this precarious and dangerous world. Heaven is the marriage of God with his beloved as community, or his beloved as a personal soul. Other metaphors of heaven are temple, womb, nut, umbilicus, or mandala; related images include book, ladder, bridge, clouds, gates, and court.

The role of space and time in the concept of heaven is related to the presence of bodies there, which requires that it be in some sense a place. Jewish tradition has always held that life in the other world is life in the body. Further, the much ignored fact is that neither the New Testament nor the early Christian writers ever used the term "immortal soul" or "immortal spirit." The early Christians, like the rabbis, understood that union with God was union of the whole human, both soul and body, with him. Christian tradition continued to assume this union until, in the third century C.E., Platonic ideas of the soul's great superiority to the body promoted the idea of the survival of souls apart from bodies.

The resurrected body was viewed as in some way identical with this earthly one, one that eats, excretes, breathes, circulates the blood, and fires neurons. The resurrected Christ ate fish (Lk 23.42–43). A body that does not eat or drink could not function. The resurrected body is a different sort of body, a glorified body, but unless it functions as a body it resembles less an earthly body than a Platonic disembodied soul. Will our resurrection body be at our physical or intellectual peak? Will a mother encounter her child as a baby or as a grown person? Beneath these questions lay a consensus that the body in heaven would be at once a physical body and a body freed from its limitations; it would possess the qualities of completion and fulfillment.

Humans on this earth have no way of knowing absolute truth about heaven, what heaven "really is." We can know absolutely neither through revelation nor through intellectual investigation, since the Bible gives hints, but no thorough analysis or picture of heaven. Intellectually, wisdom begins with understanding that human reason cannot get to the absolute truth about anything at all. We have increasing difficulty with concepts as the external referents become more abstract: the concept of "cat" has more concrete borders than that of "parliament," and "parliament" is more concrete than "heaven."

Though we are unable to know absolutes, we can have a clear and sure knowledge of concepts, the phenomena we form in the tension between our minds and the things outside our minds. We do not know things-in-themselves, so our only knowledge is the knowledge of phenomena, a knowledge that humans create or invent rather than discover. Since we create concepts, we can know them, and in this sense the knowledge of the concept of heaven is as sure as the knowledge of, say, the concept of democracy. Though intellectual investigation can never determine the absolute nature of heaven, it can determine the human concept of heaven.

The concept of heaven is expressed in artworks, theology, narrative, poetry, liturgy, and folklore. It may also be approached through social history or depth psychology; the best approach to the intellectual search for the meaning of heaven is through the history of concepts, which encompasses and incorporates insights from all disciplines. The concept of heaven is best defined as what humans have thought about heaven; it is most fully understood in its history.

The concept of heaven is broader than the theological tradition of heaven. The theological tradition is itself broader than abstract or academic theology, for it embraces not only formal theology but the life and thought of the entire community. Tradition is not repetition, but the transmission of a living reality, which must be renewed and rethought as the community develops.

Theological tradition claims that over time the tradition develops under the guidance of the Holy Spirit and ends by telling the equivalent of truth as God knows it. The history of concepts respects but does not endorse that claim. One cannot assume that the concept of heaven progresses inevitably until it becomes complete; it may continue to open out perpetually. The history of concepts is neither confessional nor reductionist. It does not claim that any concept corresponds to absolute truth, yet it rejects the assumption of contemporary materialism and skepticism that heaven is an illusion lacking external referents. It avoids draining the life out of people in the past by imposing modern worldviews and categories on them; rather, it seeks to encounter real people, to engage their ideas, and to love them.

None of this can be done without taking seriously what these people said and wrote. The author's intention remains the most important element in understanding a text, and engaging the author in loving dialogue as a real person escapes the dead heart of reductionism and the dead hand of deconstruction.

Concepts develop through time. Some concepts die; others narrow down; others stagnate. The concept of heaven opens. It opens up in the cosmos in ever-widening circles and opens down in the human character into the deepest self.

✣ 2 ✣

Elysium, Jerusalem,
and Paradise

THE Christian heaven is essentially Jewish in idea and image
but was also influenced by Greco-Roman culture. In classical
Jewish and Greco-Roman cultures, death was originally the
door to a tenuous continued existence. In Greco-Roman religion, the souls of all the dead descended to the shadowy and
unsubstantial Hades. Later the underworld became a happier
place. The belief that all the dead became shadows gradually
shifted to the pious view that heroes—the virtuous and noble,
loved by the gods—would have better lives than others in the
future world. The underworld was the source of gold and jewels, signifying that no gross matter persists in the realm of the
blessed dead but only what is pure. Source of fertile crops pushing their way upward to the sun, the underworld also symbolized rebirth. Later the blessed were believed to ascend to the sky,
leaving the earth, especially Hades beneath its surface, as a place
of punishment. Ancient Jewish and Greek cultures affirmed a
perfect age in the past. The Jewish Garden of Eden was matched
by the Greco-Roman golden age or age of Saturn, a distant eon
of simple, noble rest and comfort, free from war, famine, and
other evils. The Greco-Roman notion that the happy fields of the
blessed dead recapitulate this golden age parallels the Jewish
idea that the kingdom of God, which will come at the end of
time, will recapitulate Eden.

The happy life of the blest in the classical Elysian Fields or Isles of the Just was merited by their actions on earth. Christians later assimilated the idea of merit, combining the Roman model of patriotism and heroism with the Jewish model of faithfulness to the Covenant. Even more easily assimilated was the Stoic idea that we are judged not by our social rank but by our habits of soul. The Christian cardinal virtues of temperance, prudence, fortitude, and justice stemmed from Aristotle. Augustine later would argue that these virtues are modes of charity and would present them as both natural and supernatural.

The Greco-Roman philosophers' emphasis on the virtue of the intellect melded with the Jewish love of wisdom to encourage the Christian belief that in heaven earthly knowledge would be perfected and fulfilled. Christian thinkers transferred to the concept of heaven those attributes that the philosopher Parmenides (513–448 B.C.E.) had assigned to absolute Being: both are eternal, without beginning, needing nothing, beyond passions, indestructible, unchangeable, and invisible.

Greek and Jewish attitudes toward the body, however, were quite different. Whereas the Jews conceived of soul and body as a living unity, Plato (428–347 B.C.E.) and most of his followers perceived a human being as essentially linked to the spiritual world, with the body as a mere temporary appendage. Christianity would attempt, without notable success, to reconcile these Greek and Jewish views.

Greco-Roman writers who influenced Christian thinking on this point include Plato, Cicero (106–43 B.C.E.), Plutarch (50–120 C.E.), and Vergil (70–19 B.C.E.), Vergil becoming Dante's guide through Inferno and into Purgatorio. Plato's dialogue *Phaedo* claims immortality both for the *psyché* (the life force in all living things), and for *nous* (mind, which exists only in humans). Psyche and nous together constituted "soul." For Plato, the immortality of the soul derives from its natural affinity to the divine. In Plato's *Gorgias* the dead come to a meadow to be judged according to their deeds, sent to reward or punishment, and then reincarnated. In his *Phaedrus*, the soul soars upward into the heavens but, unable to reach the dwelling of the gods, falls to earth and is reincarnated; after numerous lives of purification, it will eventually be united with the divine. Memory and love for the eternal from which the cosmos originally sprang draw the soul upward. Everything in the cosmos has longing (*eros*) to return to the One; the cosmos itself, a living creature with "world-soul" and body, yearns for return. Christians adapted the Platonic idea of "eros," affective love, to their belief that both knowledge and affect characterize God's relationship with us and ours with him. For Plato, love is never exhausted; it generously begets ever more love. Love for a particular human, for humans in general, for the cosmos, is what allows us to understand, to have *epistēmē*, knowledge. The purpose of life is to know and to love, and one is impossible without the other. Together they bring joy to the soul and union with the divine.

For Plato, human love is intensified and deepened by our innate ability to think and to choose. An attentive soul understands its kinship with the divine; by separating itself through contemplation from the love of material things, it becomes divine. The idea of spiritual ecstasy derives from Plato's term *ekstasis*, standing outside or beyond oneself, in union with the divine.

Cicero (106–43 B.C.E.), the practical Roman philosopher, lawyer, and politician, followed Plato and the Stoics in promoting the idea of reward and punishment in another life as an enticement to civic virtue. Those who served the Roman Republic with distinction became immortal heroes, fulfilling their destiny on earth and then being raised to heaven. Calling all citizens to virtue entailed extending the prospect of blessedness beyond great leaders to the people as a whole, so that the heavens were almost entirely filled with people—or at least with Roman citizens.

Five centuries after Plato, the Neoplatonists formed an essentially religious system based on his philosophy. For Plotinus

(203–62 C.E.), everything in the cosmos yearns with affective intensity for the vision of the One Truth. But since no creature—certainly no human being—can understand or describe the One, each must be satisfied with a degree of understanding commensurate with its ability. Proclus (412–85 C.E.) made eros a universal yearning that binds the cosmos together and draws it to the divine.

Christians assimilated to their concept of the world of the blessed a number of Greco-Roman motifs. In Greco-Roman texts and images, the locus amoenus is a garden, a pastoral landscape, or a group of idyllic islands. From the time of Homer (ninth century B.C.E.), poets described a land of music, dancing, sunny meadows, flowers, fountains, and sweet refreshment and repose in shady groves, a land in which death and disease have no dominion and no one lacks anything. Latin writers fancifully connected the locus amoenus with *lucus*, a grove. Sunshine and shade, a foretaste of the poet Hopkins's "Glory be to God for dappled things." Each writer focuses on what offers relief from the rigors of his own climate: northern writers bask in the sun; southern writers are refreshed in the shade. Vergil's garden is an idealization of the Italian countryside, its plains grown golden with grain, its vineyards hung with ripe and juicy grapes, its oaks dripping honey, its sheep obligingly changing the color of their fleece from white to purple to yellow to scarlet so that we may vary our clothing. Wolves and lambs lie together, leopards and kids, vipers and infants. Earth and trees and cattle yield their fruits of wine, honey, milk, and grain.

The locus amoenus was sometimes equated with the luxurious garden of Venus, sensuously bursting with opening flowers and moistening springs, and offering delicate food and drink and noble conversation. The combination produced the imagery of Elysium (the Elysian Fields). Elysium is located either on earth, or in the sphere of the moon, or among the stars. Often it is in the Blessed Isles of the West, a motif that appears as early as Homer's *Odyssey* and is later common in Celtic mythology. Elysian imagery reinforced the already powerful Jewish vision of gardens, groves, and glory. The poet Pindar (fifth century B.C.E.) identified the ruler of the Islands of the Blest with Cronos (Saturn), the king of the Golden Age, thus conflating blessed time with blessed place.

The usual location of the land of the blest was the sky. The sky (Greek *ouranos*) was originally a god, later the home of gods. The Pythagoreans (sixth century B.C.E.) were the first Greek philosophers to advance the doctrine of immortality in the heavens. Cicero's "Dream of Scipio" fixed the land of the just in the Milky Way. The stars were associated with the souls of heroes and with fire, the element that reaches upward. Stoics believed that souls, because of their lightness, their inner desire to ascend, rise like fire to join the fires of the sky. Neoplatonists argued that the liberated soul becomes pure *nous* (intellect or mind) and ascends to the sun. The public religion of the Roman Empire symbolized power and authority by ascent: up the steps to the high dais to the throne itself and to the god-emperor upon it.

The sense that up is better was common in ancient Near Eastern religion. In Greco-Roman thought it was reinforced by Aristotle's physics. Christian philosophers adopted his system, especially as refined by the geographer Ptolemy (second century C.E.). In this system the universe consists of nested, or concentric, spheres. (No educated person believed that the earth was flat.) At the center of the cosmos is the sphere of the earth, surrounded by a sphere of air and, above that, a sphere of "purer air," called *ether*. Above the ether were the planetary spheres. Encircling the earth in ascending order were the spheres of the moon, Mercury, Venus, the sun, Mars, Jupiter, and Saturn. Beyond them were, first, the sphere of the fixed stars and then, at the outer skin of the cosmos, the sphere of the *primum mobile*, which imparted rotation and all movement to the spheres under it. Ptolemy first posited the primum mobile to account for irregular movements in the eighth sphere, the slight movement of stars owing to the procession of the equinoxes. The cosmos is thus a great sphere containing all spheres.

In this system, adopted by Christianity and later employed by Dante, any movement from the earth is by definition both outward and upward motion. Whether we stand in Rome or at the antipodes, going out from the earth is going up into the heavens. The classical and preclassical religious background imparted the idea that as one approached the primum mobile, the spheres grew purer, less material and more spiritual. Down at the center, the earth is the deepest, densest, darkest, most material place in the universe. Heavy elements such as water and earth sink naturally downward, while air moves naturally upward, and fire strives to reach up beyond air to the ether and beyond. Past the outermost sphere, the primum mobile, is the empyrean, the place of pure fire (Greek *pyr*). The soul's true home, like that of light and fire, is in the empyrean with God.

Stoic souls mounting upward found the ether (or else the sphere of the moon) a congenial place where they could remain in rest or equilibrium. These souls were globes of firelike substance indwelt with intelligence and will. Physicists and philosophers set the moon as the boundary dividing the laws of physics. Physical laws worked differently below the sphere of the moon than in that sphere or above: motion below the moon tends to be rectilinear; motion above to be circular. Below the moon, elements rise and fall; in the moon and above they rise, except as they are constrained by the spheres into rotation. The physical distinction was matched by the philosophical distinction between the sublunary region and the region from the moon outward: below are impermanence, decay; above are immortality, peace, harmony. For Dante later, the moon would be the first and lowest level of the heavenly paradise.

The exact number and arrangement of the spheres differed. Plato's *Timaeus* posited eight spheres, an arrangement generally followed by the Stoics and the Neoplatonists. Cicero offered nine, including the earth. Plutarch had only three. Hermetic literature (first to third centuries C.E.) portrayed seven spheres, guarded by demons through which the soul must mount to reach the eighth sphere, the dwelling of God. Mithraism (first century B.C.E. to third century C.E.) envisioned a symbolic ascent through seven planetary spheres by means of a ladder constructed of seven different metals.

In such spherical systems, each sphere sounds its own musical note, and together they produce a celestial harmony that represents the perfect coordination and glory of the cosmos. This harmonic view, later adapted by Christians through the writings of Boethius, made music an essential part of the architecture of heaven.

Light, splendor, or glory was the most common characteristic of the classical heaven. Ancient Near Eastern rulers were associated with the sun and the god of the sun. The synonyms that Cicero used for *gloria* elide majesty and rank and fame with bright and shining light. The sun is a god, a source of light and a sign of the intelligence that draws human reason back to its original source. To see such a god was to be dazed, even slain, by the light emanating from his power. Greco-Roman immortality was a combination of earthly power and might with the internal light of god-given character.

The Christian confusion over the relationship between spirit, soul, and body originated in persistent Greek philosophical inconsistencies about the terms *psychē*, *pneuma*, *sōma*, and *sarx*. These terms resist definition, because they frequently shifted in meaning. The root meaning of *psychē* is something like "life principle," but it could also mean a spirit able to exist independently of the body. *Pneuma*, originally "breath," also can mean that which gives life to a body (human or animal), or it can mean an independent spirit (as in the Christian *Hagion Pneuma*, Holy Spirit). *Pneuma* and *psychē* are interchangeable in some writers and separate in others, with the resulting permanent confusion in Western languages between "spirit" and "soul." A modern word that would embrace both *psychē* and *pneuma* is "the self." Usually, though not always, *sōma* is the body animated by soul, while *sarx* is the unanimated body.

For the Pythagoreans, soul originated in the heavens as a spark, which descends into the body at conception and then reascends after death. This philosophical tradition was tied to the religious tradition of Orphism, in which each human being is a duality of gross, corrupt matter and divine soul. The body is the prison of the soul, and it is our moral duty to liberate ourselves from it. Orphic tendencies appear in Plato, whose *Republic* mentions something that neither Jewish nor early Christian thought had much use for: the immortal soul (*athanata psychē*). In our present state, we are souls inhabiting bodies, but the soul, once abstracted from body and purified, partakes of immortal and eternal being. Our real self is not our soma or sarx (body or flesh), but our psyche (soul or spirit). A person who in life has been too attached to the body and the material world will in death wander as a ghost until reincarnated; one who follows wisdom will rise in spirit to the realm of the divine.

Cicero too insisted on a division between the body, which perishes at death, and the eternal, immaterial soul. Souls purged of their dross by wisdom join the gods or even become divine. This idea, which Cicero expressed in the *Tusculan Disputations*, would later tug Christian thought in a dualist direction. The Neoplatonists held that the eternal One first emanates nous (mind), which emanates soul, which emanates lower beings in which soul and matter are mixed. The more material a being is, the less good and less real it is. "Salvation" reverses emanation by the return of body to soul, of soul to mind, and of mind to the One. Souls yearn upward or downward according to their inclination to purity or to corruption.

Jewish views of heaven were quite different. They first appear in the Hebrew Bible (the Christian Old Testament) before 250 B.C.E.; they develop much further in the so-called "intertestamental period" (about 250 B.C.E. to about 150 C.E.). Writings of the latter period include the translation of the Hebrew Bible into Greek (the Septuagint), adaptations of the Hebrew Bible into Aramaic (the Targumim), and the apocrypha and pseudepigrapha, written in Hebrew, Aramaic, and Greek. In the rabbinic period (from about 70 C.E. onward), mutual but limited influences between Judaism and Christianity continued.

The Jewish conception of Scripture is quite different from the Christian, which divides revelation into the Old and the New Testament and has usually assumed that the latter largely supersedes the former.

The Jews historically have referred to the biblical text as *Tanak*, an acronym for its three divisions: the Torah (teachings, laws), the Nevi'im (prophets), and the Ketuvim (other books). Of the three, Torah is the absolutely authoritative revelation of God to Moses. At its narrowest, "Torah" means "the Law" and refers to what the Christians called the Pentateuch, the Five Books of Moses: Bereshit (Genesis), Shemot (Exodus), Vayikra (Leviticus), Bamidbar (Numbers), and Devarim (Deuteronomy). In the first two centuries C.E., Torah was given a wider meaning by the rabbis, who believed that God had given Moses two equally authoritative Torahs, the *torah she-beketav*, or written Torah, and the *torah she-ba'al peh*, or oral Torah, the oral Torah having been passed down from Moses through the generations to their own time. In the first decades of the third century, one of the most renowned rabbis, Judah the Prince, united much of the oral Torah in a single compilation, the Mishnah (the Teaching). Judah the Prince's Mishnah was elaborated by the Jewish communities in Israel/Palestine and in Persia, which they called "Babylonia." The elaborations were eventually codified in the fifth through seventh centuries as the Jerusalem Talmud and the Babylonian Talmud.

The dating and authorship of the Hebrew Bible is vigorously debated. The oldest materials date as far back as the eleventh century B.C.E. The reforms of Josiah in 622 B.C.E. established some of the texts, but most recensions occurred in and after the Babylonian Captivity of 586–538 B.C.E. The distinction between revelation and inspiration is essential in Jewish and Christian thought. Many writers may be divinely inspired, but revelation is restricted to the Bible alone. The Biblical writers received not only inspiration but also direct revelation of truth from God.

Throughout the Biblical period, Jewish religion emphasized community. God chooses and saves the people of Israel as a whole. It also emphasized this world. The Lord is the Lord of the living. The dead either perish entirely or go to Sheol, a shadowy and insubstantial underworld. This was the dominant, Deuteronomic tradition, but other views existed. A strong counter-current suggested that the blessed dead enjoy a transcendent, glorified, and even spiritual state. Good and evil persons are separated not on the basis of abstract justice or civic virtue but on the basis of faithfulness to the Covenant.

The Covenant is the center of Jewish religion. The Lord made his Covenant with Noah; with Abraham, Isaac, and Jacob; and with Moses. Israel are the Lord's chosen people, whom he blesses so long as they remain faithful to the Covenant. God wishes to gather all the descendants of Abraham, Isaac, and Jacob to himself. But the writers of the Hebrew Bible observed that many Jews were unfaithful to the Covenant. Only the faithful, the *qehel Adonai*, the "Lord's remnant," are saved. The qehel excludes unfaithful Jews as well as gentiles and Samaritans. The qehel is egalitarian: kings can go to *Ge-hinnom* (Gehenna, the pit of fire), while beggars true to the Covenant are forever with the Lord. A *hasid*, a righteous one, is one who has *hased*, loyalty to Torah. Since the faithful often have less happy lives on earth than the unfaithful, the merits of the righteous must be rewarded in another life, for it is unthinkable that the Lord could be unjust.

The Jewish idea of reward in another world goes back at least to the seventh century B.C.E., and the distinction between faithful and unfaithful Jews increased in the sixth century during the Babylonian Captivity, when much of the Hebrew Bible was written down. The suffering of the people of Israel during the Captivity helped shift the focus of Jewish hope from blessedness on earth to blessedness in the other life.

The separation between the good and the evil dead produced modifications in the idea of Sheol. Part of Sheol was identified with Gehenna, the valley near Jerusalem where rubbish was dumped and continuously burned. In Gehenna, Jews who do not keep the Covenant burn perpetually after their death. Another part of Sheol remained the shadowy abode of the mediocre. A third part, reserved for the qehel, became a place of rest and comfort. Like Hades, Sheol was too dark and gloomy a place to accommodate the souls of the righteous for long, and a tendency gradually developed to move them out, to paradise, or to the heavens, or to a future, eschatological world that has been transformed or renewed. "For I am about to create new heavens and a new earth; the former things shall not be remembered or come to mind. But be glad and rejoice forever in what I am creating; for I am about to create Jerusalem as a joy, and its people as a delight" (Is 65.17–18). Heaven and earth are inseparable parts of the cosmos, so when the cosmos comes to an end they both pass away. The new heaven and earth are either a wholly new cosmos or a renewal of the original cosmos that human actions have deformed. Sometimes Jewish cosmology divided the world into three parts instead of two: Sheol beneath the earth; the surface of the earth; the heavens above the earth. Since the blest did not belong in Sheol, tradition came to place them on the earth or above it.

As Israel was shaken by invasions, deportations, and oppressive rule by other nations, faith in corporate salvation waned, as did belief that goodness would be rewarded on earth. A more otherworldly orientation appears in later Biblical books, such as Daniel. This direction is even clearer in the Targumim. The original text of 1 Samuel 2.6 is "The Lord kills and brings to life; he brings down to Sheol and raises up"; Targum Jonathan appends: "to eternal life." It adds to the words "The Lord will guide you continually, and satisfy your needs in parched places and make your bones strong" (Is 58.11) the phrase "and your body will enjoy everlasting life." The same direction is found in the Septuagint, the Greek translation of the Hebrew Bible (third century B.C.E.). The Septuagint adds to Job 42.17, "And Job died, old and full of days," the words "It is written that he will rise again with those whom the Lord raises up." Jewish funerary inscriptions of the last century B.C.E. indicate that the individual was believed to have a personal relationship with the Lord that continued after death. The old Deuteronomic view yielded to belief in personal immortality and reward in heaven.

The complications of Greek thought regarding spirit, soul, and body had little resonance in the Hebrew Bible, where no such term as "incorporeal" appears. The words *ruah* (breath of life) and *nephesh* (life) have sometimes been translated as "soul" but are best considered terms for the animating principle of the body; they are not separable from it. The fluttering shades of the primordial Sheol were called *rephaim*.

Jewish religion and poetry sang the beauty of the physical cosmos and its living love for God: "Make a joyful noise unto the Lord, all the earth: make a loud noise, and rejoice and sing praise. . . . Let the sea roar, and the fullness thereof; the world and they that dwell therein. Let the floods clap their hands: let the hills be joyful together" (Ps 98.4–8). Bless the Lord, all things that he has made: give glory and eternal praise to him. Angels and heavens bless the Lord; sun and moon; stars of heaven; showers and dews; winds, fire, and heat; frost and cold; ice and snow; night and day; light and darkness; lightning and clouds; mountains and hills; springs, seas, and rivers; fish and birds; animals wild and tame, bless the Lord, give glory and eternal praise unto him (Dn 3.57–88).

As the idea of immortality took hold, a tension grew between the faith that the just will live with the Lord in their bodies and the observation that the body is subject to corruption and goes to the grave or pit. The Book of Daniel (165–164 B.C.E.) contains the first clear reference to resurrection in Jewish thought: at the end of the world "those who sleep in the dust of the earth shall awake, some to everlasting life, and some to shame and everlasting contempt" (Dn 12.2). Many rabbis excluded all resurrected Gentiles from a part in the new Jerusalem. Some argued that all Jews would be saved, but most restricted salvation to the faithful. By the first century B.C.E. the Pharisees (the dominant, rabbinical element in Judaism) affirmed that the body would rise from the dead in glory to remain with the Lord forever. At the moment of death the faithful Jew either enters the final state of blessedness or else awaits reunion with the body and then enters Jerusalem. The bodily resurrection was confirmed by the Pharisees at the Council of Jamnia in 90 C.E. and has remained orthodox Jewish belief.

The place of resurrection will be the Mount of Olives. The literal, metaphorical meaning of the Mount of Olives includes all Jerusalem, or the whole land promised to Israel from the Mediterranean to the Euphrates, or even the whole earth. The Biblical view is that heaven is the place of God. Humans do not and cannot live there. But the Jews of the last few centuries B.C.E. felt the need to bring the righteous into heaven somehow. Early apocalyptic literature accomplished this by making them angels or priests in the heavenly Temple. In the second century C.E., Mishnah Sanhedrin 10.1 (*Chalek*) condemns anyone maintaining that the resurrection of the dead is not in Torah. In the fourth century C.E., Babylonian Talmud Sanhedrin said that those who deny the resurrection of the dead will not be resurrected (90a–b).

All who rise must be judged. On the last day, the Messiah will come in glory to the earth and sound the trumpet (the shofar), raising up the dead. The Day of the Lord is a day of wrath as well as a day of joy, for he judges each person according to his or her character in life. The faithful, purified and cleansed, will shine like the brightness of the sky. On the Day, the bodies of all faithful Jews will be summoned to Jerusalem for resurrection and judgment. Enoch, Elijah, and possibly Moses have already been taken up into heaven. The only explicit account of ascension in the Hebrew Bible is that of Elijah, who mounts to heaven in a fiery chariot as his disciple Elisha, witnessing the event, cries out: "My father, my father! The chariots of Israel and its horsemen!" (2 Kgs 2.11–12).

Jewish images of heaven centered on the Temple, the court (implying both royalty and justice), and the garden. The emphasis upon the Temple was associated politically with the party of the priests; that upon the court with the party of the kings. Ezekiel (40–48) fuses the imagery of the Garden of Eden with that of the Temple. Given the prominence of Temple imagery in the Hebrew Bible, it seems odd that sacrifice, the main business of the earthly Temple, seldom appears in Jewish accounts of the heavenly one. Only late texts such as 3 Baruch (first century B.C.E.) and the Christian Book of Revelation refer to sacrifice in heaven, and then only as the offering of good works.

The resurrected righteous were usually believed to dwell either in Jerusalem or in paradise. The Jews placed the kingdom of God on earth rather than in the heavens. Paradise, the Garden of Eden, was the shady and fruitful orchard at the beginning of the world. The origin of the word is Old Persian *pairidaeza*, referring to the enclosed garden of the Persian king. Hebrew made this *pardes* (Greek *paradeisos* and Latin *paradisus*). But *pardes* appears in the Bible only three times (Eccl 2.5; Sg 4.12; Neh 2.8), and never in connection with Eden. In the Hebrew Bible it meant a garden, a park, or a forest. The equation of paradise with Eden came only in the second century B.C.E., when the Septuagint translated both Eden and *pardes* as *paradeisos*. The rabbis used *pardes* as a synonym for Gan Eden, a place of bliss for the faithful dead, the opposite of Gehenna. In the rabbinical tradition, *pardes* designated the blessed part of Sheol where good souls await the resurrection.

Jerusalem (Zion) is another home of the blessed. In the overt sense, these terms are geographical. Before King David captured Jerusalem, Zion was a small Jebusite fortress below what later became the Temple Mount. When David brought the Ark of the Covenant into Jerusalem, the City of Jerusalem became the Lord's dwelling place on earth and the center of worship. When Solomon moved the Ark into the newly built Temple, the term Zion was transferred to the Temple Mount. From the time of Solomon, Zion by metonymy represented Jerusalem and even all Israel. As the Second Temple was being built (538–516 B.C.E.), the prophet proclaimed that Jerusalem was the center of Israel now and in the future: "Thus says the Lord: I will return to Zion, and will dwell in the midst of Jerusalem" (Zec 8.3). Jerusalem, the capital of Israel under David and Solomon, and of the kingdom of Judah thereafter, represented the holy city of the messiah, the anointed king. Unlike Christians, who emphasized the symbolic sense of Jerusalem, the prime sense for Jews remained geographical: the city itself. There stood the throne of the kings, who are representatives of the true king of Israel, the Lord himself. God's holy Temple was there, with the Ark of the Covenant in its Holy of Holies. Zion is the faithful city, the holy mountain, the mountain of the Lord Almighty. In Jerusalem the resurrection and judgment will take place. "Next year in Jerusalem" remains a promise of the Passover seder, for the return to Zion is identified ontologically with the Passover and with the Exodus story of Israel's original entry into the Promised Land, whose imagery of rivers of milk and honey blends with that of Eden's cool orchards.

In the symbolic sense, Zion is God's kingship; his invincible power; his dwelling and throne; his benevolence and judgment. Zion is the triumph of the Lord God over the enemies of Israel and also the reign of peace, which can come only when the Lord rules all. During and after the Babylonian Captivity, the loss of Zion became the sign of God's punishment of the Jews, of Israel's disgrace and mourning, of God's rejection. But Zion also represented, in the midst of grief, the promise of God's return, when Jerusalem will become the bride of the Lord raised up in glory in the middle of the earth.

The glorified earthly Jerusalem was the model for, and gradually merged with, the heavenly city of Jerusalem. The idea that the just have the heavens as their eternal abode appears in the Hebrew Bible only indirectly by association with God and the angels. The Ark and Temple do not appear in heaven until after the Biblical period. The Hebrew word for heavens is the word for sky: *shamayim*, from *shama*, "the high place." Metaphorically it is the place of God and of the angels and was sometimes used as a synonym for God. By the second century B.C.E., the heavenly Jerusalem was the eternal abode of the just.

Jewish heaven mingled agricultural, pastoral, and urban elements. "On the banks on both sides of the river will grow all kinds of trees for food. Their leaves will not wither nor their fruit fail, but they will bear fresh fruit every month, because the water for them flows from the sanctuary. Their fruit will be for food, and their leaves for healing" (Ez 47.12). Such images were particularly poignant for a people living in a desert. The city is on a mountain, either Zion or Sinai. Waters flowing from it irrigate orchards and vineyards. The soil is so rich that every vine bears a thousand branches and every branch a thousand grapes. The heavenly Jerusalem is glorified time as well as place: it is the Day of the Lord, the Day of judgment and reward; it is the festival Day; it is the Day of rest, the eternal Shabbat, the sabbath of sabbaths, *shabbath shabbathon*.

The blessed dead dwell with God, but there is small precedent in the Hebrew Bible for the Christian idea that the saved see God (the beatific vision). Between the Lord and the cosmos that he created a great gap is fixed; Judaism is the exact opposite of pantheism. Yet God, though wholly distinct from the cosmos he has made, dwells in it through his Shekinah (his presence throughout his creation, his light and his glory). Jacob and Moses both see God, but God tells Moses: "You cannot see my face; for no one shall see me and live. . . . While my glory passes by I will put you in a cleft of the rock, and I will cover you with my hand until I have passed by; then I will take away my hand, and you shall see my back; but my face you shall not see" (Ex 33.20–23). We can see the Shekinah, or what the Christians would call a theophany or action (*energeia*) of God, but we cannot see his face, his essence, his Being (ousia).

Heaven grew more prominent from 250 B.C.E. to 200 C.E. in the "apocalyptic period" (from the word *apokalypsis*, un-

33

covering, revelation). Some features of apocalypticism appeared as early as the sixth century B.C.E., though the noun "apocalypse" did not appear before the Christian era. The first work to bear that title is the New Testament Book of Revelation, and even there it is unclear whether the title *Apokalypsis* was intended to connote something specifically related to the endtime or simply "revelation" in a general sense. Writings from the last two centuries B.C.E. and the first two centuries C.E. include the Old Testament apocrypha and the pseudepigrapha (writings falsely attributed to revered early figures, such as patriarchs or prophets). The apocrypha were accepted in some canons of Scripture; the pseudepigrapha were never accepted into any canon, either Jewish or Christian. That is the traditional distinction between them, but in fact they appeared at the same time and in the same milieus and are best considered together. Taken together, the apocrypha and pseudepigrapha contain a number of genres, including visions, testaments, prayers, liturgical texts, and tales.

The intent of the pseudepigrapha was to uncover hidden truths of the ancients, truths that the apocalyptic writers now grasped, because they stood closer to the end of time. An author writing in what he assumed to be the last days before the end might well believe that at last the time was ripe to unveil the full truth of what Abraham and Ezekiel had earlier intended. The writers of the Book of Enoch, for example, really felt at one with the ancient seer. "I, Enoch, saw" was not intended as a fiction but as a statement of metaphorical ontology (ultimate reality expressed through metaphor rather than overtly). In apocalypse, time moves in a fixed schedule toward its consummation, and salvation comes at the end, or beyond the end, of time.

Apocalyptic in some ways carried on the prophetic tradition, but rather than opposing the Temple and the priesthood, the apocalyptic writers considered both indispensable. What they opposed was the current priestly conduct of affairs in the Temple. In fact such complaints go back as far as the prophet Ezekiel. Though the prophets often said that God cared more about

Torah than about sacrifice, he still required sacrifice and thus the Temple priesthood (Hos 6.6). The endtime would restore the Temple to perfection. As Martha Himmelfarb put it, the conduct of affairs in the Temple was "the very essence of eschatological hope."[3] Eschatology does not replace the Temple; rather it perfects it.

The apocalyptic books were alleged revelations of divine secrets past, present, and future. Most assumed that the last days, when the cosmos would be overthrown, renewed, or replaced, were near at hand. The resurrection and last judgment were imminent. Often these events were linked with the coming in glory of the Messiah, who would rout the enemies of Israel and institute a reign of peace and harmony. Glory is the power of God manifesting itself dramatically, and glory characterizes the new kingdom, age, or reign that melds this world with the other world, past with future.

Apocalyptic accounts of heaven usually took the form of a visionary or dream journey. The writer, having assumed the persona of an acknowledged seer, is granted what he or she presents as a true revelation. A wind, a cloud, a bird, an angel, or a chariot of fire lifts the seer into heaven. Welcomed into the celestial paradise by angels and clothed in glory as an angel or as a priest, the seer at the end returns to earth to report the vision.

In these accounts the number of heavens varied from one through seven (the latter corresponding to the seven planetary spheres). Even ten appeared, though only in the Secrets of Enoch. The differing numbers express neither contradiction nor chronological development, but only variations in the ontological metaphor. In the heavens the blessed shine like stars. They dwell in a celestial Jerusalem. There one finds a mountain, rivers, trees, and the gates of the dwelling of God, the Temple and the throne. The seer delights in fresh scents and sweet song. He witnesses the judgment of mortals. He can approach God,

---

[3] Martha Himmelfarb, *Ascent to Heaven in Jewish and Christian Apocalypses* (Oxford, 1993), 28.

but he cannot see God's face; he can see only what surrounds God: "glory, purity, light, power, the throne, and especially the impenetrable brightness."[4]

Apocalyptic theology displayed two basic attitudes toward the body. The first supposed that the future resurrected body is identical with the present body decaying in the grave, so that at the resurrection limbs, organs—the entire body—will be restored. The other view supposes the transformation of the body. The body is raised from the grave just as in the first view, but then it is transformed into a spiritual body that dwells in a renewed and perfected cosmos. These bodies shine as gloriously as the angels.

The Book of Enoch is composed of five sections by different authors writing from about 250 to 50 B.C.E. The crucial section for the concept of heaven is "The Book of the Watchers," composed about 200 B.C.E. The Secrets of Enoch (2 Enoch) dates from the first or second century C.E. "Watchers" contains the first of many Jewish and Christian ascents to heaven, along with the first clear insistence that the just will live happily in another world. It merges the earthly city of Jerusalem with the celestial city, the eternal dwelling of God and the elect. The story derives from the legend that Enoch, son of Jared, did not die but ascended into heaven: "Enoch walked with God; then he was no more, because God took him" (Gn 5.24).

"Watchers," written by two authors, takes the evil "Watcher Angels" of Genesis 6 as the evil priests of the writers' own times. It contrasts them with the good angels (priests) of the eschatological Temple, who represent ideal priests. The text, written by persons who believed that they were seeing and reporting a true revelation of heaven, shows that the joy of the blessed in the next life surpasses all joys in this. To see and "know" a vision of the other world and to make it intelligible to others, the prophet must be a poet and the poet a prophet, speaking of the ineffable

[4] Quotations from Enoch are from the translation by E. Isaac in James H. Charlesworth, *The Old Testament Pseudepigrapha* (Garden City, N.Y., 1983–85), vol. 1.

in metaphors that are true. "Enoch," says the text, "the blessed and righteous man of the Lord, took up [this parable] while his eyes were open, and he saw."[5]

Enoch learns that the righteous dwell in peace and light on a transformed earth covered with fertile fields, orchards, and vineyards. Every seed brings forth rich harvest, and every olive produces many presses of oil. Enoch is taken up to the heaven in the skies.

> In the vision the winds were causing me to fly and rushing me high up into heaven. And I kept coming [into heaven] until I approached a wall which was built of white marble and surrounded by tongues of fire. . . . And I came into the tongues of the fire and drew near to a great house which was built of white marble, and the inner wall[s] were like mosaics of white marble, the floor of crystal, the ceiling like the path of the stars and lightnings between which [stood] fiery cherubim, and their heaven of water, and flaming fire surrounded the wall[s], and its gates were burning with fire. [It was commonly believed that after the fall paradise was protected by a two-edged sword wielded by the cherubim, which was also a wall of fire that only Enoch and Elijah were allowed to penetrate.] And I entered into the house, which was hot like fire and cold like ice, and there was nothing inside it; fear covered me and trembling seized me. And as I shook and trembled, I fell upon my face, and saw a vision. And behold there was an opening before me [and] a second house, which is greater than the former, and everything was built with tongues of fire. . . . It is impossible for me to recount to you concerning its glory and greatness. As for its floor, it was of fire and above it was lightning and the path of the stars; and as for the ceiling, it was flaming fire. And I observed and saw inside it a lofty throne—its appearance was like crystal and its wheels like the shining sun; and [I heard] the voice of the cherubim; and from beneath the throne were issuing streams of flaming fire. It was difficult to look at it. And

[5] *The Book of Enoch*, trans. E. Isaac, in James H. Charlesworth, *The Old Testament Pseudepigrapha* (Garden City, N.Y., 1983–85), 1:20–21, 49–50.

the Great Glory was sitting upon it—as for his gown, which was shining more brightly than the sun, it was whiter than any snow. . . . The flaming fire was round about him, and a great fire stood before him.

Later Enoch sees a mountain like the throne of God, "which is of alabaster and whose summit is of sapphire." This is the throne on which "the Holy and Great Lord of Glory, the Eternal King, will sit when he descends to visit the earth with goodness." There too, toward the northeast, near the house of the Lord, is the sweet-smelling tree of life to be enjoyed at the endtime by the just and meek. "And then the just and the meek shall rejoice, and they shall enter into the sanctuary, and the sweet odor of this tree will permeate their bones, and they will live a long life on earth, as the patriarchs did." Then Enoch "saw a dwelling place underneath the wings of the Lord of the Spirits; and all the righteous and the elect before him shall be as intense as the light of fire. . . . There [underneath his wings] I wanted to dwell." Enoch sees the Old One, the Ancient of Days, whose hair is as white as wool. The image derives from Daniel: the Ancient of Days with "raiment white as snow, and the hair of his head like pure wool" (Dn 7.9–10).

Enoch's visions merge the earthly and the heavenly paradise.

I saw . . . a structure built of crystals; and between those crystals tongues of living fire. And my spirit saw a ring which encircled this structure of fire. On its four sides were rivers [the four rivers of paradise] full of living fire which encircled it. . . . Moreover, seraphim, cherubim, and ophanim . . . also encircled it. . . . And I saw countless angels . . . encircling that house.

The literary parallels between the accounts of visionary experiences in Biblical and apocalyptic books "does not necessarily mean that the account is entirely a literary creation rather than a reflection of experience."[6] The visionary naturally expresses his vision in cultural idioms familiar to him.

[6] Himmelfarb, *Ascent to Heaven*, 111.

Although there is no unanimity in rabbinic teachings about the afterlife, the rabbis generally set aside such apocalyptic dreams. Some rabbis perceived the kingdom of God as present and growing in this world. The terms "new Jerusalem" and "Jerusalem built in heaven" do occur (Targum on Ps 122.3). On the whole, however, the rabbis held the view that Zion would be reconstructed on earth. The resurrection of the body and the judgment will take place in the geographical Jerusalem at the end of time, and there the Kingdom of the Lord will be established.

The already established belief in the resurrection obtained almost universal acceptance when the Sadducees, who had opposed it, were eradicated after the destruction of the Second Temple. Influential rabbis supported the idea of the resurrection; the Babylonian Talmud repeatedly affirmed it; and the Mishnah warned that anyone denying it would suffer eternal punishment in Gehenna. But this Jewish emphasis on the resurrection of the body was radically different from the Greek emphasis on the immortality of the soul. The central difficulty for Christianity was its effort to fuse these two ideas.

⁂ 3 ⁂

The Heaven of the
Early Christians

THE ROMAN destruction of the Temple and the extinction of Judean autonomy after the rebellions of 66–70 and 132–35 disrupted Jewish religion and left the growing Christian movement the main target for the wrath of the Roman state. Jewish and Christian law forbade Jews and Christians to recognize or participate in the Roman civil cult of the emperor and other gods. Roman civic religion considered the Christians, who were eagerly seeking conversions in a society where adherence to the state religion was an integral part of citizenship, to be atheists and traitors.

However monolithic Christianity may have looked to the Romans, the early Christians were in fact minimally organized, and only in the second century did the lines between orthodox and heterodox begin to be drawn. The most important distinction was that between the majority of the Christian community and the gnostics. Christian gnosticism, a powerful movement in the second century, departed sharply from majority belief on a number of central questions, especially on the nature of body and soul. The gnostics held the dualist belief that the material body is the evil prison of the soul, which must break free of matter in order to be saved.

No single view of heaven exists in the New Testament, which left many questions unresolved and open to debate in succeeding centuries. The Epistles and Gospels say little about a celestial paradise, because the earliest Christian writers were expecting the imminent return of Christ and the end of the world. The end of the world would be the consummation of the salvation history inaugurated by the original Covenant with Israel. At the endtime, Christ would unite Jew and Gentile, circumcised and uncircumcised, in the realized Kingdom of God or Kingdom of Heaven.

The Christian notion of salvation derived directly and fully from the view expressed in the Hebrew Bible and the Mishnah. Christianity continued to emphasize the salvation of the community and broadened it immensely by transforming the qehel, the saving remnant of Israel, into the ecclesia, the community of all believers in Christ, both Jews and Gentiles. The ecclesia, or church, does not mean what later came to be called the hierarchy, or even the entire organization of those professing to believe in Christ; it means the communion of saints, the community of all those saved throughout time past, present, and future. The word "saint" is used in this book not to designate an officially canonized person, but to mean one who is a member of Christ's eternal body. The body of Christ is an ontological metaphor of the highest importance throughout Christian thought. It represents, and in the deepest sense it is, the earthly body of Jesus, the glorified body of Jesus, the consecrated Eucharist, and the ecclesia (church), the community of those who love God.

The salvation of the community does not mean that the individual is submerged; witness the parable of Dives and Lazarus and Christ's promise to the good thief. Rather, one joins with God and with the ecclesia in the communion of saints without losing one's identity. Individuality remains as an incandescence amidst the great glow of light.

The early Christians believed that the union of the community in God will occur at the end of time, which they thought was at hand. It also occurs right now. It is now because for God every moment is now. It is also now for the reason that Christ has come and brought the kingdom of heaven to earth. Heaven comes down and transforms the earth rather than hovering above the earth, waiting for the saved to arrive. Heaven is also now because Christ's saving action is eternal and extends to past, present, and future. The just who lived before Christ, particularly the faithful Jews, are saved by Christ equally with those who live after him. The ecclesia is a community that exists eternally with God, embracing all ages from the beginning to the end of time. The kingdom has already come: heaven is now. More fully, it is both now and also not yet. The kingdom has come; the kingdom is here; the kingdom will come in fullness. Christ has died; Christ has risen; Christ will come again. Christ did not end this world at his first coming; he will end it when he comes again.

The end of the world has two important meanings. This world, sometimes called this age, is not primarily a term of physical cosmology, not a term of space or of time; rather it denotes the ruined state of humanity before the Redemption, or, better, because the term is not time-bound, the ruined state *without* the Redemption. The process of redeeming this ruined state began with the Old Covenant and will end at the second coming of Christ, which is followed immediately by the resurrection of the dead. The eternally meaningful and effective series of acts in this process is the Incarnation and Passion (suffering) of Jesus Christ. The New Age—identified with the City or Kingdom of God and with heaven—is now in the process of replacing the Old Age, the kingdom of Satan, a process to be completed at the Second Coming. This saving of the community over time is mirrored by the saving of the individual over time, which begins at baptism, advances with *conversio* (the turning of the heart to God), and is consummated at the Last Judgment. The New Testament speaks of three deaths: the spiritual death caused by sin, the physical death of the body, and the spiritual death *to* sin that is the prerequisite of true life. True life is fulfillment with God in heaven.

The New Age is the New Zion or Jerusalem, the New Covenant, the new heaven and earth, the eternal realization of the body of Christ. It is the transformation of this world into heaven, or a renewal of this world, or a return to the happy original state of humanity before Adam's sin. Christ is the New Adam, transforming the old. Heaven is a return to paradise, and the imagery of the earthly paradise and celestial paradise are drawn together by typology, allegory, and eventually artistic representation. But theologically the earthly paradise is transformed into the eschatological and eternal paradise in which the potential for sin and ruin—for another "fall"—has been taken away. Already found in the New Testament (Lk 23.43), this distinction between the earthly and the heavenly paradise became standard. The earthly paradise or Eden exists at the beginning of the world; the heavenly paradise at the end.

Heaven is the transformed City of Jerusalem as well as the transformed Garden of Eden. The earthly Jerusalem that the Lord promised to Abraham and his descendants is a city renewed as the center of the reign of God on earth, or transmuted into the heavenly Jerusalem promised to the members of Christ's body. The term "the Jerusalem above" or heavenly Jerusalem is used by both John and Paul. A historian would say that the earthly Jerusalem was the human model for the idea of the heavenly city. But in terms of metaphorical ontology the heavenly Jerusalem is the prototype from which the physical city was copied; at the same time it is the city that God constructs at the end of the world, which is the community of the faithful. The image of the earthly city points toward the union of the community with Christ in heaven. It is the fulfillment of the classical state (Greek *polis* and Roman *civitas*) and the Jewish Zion, combining the community of the polis, citizenship in the world empire, and the holy city of the throne of David. Jerusalem, no longer under bondage to the Devil, is free to love God. Its inhabitants live not as subjects but as free citizens of a free city.

The citizens of heaven enjoy what later would be called the beatific vision, which means not only seeing but understanding and loving God and his creatures in peace and harmony and with dynamic and growing intensity. Christian tradition had to cope with an apparent contradiction in the New Testament in that "No human sees or can see God" (1 Tm 6.16) and "We shall see him as he is" (1 Jn 3.2). The problem was later mitigated by the Eastern Christian distinction between the ousia of God, which we cannot see, and the energeia or manifestation of God, which we can. In Eastern Christianity, *theosis* ("divinization": becoming divine through God's grace) is more important than the *visio* ("vision") emphasized in the West. The New Testament declares that through grace we may become participants in the divine nature (1 Pt 4). Divinization is the recovery of the full image and likeness of God that humanity lost with Original Sin and will regain when heaven comes down to embrace earth.

New Testament and other early Christian writers drew their ideas about soul and body from both Jewish and Greek thought, though Christian reflection transformed those ideas in original ways. The mutual influence of rabbinic and Christian scholars persisted, though attenuated and with many disruptions, through the Middle Ages.

Since early Christians wrote in Greek, they used the Greek vocabulary of *pneuma, psychē, sōma,* and *sarx. Pneuma* and *psychē* can each be translated as either "spirit" or "soul," and the distinction between the two has never been clear. *Sōma,* or body, contrasted with *sarx,* unanimated flesh, often meant the whole personality, body and soul, the self. The gnostics, on the other hand, sharply divided the human person into soma, psyche, and pneuma in a hierarchy of soma people, who could not be saved, psyche people, who might be saved, and pneuma people, who were certainly saved. No clear distinction between psyche and pneuma appeared in Hellenistic Jewish thought or among New Testament or other orthodox Christian thinkers. Though the Jewish philosopher Philo of Alexandria (20 B.C.E.– 50 C.E.) used a conceptual distinction between higher and lower "parts of the soul," he meant only to distinguish the vegetative from the rational soul, a classical distinction for which the word "mind" would be a more modern equivalent than "soul." The Christians followed the Jews in insisting that the human personality is a single psychosomatic entity.

Besides the nouns *pneuma* and *psychē*, Paul used the adjectives *psychikos* and *pneumatikos*. He contrasted the terms when he wrote to the Corinthians, perhaps because some of them were holding views akin to gnosticism. He distinguished between *sōma psychikon* and *sōma pneumatikon* (1 Cor 15.44). *Sōma psychikon* is a term compatible with Greek philosophy, and the word "psychosomatic" is familiar to modern ears. By a "psychic body," Paul meant a body animated by life, and the term applied to humans, animals, and even plants. Paul calls Adam a living "psyche" (*psychē zōsan*). Christ, however, as the Second Adam, is a "live-giving pneuma" (*pneuma zōopoioun*): Paul understood pneuma as superior to psyche. A third and lower category would be a purely material body, *sōma choïkon* or *sōma hylikon*, but Paul avoided the terms. It is possible that he intended *sarx*, "flesh," for such a lower category, for he declares that flesh and blood (*sarx kai haima*) cannot inherit the kingdom (1 Cor 15.50).

The phrase *sōma pneumatikon*, however, was as odd in Paul's time as it is in ours, combining as it did two such different concepts as pneuma and soma. Paul's use of the phrase turned out to be crucial in the Christian view of the nature of humanity and of body and soul. Paul's overt intent is unclear. The translation "spiritual body" is poor, because of the ambiguity of the term "spiritual," especially since Paul sharply contrasted psyche and pneuma, which can both be translated "spirit." Nor does "ensouled body" fit. The difficulty is reduced (though not much clarified) by using a term closer to the original Greek: "pneumatic body" for *sōma pneumatikon*, as with "psychic body" for *sōma psychikon*. Paul refuted the Corinthians' belief that the kingdom had already arrived by insisting that at the endtime we shall experience a qualitative change from the "psychic" state to the "pneumatic." This may mean that bodies presently subject to sin and death will be free of them in heaven. Or it may resemble the rabbinical distinction between the present body and the resurrection body; that is, the pneumatic body will realize the potential of the present psychic body.

The New Testament follows the Old Testament in viewing the human personality as a unit rather than separating it into soul, spirit, and body. The entire human being is saved. Yet the unavoidable fact that the body decays after death forced speculation along one of two paths: if the whole person is saved, then salvation cannot occur until the whole person, body and soul, is reconstituted at the resurrection; if, on the other hand, the person is saved at the time of death, then the state of salvation must be a disembodied one. There is little Jewish precedent and no New Testament support for this second option. The term "immortal soul" nowhere appears in the New Testament, and the term "immortality" is applied only to the resurrected body. Perpetual life (*zoē aiōnios*) or imperishability is a better term than immortality for the New Testament concept of heaven.

In declaring that flesh and blood cannot inherit the kingdom, Paul seems to question the very possibility of a saved body. Yet he immediately proceeds to assert the salvation of a transformed, "imperishable" body (1 Cor 15.51–53). Soma and even sarx will be saved; Paul is determined not to allow any mind/body dichotomy on earth or in heaven. There can be no life without a body. Indeed, the main reason that the Athenians rejected Paul was his determined proclamation of bodily resurrection, which flouted all the assumptions of Platonism and Stoicism. At the sound of the shofar, the dead will be raised imperishable and immortal: the body puts on the clothing of imperishability and immortality.

Given the overwhelming testimony to the salvation of the body in both Jewish and Christian Scripture, the separate immortality of the soul is incompatible with Biblical teaching. The fathers, however, often endorsed immortality as an accommodation to Greco-Roman idealist philosophy, to which bodily resurrection appeared crude and absurd. Though Christians rejected the Platonic notion that the soul was immortal by nature, they declared immortality a divine gift. Thus Christian tradition embraced two conflicting ideas, proclaiming both the resurrection of the body and the immortality of the soul. This was ironic, for "the idea of the immortality of the soul came eventually to be identified with the Biblical doctrine of the resurrection of the body, a doctrine one of whose original polemical targets was the immortality of the soul."[7]

The general resurrection is patterned on Christ's, though he alone of humans is God. Christ rose in a real body: he ate fish and let Thomas touch his wounds (Jn 20–21). It was his own physical body, yet qualitatively changed from the body he was born with and even from his body at the Transfiguration. It could appear quite different from his body in this life, for the disciples did not recognize him on the road to Emmaus. In the overt sense, Christ's body is the physical body of Jesus the carpenter. In metaphorical ontology it is the transfigured body, the resurrected body, the ascended body, the Eucharist, the communion of saints, the ecclesia. The meaning of corporeality can be multiplied and expanded, but on no account can physical corporeality be subtracted. Thus, our resurrected bodies, however different, are the physical bodies we are now. It is these very bodies that become imperishable, incorruptible, and immune from illness, weakness, or blemish.

The new body somehow emerges from the old body. The earthly body is replaced by or exchanged for the spiritual body; or the physical body "puts on" (Greek *enduein*) the spiritual body as if the earthly body were an undergarment; or the present body is transformed; or the psychic body is the seed of the pneumatic body, sprouting and growing into its true pneumatic self. It is not a disembodied soul or spirit; it is in some essential manner the earthly body, however changed. The change, already begun by baptism and conversion, is completed at the Last Judgment, after which the body is fulfilled, perfected, glorified, and eternal in heaven. Later exegetes often ignored the seed/development imagery in favor of a theory of the reconstitution of every atom of the present earthly body.

---

[7] Jaroslav Pelikan, *The Emergence of the Catholic Tradition (100–600)* (Chicago, 1971), 51.

The imperishability of the human body is related to the salvation of the whole cosmos. Human solidarity with the cosmos is indissoluble, for the human soma psychikon is part of the created universe. The New Testament posits no duality between matter and spirit. The eternal life of the cosmos lies in the fact that all spacetime is with God, so that all that ever has been, is, or will be, simply *is* ("be's") eternally in God. The cosmos that God has created from himself returns to him in an end that recapitulates the beginning. The eschatological state of the cosmos is not its state when the last star fades and the last quark dies; it is the completion of its transformation into glory. New Testament writers were uninterested in spatial or temporal considerations, expecting as they did that the end was near and that eternity would soon irrupt into time.

For Christians and Jews the sacred nature of the cosmos does not mean pantheism, for pantheism equates the cosmos with God and so limits God to the boundaries of the cosmos. In the Christian tradition, God both transcends the cosmos and is immanent within it. A powerful current in that tradition is panentheism, which must be clearly distinguished from pantheism. Panentheism is the view that the cosmos lies within God, thus being divine. Far from limiting God to the boundaries of the cosmos, panentheism posits a finite cosmos "inside" God, who is unbounded and infinite. Since God created the cosmos from nothing at all, he created it from himself. Therefore the whole world is a theophany, a manifestation of the eternal Word (Logos). The descent of heaven, when God will be all in all, fuses his transcendence and immanence.

The value of matter is linked with the resurrection of the body. Paul insisted on embodiment at the general resurrection, but he was not clear as to whether, or how, the soul existed between death and resurrection. The term "interim state" was introduced by Tertullian (160–225), though the concept had been implied in the New Testament. The community expected the Second Coming at any moment and believed that the time between death and the Last Judgment would be negligible. Still, saints who had already (such as the martyr Stephen) died needed to be accounted for. The alternatives are these: (1) At the moment of death one passes into eternity with God; because in God all times are one, the moment of one's death is the moment of one's resurrection, so body and soul are not separated. (2) At the moment of death the soul is separated from the body until the endtime. (3) At the moment of death the soul undergoes a "particular" (personal) judgment. If saved, the soul enters without any delay into the beatific vision, or else it rests in peace until the Last Judgment and resurrection, when it will at last enjoy the beatific vision. (4) The emphasis is on the whole community: either the community is in heaven now, and the parousia will complete this state; or an earthly kingdom of Christ forms a transition between the parousia and the end of the cosmos.

Paul believed that the martyr Stephen and others who died before the parousia were *gymnoi* (naked in the sense of being unclothed by a body), and Paul feared being *gymnos* before receiving his resurrection body (2 Cor 5.3). The soul in the interim state is said to "be in the bosom of Abraham" (Lk 16.22) or to be "asleep." Sleep in this context does not imply unconsciousness. The souls of the just are asleep, not by being unconscious, but by being indifferent to this world and alive to the real world of Christ. The souls of the just enjoy their union with Christ, for they are members of his body and cannot be separated from him. This state of being, already perfect, is rendered more perfect by the resurrection.

The sociology of the kingdom of heaven is characterized by the freedom of its citizens, by equality (the equal blessedness of all members of Christ's body), and by hierarchy (some are closer to God than others). All are perfectly fulfilled, and some have greater intrinsic potential for fulfillment than do others. This triple sociology would be played out in many ways for centuries. Later Christians, after the establishment of Christianity as the official faith of the Roman Empire, were tempted to ascribe to heaven a hierarchical arrangement reflecting that of earth, with emperors, princes, and bishops at the top. But at the top of the

New Testament hierarchy are humility, poverty, mercy, love, and martyrdom, not worldly power and prestige. The New Testament is unclear whether angels "outrank" humans and uncertain about the hierarchical structure of the angelic orders. But ranks, whatever values they represent, are of no importance at all to God. All whom he loves are equally precious to him. Heavenly beings would descend to lower spheres to speak with Dante while at the same eternal moment staying in their true place in the empyrean with the Trinity.

⅄ The Apocalypse or Revelation of John the Divine, unlike the rest of the New Testament, was intended mainly in the symbolic sense. It was never intended as a literal guide to the future. The Apocalypse is carefully crafted, rooted textually in the Old Testament, and metaphorically coherent. God reveals to the human being John what is beyond human knowledge. John enters the stream of events without affecting them, unlike Dante, who interacts with them. Yet Dante frequently harks back to John, not least in his triple exclamation "I saw" (*io vidi*), echoing the repeated *vidi* of the Apocalypse.

The Apocalypse reveals that the world is soon to be renewed. The divine figure on the throne says that he is "making all things new" (Rv 21.5). "Then I saw a new heaven and a new earth; for the first heaven and the first earth had passed away. . . . And I saw the holy city, the new Jerusalem, coming down out of heaven from God, prepared as a bride adorned for her husband" (Rv 21.1–2). It is renewed and completed. The figure on the throne says, "It is finished! I am the Alpha and the Omega" (Rv 21.6). This echo of the last words of Christ on the cross means that the world is consummated; heaven is here.

> The New Jerusalem has the glory of God and a radiance like a very rare jewel, like jasper, clear as crystal. It has a great, high wall with twelve gates, and at the gates twelve angels, and on the gates are inscribed the names of the twelve tribes of the Israelites. . . . And the wall of the city has twelve foundations, and on them are the twelve names of the twelve apostles of the Lamb.

The angel who talked to me had a measuring rod of gold to measure the city and its gates and walls. The city lies foursquare, its length the same as its width; and he measured the city with his rod, fifteen hundred miles; its length and width and height are equal. (Rv 21.11–16)

The shape of the heavenly city is modeled on the Ark of the Covenant, the Temple, and the Temple Square (Ez 45, 48; 1 Kgs 6). The New Jerusalem is a sacred space whose boundaries are the boundaries of creation itself, for what is outside it is not anywhere at all.

John's heaven, unlike that of the Jewish pseudepigrapha, lacks a temple. "I saw no temple in the city, for its temple is the Lord God Almighty and the Lamb" (Rv 21.22). The wall of the city "is built of jasper, while the city is pure gold, clear as glass. The foundations of the wall of the city are adorned with every jewel. . . . And the twelve gates are twelve pearls, each of the gates is a single pearl, and the street of the city is pure gold, transparent as glass" (Rv 21.19–21). The "four-horned golden altar before God" (Rv 9.13) corresponds to the one that stood in the Tabernacle and the Temple in the holy place of Israel (Ex 27). At the center of the heavenly city is the garden where God sits on his throne. Temple, throne, and garden bring together the images of heaven as tabernacle, city, and paradise. "Then the angel showed me the river of the water of life, bright as crystal, flowing from the throne of God and of the Lamb through the middle of the street of the city. On either side of the river is the tree of life with its twelve kinds of fruit, producing its fruit each month; and the leaves of the tree are for the healing of the nations" (Rv 22.1–2). The waters of life flow from the source of life and light, while the waters under the earth, which represent chaos, formlessness, and death, vanish or are purified into a clear sea of glass or crystal before the throne. The leaves and the fruit offer healing and wholesome nourishment.

God on his throne is the true king of Israel, the king of all nations, king of all the cosmos. "Then I saw a great white throne and the one who sat on it; the earth and the heaven fled from his presence, and no place was found for them" (Rv 20.11). The terrible presence of God's glory on his throne is under the canopy of his mercy, the rainbow. Angelic, priestly figures surround the Lord, praising him, falling to the ground, and casting the crowns of their glory before his throne.

God is king and judge, but merciful in judgment, and he is also the bridegroom welcoming his bride Israel, now transformed into the ecclesia. "Every creature in heaven and on earth and under the earth and in the sea, and all that is in them" sing to the Father on the throne and to his Son the Lamb, "blessing and honor and glory and might forever and ever" (Rv 5.13). This eternal and joyous song expresses God's singing silence. It is the primal silence before time, which silence sang in the creation, and the silence of the end, which silence sings in the re-creation. The living and the dead are brought before the throne and "judged according to their works, as recorded in the book of life" (Rv 20.12). God judges each according to his or her character, that is, their basic inclination to love God or to turn away from him. The Lord takes the martyrs robed in white and others who love him to dwell with him forever; he sends those who choose not to love him away eternally.

The New Testament canon excluded as apocryphal a number of books, some on the ground that their message was gnostic and did not accord with the community's idea of Christ's life and mission, some because their claim to legitimacy was vitiated by fiction. Such works might contain some truths, even inspiration, but the community would not guarantee them as divine revelation. The "fathers of the church" were the earliest post-apostolic theologians. The Christian apocrypha and the fathers can on the whole be considered together as representing second- and third-century thought; on the other hand gnostic literature (including gnostic apocrypha) and vision literature are quite different, and I take them separately.

Gnosticism (as opposed to gnostic thought in general, some of which was Jewish) was a variety of Christianity that faded by the third century, although it enjoyed repeated revivals later. Christian gnosticism was rooted in apocalyptic Judaism, Persian Mazdaism, and Platonist philosophy, but it sprang from the inherent tension within Christianity between monism and dualism. Christianity is essentially monist in its affirmation that there is but one God and that everything that is proceeds from him. God made the world and pronounced it good. Yet terrible evils occur. If God causes, or at least chooses to permit, evil, it seems that he is not entirely good. If evil occurs without God's permission, it seems he is not all-powerful; something other than God must initiate and prolong evil, such as Satan and human sin. This idea was a step away from absolute monism. A spectrum of thought exists between absolute monism and absolute dualism. Both gnosticism and Christianity lay between the two ends, but orthodox Christianity remained much closer to the monist end than did gnosticism. Still, Christianity is far from monism. Satan was a creature of God, an angel who chose to sin of his own free will. Humans also freely make evil choices that God does not ordain.

The gnostics were much closer to the dualist end of the spectrum. The Devil, the source of evil, is God's immensely powerful opponent. For some gnostics, he is a wholly independent deity, an anti-God. God created spirit, which is good, but a "demiurge" (a subdeity, often identified with Satan), created matter, which is evil. A human being is a spark of divine spirit that Satan has entrapped in loathsome flesh. Our duty is to escape the flesh and return our spirit to God. We can achieve this only by embracing *gnôsis*, divinely revealed knowledge. Since bodies are disgusting and evil, Christ did not have a body, nor will our own bodies rise again. Christ, in order to communicate with us wretched humans, took on only the appearance of a body. He saves us not by becoming flesh and dying on the cross, but by serving as an angelic, bodiless messenger, bringing from God the gnosis that we must escape our prisonhouse of flesh. The liberated soul ascends through a series of spheres, hindered by demons but aided by angelic guides. As it mounts it sheds its bodily integument and, having cast all filthy matter aside, shines forth as pure pneuma and reunites with the pure, spiritual Light from which Satan had kidnapped it.

Gnostic views were banished by the fathers. The "apostolic fathers" of the first two centuries, like the New Testament, said little about the celestial paradise, because they expected the general resurrection at any moment. As time went on and the end of the world was delayed, the fathers had to consider the state of the holy people after their death and before the endtime. Persecutions and martyrdoms forced victims and their friends to face a painful and immediate transition to another world.

The Christians held that the death of the body is not the end of life; it is the beginning of new life with Christ. Thus saints are commemorated not on the day of their physical birth but on that of their physical death, their birth into heaven. The delay of the Second Coming also increased the tension between the idea of the personal judgment at the moment of death and the Last Judgment. Clement of Rome, writing about 95, said that Peter and Paul went directly to "the holy place," but he may have meant either in spirit or in body. Only Enoch, Elijah, Moses, Mary, and Jesus are already bodily in heaven. The idea that Mary was bodily in heaven began at least as far back as the fourth century and is hinted at in the third-century Gospel of Bartholomew, where the Lord tells her that her body will be taken up to paradise and her soul into the heavens. In Bartholomew, Mary's eminence is clear, but the state of her departed soul and body is still ambiguous. As for the other blessed dead, their souls await the resurrection, but the fathers disagreed as to whether the blest could actually be in heaven before the endtime. Most of the fathers assumed that they already were somehow in heaven, but Justin Martyr (d. 165) believed that souls at death cannot enjoy eternal life in heaven before the resurrection.

The fathers agreed that resurrection and salvation are acts of divine will. No one is saved who is not chosen (elect); the resurrection revives the *reprobi* (those not chosen) as well as the elect, but only the elect will dwell with God in heaven; the rest are ruined eternally. The merits of the martyrs place them highest in God's favor, an idea rooted in Jewish tradition. Both Justin and Ignatius (d. 107) hoped for heaven as reward for their own martyrdom. Merit is the result of divine grace: a martyr is a martyr because he or she has accepted God's will. Some are higher in heaven than others because grace has endowed them with keener intellect and a more intense desire for God.

Justin set the Judeo-Christian resurrection of the body against the Greek immortality of the soul. He insisted on the resurrected body and its identity with the present body. This was in part a response to the gnostic denial of the body's value. Justin argued that the salvation proclaimed to humanity is proclaimed to human flesh. The body inherits the kingdom; even more, the kingdom inherits the flesh. Irenaeus (second century) reaffirmed this view strongly, but his near-contemporary Athenagoras attempted to quell Greco-Roman philosophical objections by accommodating bodily resurrection to the immortality of the soul. On the one hand, he accepted the resurrection of the body; on the other, he claimed that in heaven, even after the resurrection of the body, we shall live with God as heavenly spirits.

Irenaeus summed up the tradition as it was in his time. All the blessed in heaven will see Christ, the glory of the communion of saints, and the renovation of the world. They will dwell in their true home, where with Christ they enjoy eternal peace and comfort. Paradise, the heavenly city, the celestial abode, and the reign of God come together at the endtime, when the Word of God restores the cosmos to himself. We were originally created in Eden in God's image and likeness, and the grace of the Holy Spirit will restore and further perfect that blessed state. The image (*imago*) is the natural image of God intrinsic in every human soul; the likeness (*similitudo*) is the potential, through grace, of becoming like him in eternal life.

Irenaeus defended the psychosomatic integrity of the human being as unified body and soul against the gnostic belief that the soul is saved independent of the body. The Holy Spirit grafts eternal and immutable life onto our earthly bodies, changing them into spiritual bodies. As Christ descended into the shadow of death until the third day, so the souls of the just will pass into an invisible place God has designated for them and there await the resurrection. When at last we rise in our bodies, we will see God and be taken into him, for "those who see God are within God, sharing His glory" (*Against Heresies*, 4.20.5). Irenaeus set the pattern for Origen (185–254), Lactantius (260–330), and Augustine (354–430) in arguing that in the other world we remember our past life. Part of our purgation is the memory of our sins; once purged, all our joy on earth commingles with the joy of being in the company of God.

Most Christians learned from liturgy more directly than from theology. The liturgy of the sacraments, particularly the Eucharist, brings us into the eternal now even as we await, in time, Christ's return. The liturgy connects us with the whole ecclesia, with the congregation of all who love Christ, past, present, and future.

Direct references to heaven are rare in the earliest liturgies, though an early formal prayer asks for eternal joy in the society of the martyrs. The Odes of Solomon, a collection of early Christian hymns (first or second century), declare:

> I have been freed from vanities, and am not condemned. My chains were cut off by His hands; I received the face and form of a new person, and I walked in Him and was saved. . . . And I stripped off darkness and put on light. . . . And abundantly helpful to me was the thought of the Lord, and his incorruptible fellowship. And I was lifted up in the light, and I passed before his face. And I was constantly near him, while praising and confessing him. . . . And immortal life embraced me and kissed me.[8]

The fathers explored the landscape of heaven. In Lactantius' poem about the earthly paradise, *About the Phoenix*, the Greek

---

[8] *The Odes of Solomon*, trans. James H. Charlesworth (Oxford, 1973), 74–75 (Ode 17.1–4).

phoenix rising from the dead becomes a metaphor of Christ. In paradise, Lactantius said, spring is the only season, spices emit sweet scents, water flows from a spring or fountain, trees bear luscious fruit, and flowers bloom in green meadows. Lactantius introduced the palm tree into paradise, associating it with the Roman palm of victory and the palms of glory strewn before Christ on his entry into Jerusalem.

Christian pictorial art emerged in the third and fourth centuries, with motifs of meeting Christ, reception by angels, and life in community with those who love the Lord. Heaven is a place of peace, refreshment, light, and beauty, an eternal home where we rest free from the stress of life in this world and where we realize our potential for joy. Life on earth is a journey, short or long, toward that home. The art illustrated and concretized the traditions: a dove's flight representing the upward migration of the soul; a praying figure (orans) surrounded by doves; a starry sky representing the clarity and infinity of the real world; a paradise with trees, lawns, flowers, fountains. The saved are seen in this garden either in human form or as doves, and the phoenix and the peacock appear as symbols of eternity. A vine suggests the rich harvest and the plenty of the heavenly country. A house symbolizes the home of those who love Christ; often a soul is shown entering or at the door. Crowns of roses, laurels, or palms appear, as do cups, lamps, torches, and rich clothing and jewelry, representing the glory of the Lord covering those who love him.

Heaven is rich and detailed in many dreams or visions rooted in the apocalyptic tradition. One of these, almost included in the canon of the New Testament, is the *Shepherd of Hermas* (ca. 150). Whoever the actual author, his persona (character), "Hermas," saw the heavens open, revealing the martyrs crowned in the company of angels and living joyfully with the Son of God. The most important texts that followed are the *Vision of Paul* (second to fourth century), the Christian version of the Jewish *Ascension of Isaiah* (possibly third century), and the

Passion of Perpetua (third century). These texts often contain accounts of heaven and hell, intended not as intimidation but as encouragement for believers facing persecution. Martyrs are highest in heaven, followed by confessors (those who persevered in their faith in the face of persecution yet enjoyed a natural death).

The visions narrate the story of a persona who, like Hermas, sees heaven. The persona of the seer may be the author or alleged author of the text, reporting on his or her return what had been revealed. Or the persona may be someone other than the author. In the overt sense, the seer goes on a voyage to the otherworld, usually via a vision or a dream. In the symbolic sense, it matters little whether the journey is a "real" one, a visionary one, or a dream, or whether the seer is alleged to have had the vision while in the body or while out of it. Any report of having seen the otherworld may be termed a "vision" in the general sense. Characteristically, the vision recounts the persona's experience of being removed by divine agency from everyday surroundings into another kind of space and time. The seer learns divine secrets, which he or she reports in descriptions meant to be understood both in the overt and in the symbolic sense. The visions are markedly similar: a judge on a holy mountain, pastoral scenes, meadows, fields, trees, fruit, flowers, fragrance, bright and kindly light, and the saved of the Old and New Covenants, shining white with glory as did Moses on Sinai and Jesus at the Transfiguration.

The visions were controversial, for the bishops and other representatives of order and authority wanted to draw a clear line between revealed Scripture and all other texts. Writings beyond Scripture could be divinely inspired, but their authenticity as revelation of divine truth could not be guaranteed. Yet the visions were popularly accepted as the revelations their authors claimed them to be.

The Vision of Paul, translated into Latin by the fourth century, was the key text for later medieval vision literature. Paul is led by an angelic guide on a complicated and confusing journey in which he sees hell and then several blessed abodes. The narrative shifts back and forth between visions of bliss and visions of punishment, but the overall wealth of images and concepts is more important than the distinctions drawn between the various heavenly abodes. The angel takes Paul to the door of the third heaven, "and I looked at it and saw that it was a golden gate and that there were two golden pillars before it and two golden tables above the pillars full of letters. And again the angel turned to me and said: Blessed are you if you enter in by these gates"[9] (an idea later inverted by Dante: "abandon all hope, you who enter" [*Inferno*, 3.9]). The letters are the names of the righteous, inscribed in heaven while they still dwell on earth.

Entering the gates of paradise, Paul meets the ancient, hoary Enoch, whose face shines like the sun. After warning Paul not to tell what he has seen in the third heaven, the angel descends with him to the second heaven and the earthly paradise, where the souls of the just await the resurrection. There Paul sees the four rivers of paradise, flowing with honey, milk, wine, and olive oil. On the banks of each river he meets the blessed dead who have shown a particular virtue in life: honey for those who have renounced their own will for God's; milk for the innocent and chaste; wine for the hospitable; olive oil for those who have sacrificed earthly rewards for God. This sort of "principle of enumeration—naming four virtues, grouping their adherents into lands where each virtue is pursued—is a fundamental structural element" in vision literature as late as Dante and beyond.[10] The angel sets Paul in a golden boat, "and about three thousand angels were singing a hymn before me until I reached the City of Christ." In a forest standing before the city, repentant sinners

---

[9] *Vision of Paul*, in *New Testament Apocrypha*, ed. and trans. Edgar Hennecke and Wilhelm Schneemelcher, 2d ed. (Westminster, Md., 1991), 2:771–77.

[10] Alan Bernstein, *The Formation of Hell* (Ithaca, N.Y., 1993), 296.

wait in the interim between death and resurrection. Paul sees a
city with twelve walls, each wall exceeding the next in greatness
as he proceeds toward the center:

> I saw in the midst of this city a great altar, very high, and there
> was [David] standing near the altar, whose countenance shone as
> the sun, and he held in his hands a psaltery and harp, and he sang
> psalms, saying Alleluia. And all in the city replied Alleluia till the
> very foundations of the city were shaken. . . . Turning round I
> saw golden thrones placed in each gate, and on them men having
> golden diadems and gems: and I looked carefully and saw inside
> between the twelve men thrones in glorious rank . . . so that no
> one is able to recount their praise. . . . Those thrones belong to
> those who had goodness and understanding of heart and made
> themselves fools for the sake of the Lord God.

Among the blessed are the Jews loyal to the Covenant, and
Mary, the Mother of God. While he is looking at heavenly trees,
Paul sees two hundred angels preceding Mary and singing
hymns. Mary salutes him and tells him that the blessed have
looked forward to his being in heaven so much that they have
granted him the extraordinary favor (granted later to Dante) of
coming there before he dies.

The Ascension of Isaiah is more carefully organized. The
prophet is taken out of his body and led by an angel to the first
heaven above the sky. "And I saw a throne in the midst, and on
the right and on the left of it were angels" singing praises.[11]
Isaiah asks to whom the praise is given. "It is for the praise of
him who is in the seventh heaven, for him who rests in eternity
among his saints, and for his Beloved, whence I have been sent
unto [you]." This heaven above the sky is the first heaven; the
angel then takes Isaiah beyond to the second heaven, where
again there is a throne and angels on the right and left. The
prophet falls on his face to worship the one on the throne, but

---

[11] *The Ascension of Isaiah*, in *New Testament Apocrypha*, ed. Hennecke
and Scheemelcher, 2:653–56.

the angel tells him not to do that till they reach the highest heaven, where God's own throne is set. Ascending, they find each heaven more glorious than the one below. The sixth is so bright that by comparison the previous five are darkness. Isaiah begs the angel not to send him back to the flesh. The angel replies: "If [you] already rejoice in this light, how much [will you] rejoice when, in the seventh heaven, [you see] that light where God and his beloved are, whence I have been sent. . . . As for [your] wish not to return to the flesh . . . , [your] days are not yet fulfilled that [you may] come here." Jesus orders that Isaiah be admitted into the seventh heaven. "And I saw there a wonderful light and angels without number. And there I saw all the righteous from Adam [onward]. . . . I saw Enoch and all who were with him, stripped of the garment of the flesh, and I saw them in their higher garments, and they were like the angels who stand there in great glory." He adds, "But they did not sit on their thrones, nor were their crowns of glory on their heads," because the blessed of the Old Testament will not be fully glorified until the Word is made flesh. At the end of the vision, Isaiah descends with Christ through all the heavens to earth and witnesses the Annunciation and Incarnation.

The Passion of Perpetua recounts two visions: her own and that of her fellow prisoner Saturus. The *Passion* is unusual in that the seer was a historical figure, the imprisoned young mother Perpetua (martyred in 203), who wrote the account herself. Perpetua saw

> a golden ladder of great size stretching up to heaven, a narrow one, so that people can mount it only one at a time, and on the steps of the scale iron tools such as swords, spears, and axes are fixed, so one must be very careful in ascending. . . . I saw a garden of immense extent, in the midst of which was sitting a white-haired man dressed as a shepherd; he was tall, and he was milking sheep. And he raised his head and looked at me and said, Welcome, child. And he called me and gave me a mouthful of cheese from the sheep he was milking; and I took it with my hands and

ate of it, and all those who were standing about said, Amen. And then I woke up.[12]

Saturus' vision involved both himself and Perpetua:

> Blessed Saturus also had a vision: he said that we had died and that we left our body and we began to be carried by four angels toward the east, and their hands did not touch us as they bore us. . . . We arrived at a wide open space with a grove; the trees bore roses and all kinds of flowers. The trees were as high as cypresses, and their leaves sang without pause. And in that orchard were four other angels brighter than those before. [They received us with honor and joy, and the first four angels set us down, and] we went on foot through the grove through the violet-covered field [and found our martyred friends. The angels said,] Come first and greet the Lord. . . . We came then toward a place whose walls were as if made of light, and in front of the gate of the place four angels were standing, and we put on white robes. We went in and we heard voices in unison saying Holy Holy Holy without cease. And there we saw a white-haired man sitting, but his face was young; we could not see his feet. On his right and on his left were four *seniores* [elders or angels] and behind them many others. And when we went in we stood with great awe before the throne, and four angels raised us up, and we kissed the man, and with his own hands he drew us up to his face. And then other angels told us to stand, and we stood, and we exchanged the peace. And the angels told us, Go and play. And they said to Perpetua, You have what you wish, and she said to me, thanks be to God.

Saturus' and Perpetua's visions can be examined as a whole. Saturus sees both of them together in the otherworld. Christ is the Good Shepherd; his flock are those who love him, particularly the martyrs. The white-haired pastor may be a combination of the Good Shepherd and the Ancient of Days (Dn 7),

---

[12] *The Passion of S. Perpetua*, trans. J. Armitage Robinson (Cambridge, 1891), 66–82.

while the cheese he offers relates to the bread of life, the Eucharist. A dream of a ladder leading up to heaven was a common sign of approaching martyrdom. Saturus, on the other hand, advances up a gentle slope. He has a philosophical conversation in a heavenly rose garden (a motif drawn from Greco-Roman elysian imagery, although his elysium is in a higher sphere than earth). The joyful (*hilares*) saints play in heaven, an image rooted both in the divine leisure of Proverbs 8 and Job 40 and in the heavenly garden of the philosophers. The sweet scent of paradise that they enjoy is found in 1 Enoch, where the tree of life exudes perfume. The fountains and pools represent baptism and renewed life.

Some elements of the *Passion* are distinctive. To be a martyr or a saint seems to transcend both gender and social status. Perpetua's lactation ceases and, no longer able to nurse, she leaves her child in the hands of her pagan father so that she herself may die for Christ. The martyrs unite as a community and become Perpetua's new and true family, recalling Jesus' words, "Here are my mother and my brothers" (Mt 12.49). Perpetua's husband does not appear in the text: in the vision literature in general, blood kin seldom greet the seer in heaven, for the ecclesia, the community of Christ, is the saint's real family.

In heaven all doubt is removed, all faith vindicated, all suffering soothed, all happiness enhanced, all loneliness transformed in the joy of community with others in the body of Christ, the living and loving union of all the faithful. In the centuries to come, Christian understanding of the otherworld would continue to open out in wider and richer metaphorical ontology.

✢ 4 ✢

Returning to God

Fᴿᴏᴍ ᴛʜᴇ second century, Christian writers, under the spell of Greek philosophy, sought a metaphysical basis for the concept of heaven. Earlier, the emphasis had been upon the experience of heaven; now it was upon the idea of heaven. When heaven became a matter of intellectual knowledge as well as of personal experience, Christian writers applied the Greek rational thought they admired to the questions of salvation: the nature of the soul and its relationship to the body, the nature of resurrection, and the nature of the return to God.

Most Christian thinkers before the fourth century shared the model of heaven enunciated by Irenaeus, but Tertullian (ca. 160–225) and his near-contemporary Origen offered striking alternative views. For different reasons, the orthodoxy of these men was questioned, and both had powerful and dangerous enemies. But there were deeper reasons than personal animosity for the tension between orthodoxy and heresy, order and dissent, in the Christian community. All movements and institutions, whether religious, political, or corporate, need two opposing qualities if they are to endure. On the one hand, they need the spirit of order, coherence, authority, and consensus, which keeps the movement from fragmenting; on the other hand, they need the spirit of dissent, inspiration, exploration, and originality, which wards off atrophy. A tree, in order to stand and flourish, needs both the unyielding structure of the inner trunk and the life-transmitting cambium layer. In societies, unlike trees, these two forces are often in conflict. Still, the life of an institution, like the life of a tree, is dependent upon both. Without dissent, the institution becomes rigid and lifeless; without order, the institution is atomized and eventually vanishes.

The struggles within the Christian community over important issues—some as central as the nature of the Trinity or the canon of Scripture—were intense, and they were necessary. They gradually formed orthodox doctrine in a discernable historical pattern. Ideas were raised, discussed, often fought over, and in that process some of them were extruded from the Christian community; other ideas, nebulous in the New Testament, were clarified and became part of the orthodox tradition. It is not possible for the historian to declare what ideas are true and what are false, but it is possible (and necessary in constructing the history of Christian thought) to determine what ideas the Christian tradition accepted as true and what it rejected as false.

As the Christian community grew in numbers and geographical range, interest in community in heaven was reinforced. Cyprian (d. 258) exclaimed over the glory and joy in heaven that will attend our meeting the fathers, apostles, prophets, and martyrs, and the pleasure we shall take (*voluptate gaudere*) in their company. Heaven is a port, a home, our native land, where we shall be reunited with those we love, and that means with everyone, for our love will be unbounded. Heaven is to be with Christ, forever, in our common homeland, amidst our friends and relations and all the lovers of God. In this life of eternal light, glowing with divine radiance, we are happy with an inconceivable joy that we know will go on forever.

Lactantius (260–330) believed that in heaven we remember our entire lives. This belief would provoke other questions in the tradition, such as whether we remember our sins and our sufferings; whether we are purged of painful memories and retain only the good ones; how that could happen without our whole personality being changed; to what extent we would then really be ourselves. What we do of good and ill, and our memories of good and ill, are inextricably intertwined in our lives; they

65

cannot be separated like pieces of a puzzle. An alternative view is that we will remember everything but without the pain or guilt, as we still see the mark of a wound that no longer troubles; we bear scars as the marks of being human, but the scars have lost their sting. We shall see not only our sin but its forgiveness, and our knowledge of the wrongness of what we have done is accompanied by the knowledge of our mutual joy with those whom we have wronged and those who have wronged us. We shall forgive by Christ's example, each confirming that he or she has no claim against anyone else.

The early writers emphasized that martyrs were in heaven, but most agreed that all baptized Christians whose lives and works bore the mark of grace were also there, as well as the Jews who were faithful to the Old Covenant before the institution of the New. Jews who failed to accept Jesus as Messiah were excluded, as were pagans and sinful Christians. (The word "pagan," which could embrace anyone from Plato to the most ignorant yokel, was invented by the Christians to exclude all beliefs and practices of people who were not Jews or Christians. Historians properly avoid the word, but since it accurately connotes the attitude of Jews and Christians toward nonbelievers I use it here.)

A special difficulty was presented by virtuous pagans who lived before the time of Christ and so had no opportunity to accept or reject him. Theologians were concerned especially about their fellow philosophers, such as Plato, who seemed to have been granted so much of the truth. Justin held for their salvation, and on the whole the fathers believed that virtuous pagans who lived before Christ are saved. God imprints the natural law upon every human mind, and some people recognize the law through the unaided and unimpeded use of their intellects. This is what Tertullian meant when he spoke of souls that are by nature Christian. Clement of Alexandria (ca. 150–215) and John Chrysostom (d. 407) said that Christ saves such persons even if they do not realize that it is he who does it. Another explanation was that God grants to certain pagans a special grace or revelation. Other theologians extended this grace to non-Christians living after the resurrection of Jesus, so long as they are sincere seekers who have no practical opportunity to learn about Christ. Origen and some of his followers may have gone even further, arguing for universal salvation. A simpler solution was apparently not entertained: Christ's sacrifice, being in eternity, is valid for all time, whether before or after him.

Tertullian, whose somewhat unorthodox views did not prevent him from being one of the most influential Latin fathers, believed that at the endtime the blessed will rise in their bodies and enjoy a thousand-year reign of Christ in the new Jerusalem rebuilt by God on earth. After the thousand years, the saved, removed to heaven, will take on the substance of angels. Millenarianism (belief in the thousand-year reign) was based on a particular reading of the Apocalypse of John and would be decisively rejected in the fifth century, yet reoccur again and again up to the present day.

Tertullian wrote the first Latin book devoted to paradise, *About Paradise*, but it has been lost. In the *Apology* he says that a barrier of fire separates heaven from the material universe. This fiery zone indicates the purging fire through which souls must pass to enter heaven. Tertullian imagined the original paradise transfigured at the endtime into the celestial paradise. Only martyrs are assured of a place in heaven. Tertullian noted the similarity between the heavenly landscape, which he called a "place of divine charm" (*locus divinae amoenitatis*) and that of Elysium. The pagans, he seemed to believe, had borrowed their ideas from the Jewish tradition.

Tertullian affirmed the resurrection yet believed that the souls of at least the martyrs go to heaven before the endtime. He affirmed the immortality of the soul (*spiritus* or *anima*). Latin writers translated Greek *pneuma* and *psychē*, and sometimes *nous*, by *anima*, *animus*, or *spiritus* without consistent distinctions. Tertullian did not intend to oppose soul to body in teaching the immortality of the soul; he meant simply to distinguish the vital principle that has left the corpse from the true personality that is the living oneness of body and spirit. The word "dead" applies only to the corpse, which has lost the vital principle (anima) that once gave it life. The soul cannot die, so the term "resurrection" can be applied only to the body.

At the resurrection, we shall have a body identical to the present one. The body is the hinge of salvation (*caro cardo salutis*). If the resurrected body is not our own earthly body, there is no point in the resurrection at all, yet if our restored flesh will no longer feel fleshly temptations, a body so freed seems more a soul than an earthly body. Tertullian had primarily sex in mind, but the elimination of sexuality would dissolve our personalities, as well as conflict with the idea that all earthly relationships will be perfected in mutual love. The fathers seldom entertained the idea of sexual intercourse in heaven, a tribute not only to Jesus' denial that there was marriage in heaven (Mk 12.25) but also to gnostic, dualist suspicion of sex. Perhaps in denying marriage in heaven Jesus, who never showed contempt for the body, meant to rebuke the exclusive possession of one person by another in heaven, where all are in love with all.

Tertullian himself elsewhere insisted that bodies, however mutilated, will recover their perfect integrity in the resurrection. If God does not raise the entire person, he cannot be said to raise the dead at all (*On the Resurrection of the Flesh*, 57). Wholeness and integrity entail lack of disease and deformity, and they ought also to entail the fulfillment of all our potentials, including parental, filial, and sexual love. Without parental and filial love, and without love between the sexes, we could scarcely be whole. Tertullian's answer was to change the meaning of "body." We will lose nothing essential in our corporeal identity, and bodies will retain characteristics such as gender, but the function of these characteristics will change. Every organ will have a function in heaven, though we cannot yet know what that will be.

Tertullian used the term *refrigerium* to denote the everlasting happiness of heaven, which the martyrs enjoy immediately at death; he coined the phrase *refrigerium interim* to denote the interim state, or "bosom of Abraham," in which other souls await the final judgment. No one, except perhaps a martyr, comes immediately at death into the presence of the Lord. The idea of an interim eventually led to the idea of purgatory, but for Tertullian the interim was not for purging but for joyful expectation of the resurrection. In the interim, souls experience joy or pain according to their characters—but not complete joy, for they lack their bodies. Tertullian fought the gnostic belief that salvation was for souls who had shed the evil body. He argued that the elect must wait for the resurrection to experience the beatific vision and fullness of joy. Christian tradition tended to follow Tertullian on this point, thus creating difficulties as to why the interim state was needed, for the personal judgment could not possibly yield results different from the final judgment, since neither the dead nor God change their minds. An effective solution—that the two moments are actually one moment in eternal or eschatological time—was for some reason found unacceptable.

The great Greek fathers of Alexandria, Clement and Origen, firmly grounded in Scripture, were also influenced by Platonism and Stoicism. Clement's affirmation of the inconsistent doctrines of salvation of the soul and salvation of the body, typical of many fathers, also intensified the problem of the interim state. Clement defined heaven as the place or state where the elect receive the vision of God, *theōria*, a kind of "seeing" or "understanding" that eventually surpasses knowledge. It is neither Platonic nor gnostic knowledge, but a divine gift of wisdom, nurtured and developed throughout a person's life.

Clement introduced the terms *theōsis* and *theopoiēsis*, "divinization," which then passed through Athanasius (d. 373) and Gregory of Nyssa (340–95) to Eastern Christianity as a whole. Both terms refer to the potential of every human being and of the Christian community in general to become divine, not in the impossible sense of participating in God's essence, but in the sense of Jesus' command to be perfected and Paul's teaching that the saved are members of Christ's body. For Clement, theosis is attained through wisdom.

The great Jewish philosopher and theologian Philo of Alexandria (20 B.C.E. to 50 C.E.) was, before his revival in eighteenth-century Judaism, more influential in Christian than in Jewish thought. Clement and Origen drew extensively on his work. Melding Greek philosophy with Jewish revelation, Philo developed an abstract idea of salvation that worked against the powerful and vivid imagery of apocalyptic tradition. Influenced though he was by the Greeks, especially Plato, Philo denied the Platonic idea that one can reach God through knowledge. God is beyond all human language. Knowledge can only help us understand that we understand nothing. God is unknowable in himself and known only in his works in the cosmos and in his relationship to us. God chooses to give that relationship to humans as a free gift, not as a right. Our response to his gift is to adhere to the Covenant. If we do, then we shall see God, not in his essence, but as he manifests himself to us. Philo distinguished between God's ousia (essence) and the energeia of his *dynameis* (manifested powers); even in heaven the just cannot see God's essence but will see God's manifestation to us. Philo held that humans had two souls—a resolution of the pneuma/psyche problem that would be rejected by Jewish orthodoxy as well as by Christianity.

Origen, the most important third-century writer on heaven, was contentious, misunderstood, and often unpopular with his contemporaries, although he had a following and later influenced the Cappadocian theologians and, still later, Cassian and Dionysius. Of all the fathers, he had the keenest sense of epistemology. Recognizing the impossibility and undesirability of attempting to understand the Bible in the overt sense only, he constructed a scheme in which Scripture was read in three senses: the somatic (overt) the psychic (moral), and the pneumatic (spiritual). This was similar to the Jewish tradition of distinguishing among *peshad*, the simple or literal meaning; *remez*, the allegorical; *derash*, the homiletical; and *sōd*, the secret meaning. Origen's schema influenced the Latin West as much as the Greek East. Rendered into Latin, his divisions were *litteralis, moralis, spiritalis*, later developed into the fourfold scheme of literal (overt), allegorical, moral, and anagogical (eschatological). In a text, the overt meaning tells what went on historically; the allegorical, what we should believe; the moral, what we should do; and the anagogical or eschatological, where it is all going. This formal scheme was a device for exploring metaphorical ontology. The contrary insistence that the overt sense of the Bible must take precedence began in the sixteenth century and intensified in the nineteenth and twentieth; it has led to many absurdities, including the assumption that revelation and science are incompatible.

Like Clement, Origen believed that humans have an inherent and natural desire to seek God, though that desire must be confirmed, enlivened, or animated by grace in order to be effective. On earth we learn through wordy enigmas, in heaven by a direct intuition, unmediated by words, symbols, and types. Origen's Platonic notion of salvation as knowledge is not the heretical gnostic view of salvation *by* knowledge. Only God's grace enables us to understand deeply both what is in nature and what is beyond nature. Even the knowledge that God grants to the saved is as nothing compared with God's own knowledge. God's knowledge utterly transcends the human capacity to know.

Our yearning for God is affective even more than it is intellectual. Origen daringly combined eros and agape, Platonic and Christian love. Eros, passionate love, usually comes to us as love for another human. Eros often transcends sexuality in devotion, sacrifice, or partnership, and it can extend to affective love of the cosmos and of its Creator. God himself is both agape (1 Jn 4.8) and eros. God desires the cosmos and draws it back to him in love. God, Love himself, engenders love in the cosmos, so that the cosmos yearns for him as he yearns for it. In theosis the blessed are glorified and become one with God. In heaven the image of God, which since the fall of Adam and Eve has been deformed, becomes a perfect realization of the divine likeness.

Another great Alexandrian, Athanasius, an influential proponent of the orthodox Trinitarian party at the First Nicene Council in 325, rejected Origen's views on the salvation of the cosmos, and others caricatured them as pantheistic. But Origen was misunderstood by writers misled by the bias of Methodius (d. 311) against him. Origen was no pantheist. He held that God exists beyond the cosmos as well as in it. God is not contained anywhere, even in heaven; he is beyond space and time. Heaven too is beyond the cosmos. In the ascent to God we shall pass above the earth and above the skies to the heavenly realm. God is not the cosmos, though the cosmos lies in God; God creates the cosmos from nothing.

Origen's doctrine of creation in his work *First Principles* expresses his complex and sometimes inconsistent view of soul and body. In the beginning, God created a number of intelligent beings, both equal and free. After creating the intelligences, God created matter. The intelligences all freely chose to depart from the divine unity, but in differing degrees, so that each sank as far away from God into matter as its choice dictated. Those that sank least remained in the ethereal realms near heaven and lived as ethereal creatures; those that sank further fell into the lower air and acquired thicker bodies. Still other intelligences fell as low as earth, where they acquired material bodies and became human.

This universe that God has created departs from him, and it will return: once fallen, each intelligence embarks on a pilgrimage back to God. Its progress back to God depends partly on its freedom and partly on providence. Human souls, like all the intelligences, are essentially immortal, since none can avoid returning to their divine source in God himself. Still, the elect, those whom God chooses, are granted more than other creatures: the fulfillment of their potential to know and love Christ in this world and the next. Origen insisted that Christ's redeeming sacrifice is necessary to salvation.

As Origen took the essence of a human being to be intelligence, the material body was not integral to his definition of a human being. A human being is composed of two essential parts: pneuma, the seed of the divinely created intelligence, and psyche, the mind in its fallen condition. These two temporarily use soma, the corporeal body. The body is a necessary vehicle, a cart that the soul uses in journeying back to God. Yet the body also blocks the soul's view of God. Origen sometimes envisioned an abandonment of matter, or at least a transcendence of matter, as the person comes back to God. The purified spirit rises above all material things to a divine vision. Though we cannot understand God as he understands himself, we shall know him to the extent of our capacity as human creatures. This full knowledge or clear vision implies the ultimate union of the seeker with the One who is sought.

Like Clement, Origen tried to combine the immortality of the soul with the resurrection of the body, which he defended vigorously. Using his sophisticated epistemology, he defended the resurrection against pagan philosophers by steering a middle course between materialism and the hyperspiritualism of the Platonists and gnostics. The essence of the body is distinct from its qualities. The unchanging essence (ousia) of the human being gives it its identity but cannot subsist except in matter. Origen also used the Platonic idea of a corporeal form (*eidos*), a term expressing the continuing identity of the earthly body with itself despite the continuous change of its material constituents from the womb to the tomb. The eidos is "the body's principle of unity, development, existence, and individuation: it shows outwardly in the features by which a person is recognized and distinguished from others."[13]

From babyhood to death, our bodies change continuously, but the unifying principle, bodily form (*sōmatikon eidos*) remains unchanged. The same is true as we continue to change after death. Death is one moment in the process of growth. The body preserves its eidos as it becomes a glorified body or soma pneumatikon. Though the resurrected body will have a different

[13] Henri Crouzel, *Origen* (San Francisco, 1985), 255.

appearance from that of the present body, the eidos assures the substantial identity of the earthly body with the glorified body. Thus bodies can decay in the earth yet be perfectly whole when resurrected. Finally, Origen employed the Stoic notion of the *logos spermatikos*, a seminal identity inherent in each human body. This logos, implanted in every body from the beginning, has the potential for growing into the glorified body. The resurrected body is as much a development of the twenty-year-old human being as the twenty-year-old is the development of the baby.

Origen sometimes held it impossible for humans to live either in this life or in the other life without their bodies. God creates bodies as the means or vehicles by which the intelligences are restored to him, and it is to restore them that Christ himself had a body. No nature except God can live without a body; no essence can manifest itself except in matter. The soul cannot be without a body. By "body" Origen sometimes meant this earthly body, sometimes a bodily vehicle of the soul between death and resurrection, and sometimes the resurrection body. After death our souls already enjoy the contemplation of God, but "the joy of Christ and the saints will not be complete until the whole [human] body is reconstituted in the heavenly Jerusalem."[14]

At some time in his life Origen may have believed that everyone would eventually be saved, an idea called "universalism" in modern thought. Origen used the term *apokatastasis*, "restoration," an idea he derived from Paul (1 Thes 4.17; 1 Cor 15.28). God brings everything into being with love and is in the process of bringing everything back to him with love. At the endtime all that God has created—the entire cosmos—returns to God and is assimilated to him. Our salvation is *aiōnios*, a term connoting eternity when applied to the Trinity or, when applied to created intelligences, perpetuity, as in the liturgical formula, *eis tous aiōnious tōn aiōniōn*, forever and ever world without end.

[14] Crouzel, *Origen*, 247.

Creatures lacking free will and intelligence return automatically to God. In the stricter sense, apokatastasis refers to the return of intelligences. Rational creatures, unlike irrational ones, have the choice of returning to God freely or of blocking his invitation. For Origen, unlike Plato, returning to God does not mean finding in ourselves the principle of reason and following it, but rather submitting to what Christ the Word (Logos) wills. Reason helps us to understand what is true and what is right, but it does not itself save the intelligences from the consequences of their initial choice to depart from God. What saves them is the cosmic fact of God's incarnation in Christ. Obedience to the Logos is not a rational process but a free act of will.

Origen subscribed to the privation theory of evil and hence could argue for the eventual salvation of all the intelligences, including the Devil. Everything that God created is good; everything that truly has existence is good. Evil does not exist as being; it exists only as lack of goodness, as holes exist in a cheese. The Devil's evil is a lack of his true nature; when his true angelic nature is restored, the evil melts away, and Satan is saved. But elsewhere Origen denied the salvation of Satan and called the idea that he believed it a mad invention of his enemies.

Theoretically the Devil might repent, but in fact his character is habituated to evil, his free will and his chance of salvation lost. If in theory it is possible to remove evil from a subject, in practice such a process would destroy the intricate wholeness of the personality. If Satan or Nero were burned clean of his evil, it would not be Satan or Nero—or Hitler or Stalin—who would be saved. The "Satan" or "Nero" restored to God would be only a characterless logos spermatikos, an irreducible seed unrecognizable as Satan or Nero. A person's character is set like a vessel drawn from the kiln. If clay that has been twisted and fired into a hideous shape is reduced to its original clay, it is recognizable only as clay, not as the hideous artifact.

Justice requires a hierarchy of reward for degrees of perfection. Sinners who need purifying will have the earthly paradise, whereas greater lovers of God will have the kingdom of heaven.

God gives some persons more potential or more grace to enjoy him than he does to others. It may be argued that all things are possible to God, and if time were infinite, perhaps all would be saved. But Origen denied both the eternity of time and the cycle of worlds. Therefore evil intelligences who are habituated to blocking God from their lives never return to him.

When the intelligences are about to return to God, they regain their pristine purity. But if that were all, there would seem no point in the whole process, nor would Christ's Incarnation have any ultimate purpose. Therefore Origen had to argue for a paradox: a return to an original state that when renewed is actually better than it was before. The concept of *reformatio in melius*, "return to a better state," appears in many cultures and institutions with historical consciousness, and it is a powerful motif in Christian thought. The celestial paradise recapitulates the original paradise but in even greater goodness and glory.

Origen's heaven is primarily an intellectual one, in which the saved soul will perceive the rational order of the cosmos as God sees it. Origen's ideas were suspect for centuries, and anti-Origenist reaction firmly established as orthodox the complete identity of the material body with the resurrected body.

❖ 5 ❖

Heaven, East and West

DURING THE fourth century two momentous innovations occurred: the Roman Empire legalized Christianity and then established it as the official religion; and monasteries became the center of Christian values and thought. With the end of persecution and martyrdom, the special honor held by martyrs in heaven was now expanded to holy monastics, both men and women. One important way in which medieval thought differed from ancient was in the approach to the classics: rather than emphasizing the overt sense of the classics, early medieval readers tended instead to compact and select them for moral, usually monastic, purposes. Monasticism centered on *metanoia* or *conversio* (transformation) through a program of asceticism designed to liberate the soul from material concerns so that it might fully open itself to God. Monastic discipline became the most common road to theosis and thus to the beatific vision.

The conversion of Rome meant that the metaphor of the Christian community as the City of Jerusalem and as the Kingdom of God was extended to the City of Rome and the Roman Empire. Christian writers considered the empire providential for the spread of Christianity, and Rome gradually became the center of the ecclesia. Still, the iconography of Christ's triumphal entry into Jerusalem on Palm Sunday, and of the entry of the blessed into heaven, was quite different from that of the imperial triumph. The Christian idea of sacral kingship was founded on Jewish, not Roman, bases (Ps 110), although it was further strengthened by both Roman and Germanic ideas of the divine ruler. At the crucial battle of the Milvian Bridge (312), Christ had given the emperor Constantine a miraculous sign, written in the sky, that the emperor would conquer. Triumph, like hierarchy, is not a theme of modern democracies, but it was a commonplace of ancient empires. The early Christians had seen the empire as the kingdom of Satan; after the empire embraced Christianity, it appeared instead as the temporal counterpart and companion of the church, with the emperor as a living representative of Christ. The political hierarchy of the imperial government corroborated and illustrated the hierarchy of heaven.

For writers between Constantine and the sack of Rome in 410, God worked his purpose in history by extending Roman rule, which brought about the Christianization of the heathen. The apparently endless triumph of the empire was assimilated to the supposedly endless rule of the church. The meaning of time is that God created the world in the beginning, redeemed it at the Incarnation, and will bring it to a triumphant end. But how would the last things come to pass? The millenarian view of some of the earlier fathers, that Christ would rule for a thousand years on earth after the Second Coming, was supplanted by the idea that Christ's reign had already begun at the Incarnation and would be fulfilled at the Judgment. Augustine's *City of God* identified the marks of the endtime: Elijah will return, and the Jews will accept Jesus as the Messiah: Antichrist will persecute the righteous and will be defeated; the dead will rise; Christ will judge all humanity; the world will be purged and renewed. Though Augustine cautioned that we have no way of knowing when or in what order these things would happen, his eschatology became the established view, and millenarianism sank into disrepute.

Theology came to the laity through sermons and the liturgy, especially through the recitations of belief first appearing in baptismal rites and then more widely and firmly fixed in the liturgy as "creeds." The creeds were intended to affirm belief in the Trinity and the church, but an important secondary concern was to insist, against gnostics, Platonists, and other skeptics, upon the resurrection of the body. The point was made again and again. "We believe that we . . . will be raised on the last day in that flesh in which we now live. . . . Not in an ethereal or in any other widely different flesh, as some assert in their foolishness, will we rise again, but, as our faith teaches, in this self-same flesh in which we live, exist, and move."[15] In fifth-century Gaul, candidates for the episcopate had to affirm that they believed in the resurrection of that very same flesh in which we now exist. These credal statements were frequently confirmed through the ages, notably by the powerful Fourth Lateran Council of 1215. Still, the unbiblical idea of immortality did not die but even flourished, because theologians who admired Greek philosophy found support there for the notion of the immortal soul but not for the Jewish concept of the resurrection of the body. The two ideas remained difficult to reconcile.

The nature of paradise was another persistent concern. Ephraim of Syria (306–73) identified the terrestrial paradise with the Temple, the Christian community, and ultimately the celestial paradise. Paradise surrounded and contained the cosmos, so that rather than "going to heaven" we are opened up to a reality that is always and everywhere. Ephraim said that the martyrs will rise with the marks of torture transformed into signs of glory. Cyril of Jerusalem (315–87) invoked an explicitly miraculous explanation of the fact that the present, earthly body itself shall rise. Our bodies do rot in the grave, *and* they will be raised with all their members by a miracle of God. Our present bodies will be glorified, so that we will no longer need food to eat or stairs to climb, and God will make our bodies shine (*splendere*; Dante would later call the blessed souls *splendori*).

About Paradise, a treatise by Ambrose of Milan (339–97), identified paradise with the heavenly Jerusalem. Ambrose

---

[15] Formula "Fides Damasi" (about 500); Letter of Pope Pelagius I (557) to Childebert I; eleventh council of Toledo (675). See Henri Denziger, *Enchiridion Symbolorum*, 31st ed. (Rome, 1960), 12–13, 110, 133.

adapted the imagery of the earthly paradise to the celestial paradise while widening the theological distinction between the two. The earthly paradise is where humans were fully human according to the body (*secundum corpus*), but the celestial paradise is where humans will be even more fully human according to the image of God (*secundum imaginem Dei*). Our joy in heaven lies in being forever joined with one another and with Christ without fear or danger of separation. Ambrose employed the erotic imagery of the Song of Songs to express the union of Christ with his community. The community is not only the invisible community of the saved but also the visible church, whose bishops and sacraments are channels of the grace that transforms us. The soul is incomplete without its body, but they are reunited at the resurrection, which guarantees the immortality of both body and soul. This scenario implied an interim between death and resurrection. In dwellings (*habitacula*) or even storehouses (*promptuaria*) the souls await with a foretaste of joy the return of their bodies at the Last Judgment.

Jerome (342–419) explained that the particular (personal) judgment of an individual at the moment of death was eternal and unalterable. He did not conclude that the particular judgment and the Last Judgment were identical, though that could have been argued in two ways: first, that in eternity the moment of an individual's death and personal judgment and the moment of the Last Judgment are one moment for God; second, that the personal and general judgments, though overtly separate, are by metaphorical ontology one and the same, for unalterable judgment occurs in the one eternal moment.

Jerome avoided such solutions. He did emphasize the communal nature of heaven: the saved are together with God and with one another. In heaven we meet those whom we loved on earth, along with Mary and all the others who love God. The ardent love we feel includes family and friends still in this life. Jerome, unconsciously betraying a bit of double motive, postulated grades of reward in heaven: "If all are equal in heaven, our humility in this life is in vain" (*Against Jovinian*, 2.33).

Christians continued to need concrete imagery as well as theological speculation, and poetry in late antiquity was rich with images of the meadows, trees, fruits, and flowers of paradise. In paradise the air is pure; it is springtime all year long, with fragrant roses and lilies and a fountain overflowing into four streams slipping over bright jewels; when a breeze stirs, the whole forest sings to God. The poetry of Prudentius (348–410) reveals the persistence of classical topoi. The soul is borne into paradise, where it dines on ambrosia and reclines on a purple couch (a metaphor especially attractive to the poor and needy). Prudentius adapted the classical banquet to the Christian themes of the Eucharist, the feast at Cana (Jn 2.1) and the multiplication of the loaves and fishes (Lk 9).

Pictorial images of Christian ideas became common from the fourth and fifth centuries onward, having been inhibited earlier by the Torah's prohibition of images, by intimidation from Roman civic religion, and by uncertainty as to how to portray the Lord. Christ is the only true image of God; human beings are created in the likeness of Christ; the likeness and image consist in reason, free will, and contemplation. But that was too airy a bread to nourish the people, many of whom were leading destitute and hungry lives; so icons of Christ, Mary, and other saints soon became a focus of worship, especially in the East.

Devotion to Mary was already well established by the fourth century, more through theology and monastic values than through popular cult. The idea of the bodily assumption of Mary goes back to the fourth century. In the fifth century, Mary's eminence was established. In 451, the crucial and definitive Council of Chalcedon, while defining Christ as both fully divine and fully human, named Mary *theotokos*: not merely mother of Jesus but Mother of God. Monastic asceticism urged reverence for Mary as Virgin as well as Mother. The idea of the assumption of the Virgin into heaven at the moment of her death was widespread in the West in the sixth century by Gregory of Tours and became as universal in the West as it was already in the East. Mary, the greatest of those whom God loves, is already bodily in heaven. The liturgical Feast of the Bodily Assumption of Mary appeared in the East in the fifth century and in the West about 700.

Ambrose and Jerome both wrote of the happy communion of the blest with Mary in heaven. Mary's place in heaven was even stronger in the East than in the West: the liturgy of John Chrysostom includes the "Magnification of Mary," Mother of God, sung after the consecration of the Eucharist:

> It is truly proper to glorify you who have borne God, the ever blessed, immaculate,and the Mother of Our God. More honorable than the Cherubim and beyond compare more glorious than the Seraphim, who a virgin gave birth to God the Word, you, truly the Mother of God, we magnify.[16]

Revered as the greatest of the saints and even higher than the angels, Mary, though always separated by an ontological gulf from the Trinity, occupies the highest place among humans in heaven. By the twelfth century, Mary, like the soul and the Christian community, was perceived as the bride of Christ. The image of Mary as queen goes back at least as far as the fifth century, reflecting the imperial theology of the Augusta (the empress), and was fortified by the theology of sacral kingship in the eighth and ninth centuries. The bodily existence of Mary in heaven combined with her royalty to make her queen of heaven under the sovereignty of her divine Son and bridegroom; this tradition was firmly established by the twelfth century.

The effusion of light around a sacred figure, found also in the iconography of other religions, entered Christian art in the third century. At that time it was limited to a halo or nimbus surrounding the head, and the only person so crowned was Christ. In the fifth century angels and saints acquired haloes. The aureola or gloriola, which shines from the outline of the entire body, also appeared around virgins, martyrs, and church fathers from

---

[16] *The Divine Liturgy of Our Father Saint John Chrysostom* (Pittsburgh, Pa., 1965).

the fifth century onward, though no theological treatment of the aureola occurred before the thirteenth century. Popular beliefs, as discerned from epigraphs, images, and sermons, were not theoretically different from those of intellectuals, but they did emphasize the concrete over the abstract. Physical images of happy repose in well-watered, fruitful, and temperate lands had wide appeal.

Among the most powerful Eastern theologians of the period were the Cappadocians Gregory of Nazianzus (330–90) and his friends the brothers Basil the Great (330–79) and Gregory of Nyssa. Their view was that God forever veils his essence (ousia) from us behind a shadow; in our ascent toward knowledge, we reach a point where the shadow blocks us. Gregory of Nazianzus said that it is characteristic of the soul to long for God with affective desire, eros. The eros penetrates deeper and deeper into the divine darkness without ever seeing clearly or reaching the center, for God has no center. No matter how we long to understand God, no matter how we long to understand the cosmos, no matter how we long to understand another human being, no matter how we long to understand ourselves, we are always frustrated. The frustration lies both in our intellect and in our love. Though even in heaven we can never comprehend the divine essence in itself, our longing will be satisfied according to our potential for understanding. We shall be united with God's energeia to the extent that our human nature can be, and we shall feel no lack. Realizing our full potential as the image of Christ, recovering the image that we distorted in our sin, we are taken up in the energeia of God and so become divine.

Gregory of Nyssa, influenced by Origen, believed that we have a divine spark within us constituting our likeness to God. Through this likeness, God draws us to him until we are united with him. Once cleansed of the mud of sin and material concerns that blurs our sight, we shall enjoy the blessed vision of God's energeia, radiant in the pure heaven of our heart. Then we shall be in ecstasy, our human nature filled with the divine qualities of glory, honor, power, and perfection. *Apokatastasis* is the return to our original paradisal nature, and it is virtually the same as *anastasis*, the resurrection of our perfected personalities in glory. Gregory of Nyssa's brother Basil of Caesarea wrote that "after the resurrection the elect will be counted worthy to behold God face to face; they will blossom like flowers in that brilliant [land], enjoying friendship with one another and with God."[17] While still in this life, we may be granted a flash of awareness of divine love; but in heaven we love with calm and unending delight.

In his *Sermons on the Incomprehensible* and other influential works, John Chrysostom (347–407) expressed the Cappadocian fathers' ideas on the beatific vision, specifying that even in heaven we can know God's *energeia* only, never his *ousia*, for God's essential nature is incomprehensible. Simple and without form, it cannot be an object of human vision.

The influence of Augustine of Hippo (354–430) in Western Christianity has been greater than that of any Christian writer since the New Testament. Aware of the limitations of the human intellect, Augustine divided theology into natural theology, akin to philosophy, with which we understand certain things without divine aid; and revealed theology, which is intellect reflecting upon the revelation of the Bible. The Bible itself is understood in four senses: the overt, allegorical, moral, and eschatological. Augustine, in trying to discern the meaning of Paul's third heaven (2 Cor 12.2), developed the view that allegorically the three heavens represent three modes of vision: *visio corporalis*, sense knowledge; *visio spiritalis*, knowledge through the imagination; and *visio intellectualis*, the intuition of substances or essences face to face. Fixing in theology the epistemology that Origen had begun, Augustine established the validity of metaphorical ontology. Earlier semantics was based upon the data of the senses, but Augustine's was based upon the language of the Bible, itself ultimately based on the Logos, the Word of God. The way to God is less through the intellect than through intui-

[17] J.N.D. Kelly, *Early Christian Doctrines* (London, 1958), 486.

tion and less through intuition than through affective love
(*amor*). Love is not merely *from* God; God *is* Love, both affective and selfless love, and the Holy Spirit is Love proceeding
from the mutual love of Father and Son.

Heaven is Christ himself, and to be fully with Christ is to be
fully in heaven. When we die, God will be our place. And that
place is eternity. Augustine moved beyond the idea of eternity as
perpetuity or endless time (*aiōn*; *seculum*) to the idea of a transcendent eternity, ever present, ever here, ever open to those
who yearn for it. This eternity is the celestial paradise, which
Augustine distinguished sharply from the terrestrial paradise.
The celestial paradise, which he called "paradise of paradises,"
is both eternal and eschatological. It is the fulfillment at the end
of time, the sabbath of sabbaths, an eighth day of creation when
we shall "rest and see, see and love, love and praise."[18] With his
strong sense of history and development, Augustine insisted that
the paradise at the end of time is a *reformatio in melius*: it will
restore, yet be superior to, that at the beginning of time. In the
first paradise we had freedom to sin or not to sin, but in the
eternal paradise we are so wedded to God that we lack even
the ability to sin.

This impossibility of sinning in no way abrogated freedom of
the will. After all, God is free even though his nature makes it
impossible for him to sin. It is by free will that we make the
eternal, unchangeable choice to sin no more. As God's nature
freely draws him to embrace us, so our nature, once released
from sin, freely draws us to embrace him. It is a truly free, and
entirely unshakable, embrace.

We shall see and recognize the resurrected bodies of those
whom we love, though those bodies will be finer than those they
had on earth. So fine will they be that the saved fill the gaps in
the angelic ranks left by the fall of Lucifer and his followers.
Augustine did not himself mean that we actually become angels,
but Gregory the Great (540–604) thought so, and eighteenth-

---

[18] *City of God*, trans. Marcus Dods (New York, 1950), 867.

century pietists would revive this minority tradition that humans become angels when they "go to heaven." For Augustine, the angels are our fellow citizens, joyfully awaiting our arrival. We shall be equal to the angels in immortality and happiness, but angels, since they cannot die, need no resurrection themselves. Augustine, translating Paul's Greek *sarx/soma* distinction into a Latin *caro/corpus* distinction, takes *caro* (flesh) and *sanguis* (blood) as referring to the body corrupted by its domination by sin, and *corpus* as something capable of being reformed and transmuted into a heavenly body (*corpus celeste*). Heaven is being where Christ is, and it is being with Christ together with others, forming a holy community or body of the saved, the ecclesia. The ecclesia is the body of Christ, not just here and now, but always and in the whole world from Adam to those yet unborn, the whole people of the blest who belong to the one city, the city that is Christ's body.

Augustine's greatest work, completed shortly before his death, as Dante's was shortly before his, is *The City of God*. Human society, by metaphor a city, is a city where the good and the evil live commingled and where one can never securely judge the interior state of any person. More real than this city, however, are two underlying cities, one the "city of this world" (or of the Devil), the annihilating anti-abode of those who are not saved, and the other the city of God, the community of those who are. The kingdom of heaven is the final realization of the city of God. Under Augustine's influence, the city became the standard metaphor in the West, while *basileia* (the kingdom of God) remained standard in the East. The communion of saints is the bond between the free citizens of the polis, civitas, respublica, congregatio, of heaven. And it is as this society, this communion, rather than as individuals, that we are saved. The celestial Jerusalem is the Christian community in all its realized potential. In heaven we are all equal in that we are all fulfilled as to our own potential and talents. But some gifts are greater than others, so that some persons, by virtue of their merits, shine more brightly in heaven than others. No one will envy another, for each will be content to desire no more than he or she has. Equality is compatible with hierarchy, for no one will lack anything essential to perfect happiness and perfect fulfillment as the image of Christ. We shall be conformed to Christ's image, not in that we shall resemble his features, but in that we shall be perfected human beings.

Augustine confirmed the resurrection of this earthly body. The exact same flesh that used to eat and drink and feel pain, and now lies in its grave, will rise again, but the flesh of the resurrected body will be different in that it will be incorruptible. Augustine had to face the mockery of nonbelievers still asking whether aborted fetuses rise, whether we shall rise with all the hair and fingernails that we have ever grown, whether those who have been eaten by cannibals will rise as themselves or as the cannibals who incorporated their flesh, whether our excrement will be restored to us. Augustine knew that the skeptics brought these subjects up for the purpose of ridicule, and he might have evaded them with a purely allegorical interpretation of the resurrection, but neither his faithfulness to Scripture nor his sense of history permitted that. He had to affirm the resurrection in the overt sense as well as the allegorical, and to do that he had to address such hostile questions seriously.

The resurrection itself is a miracle, and nothing can limit a miracle of God. Whatever the state of the body on this earth—decomposed, burnt, devoured—it will rise whole. But God works his miracles according to his own plan, not according to human reason. Wholeness is that which is appropriate to a person in his or her most fulfilled state. Accumulations of excrement or fingernails would detract from the perfected state and so will not be restored. The resurrection bodies of the saved will be perfect and entire, with all their limbs and organs, and only what is ugly, deformed, or superfluous will disappear. Every proper thing that is lacking will be restored: amputated feet, diseased lungs, deprived minds. The only exception is that the martyrs will bear their wounds as marks of honor and beauty. This implied that white people will rise white, blacks black. Men rise

as men, women as women, all in their prime. Children and fetuses rise perfected. They "receive by the marvelous and rapid
operation of God that body which time by a slower process
would have given them," and in the perfect fullness of their potential.[19] The age of our prime vigor is about thirty, Christ's age
when he began to preach, and in that bodily prime we shall also
possess all the wisdom of age and experience.

All members and organs of the resurrected body, which now
we see to be suited to various necessities, will have their own
special uses in heaven, though what these are Augustine refrains
from stating. The resurrected are able to eat or run but have no
need to. They are, after all, *somata pneumatika*, which have
every power of our earthly bodies and more—for example, the
ability to move anywhere in the cosmos in a moment.

Augustine distinguished between knowing (*intellegere*) and
seeing (*videre*). We cannot know God in himself, but we can in
some way see him. Early in life, Augustine rejected as absurd the
idea that we shall see him with physical eyes. Our earthly eyes
see God only darkly though a mirror, but our resurrected eyes
will have an unmediated ability to see God, just as the mind will
have an unmediated ability to understand him. This power in
our resurrected eyes and mind is a spiritual power, a miracle.
The beatific vision is a grace given to the deepest part of the
personality, which enables us to find our true selves in God. The
vision is a fusion of love and knowledge and surpasses both. It
is given as an ecstasy only briefly and to few in this life. Both in
this life and in the other it is beyond bodily vision, beyond symbolism; it is a direct vision of God granted to a human mind that
has been elevated to it by grace. Heaven is the ultimate realization of vision without defect and of love without weakening.
Love is bound with intellect in vision, which is not passive reception but an activity of the character. Vision is a dynamic circuit
between that which sees and that which is seen. By extension, all
understanding is a kind of vision, an active dynamic.

[19] *City of God*, 837.

A complication that Augustine inherited unresolved from the Book of Revelation is the question of the two deaths and two resurrections. On this, as on many points, his view shifted, but his mature opinion was that death, which is the temporary separation of body and soul, must be seen as the death of both. This is the first death. By the first resurrection, he meant revival of the soul by Christ's grace, an event experienced only by the saved and equivalent to baptism, metanoia, or conversio; the second resurrection, at the end of the world, is of the body and is for both the saved and the lost. The second death is the eternal ruin of the bodies and souls of the lost.

Soul and body are temporarily separated at death. The particular or personal judgment occurs immediately, and it is exactly the same as the judgment the person receives at the endtime. After the personal resurrection, the damned soul enters immediately into punishment, the saved soul into heaven. The soul's enjoyment of heaven will be enhanced at the resurrection of the body. In the interim the souls are at rest (*requies*) in the earthly paradise, awaiting the time when they shall receive their bodies again. They will have the vision of God right away after the personal judgment, though their joy will not be complete before body and soul are again united. Augustine's endorsement of the interim state fixed it finally as the dominant view.

Heaven is God within us as well as God above us: to go up we must go down and find God at the center of our true being. Heaven is blessedness and joy (*beatitudo, gaudium*), the complete fulfillment of intellect and will, of knowledge and love. Love (*amor, dilectio, desiderium*) is essential to Augustine's "seeing." Yet an essential difference exists between his view of love and that of his Eastern contemporaries. Perhaps in reaction to his own early intense experience of sexuality, Augustine's view of the vision and of love emphasized *caritas* (selfless love, the Latin translation of Greek *agapē*) more than *amor*, or, rather, interpreted *amor* as *caritas*. Unlike Origen and Ambrose, Augustine in all his vast work never wrote a commentary on the Song of Songs. In Augustine the underlying tension between erotic imagery and the monastic ideal of asceticism came close to the surface. Nonsexual, nonphysical, views of amor would now predominate in the West until the twelfth century, never, however, eliminating the affective and erotic undercurrent and never creating the alleged soul/body dichotomy often imposed on the Middle Ages by modern writers.

The Western Christian tradition is that the blessed see the Trinity, Father, Son, and Holy Spirit, face to face, to the extent that human finitude permits such a vision. We shall always seek more, and be granted more, without end. Heaven is dynamic, not static. But though God is infinite, our own potential is not. We cannot know God to the extent that he knows himself. We shall reach the ultimate fulfillment of our potential, and we shall know God to the greatest extent that we can know him. We shall see the Trinity as it is, but we can never comprehend it entirely, since God's transcendence goes beyond even our glorified understanding. Though bound tightly and eternally to God and to the other lovers of God by the free choice of our living, loving will, we shall never become one with him. The essence of salvation for Augustine was the restoration to humans of the original similitude or image (Augustine did not sharply distinguish between the two) of the Trinity. From this Dante would draw the final image of the *Divine Comedy*.

1. The heavenly Jerusalem. *Apocalypse of Cambrai* (ninth century).

2. Heavenly paradise. *Beatus Apocalypse* (926).

4. The heavenly Jerusalem as a city. *Liber floridus,*
(ca. 1200).

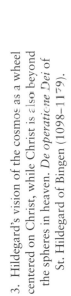

3. Hildegard's vision of the cosmos as a wheel
centered on Christ, while Christ is also beyond
the spheres in heaven. *De operatione Dei* of
St. Hildegard of Bingen (1098–1179).

5. St. Peter welcoming souls to heaven. Wall painting from Östra
Vemmerlov, Skäne, Sweden (fourteenth century).

6. Angels and saints worship Christ as the Lamb of God. Hubert and
Jan van Eyck, *The Mystic Adoration of the Lamb* (1432).

7. The terrestrial paradise. The Limbourg Brothers, *Très Riches Heures du Duc de Berry* (1410).

8. The coronation of the Virgin. The Limbourg Brothers, *Très Riches Heures du Duc de Berry* (1410).

9. Master of the Upper Rhine, *The Garden of Paradise* (ca. 1410).

10. Angels and saints praising the resurrected Jesus. Fra Angelico (fl. 1417–55), *Christ Glorified in the Court of Heaven.*

della uagina delle menbre sue
Duuma uirtu se mire presta
tanto che lonbra del beato regnio
segniata nel mio capo manifesta

11. Dante invokes Apollo. Giovanni di Paolo, illustration to the
Divine Comedy (ca. 1440).

pelle dellume suo poco sinbranca
t in sua diguita mai nō riuene
se nō rienpie doue colpa uota
cōtra mal delectar con giuste pene.

12. Beatrice explains to Dante the mystery of the Redemption. Giovanni di Paolo,
illustration to the *Divine Comedy* (ca. 1440).

13. The calling of the elect to heaven. Luca Signorelli (ca. 1441–1523). Detail from the Duomo, Orvieto, Italy.

14. The heavenly paradise as a walled garden. Follower of Robert Campin, *Madonna and Child with Saints in the Enclosed Garden* (ca. 1440–60).

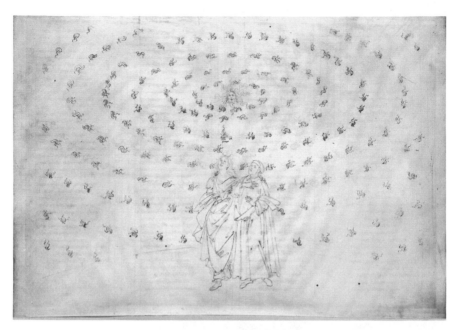

15. Dante and Beatrice before St. Peter. Sandro Botticelli (1444–1519), illustration to *Paradiso* XXIV.

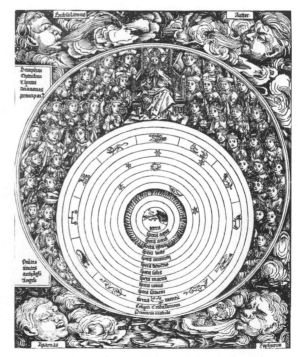

16. God enthroned with angels above the cosmos. *Nuremberg Chronicle* (1493).

17. The golden age at the beginning of the world recapitulated in the heaven at the end of the world. Lucas Cranach the Elder (1472–1553), *The Golden Age.*

18. Scenes from the earthly paradise. Lucas Cranach the Elder, *Garden of Eden* (1530).

∻ 6 ∻

Visions of Heaven

DURING THE sixth through ninth centuries, connections between Eastern and Western Christianity, though gradually attenuated, still allowed for the interchange of ideas. Both in East and West, monasteries were virtually the only centers of learning. Rejecting the earthly hierarchies of emperors, popes, kings, and bishops, monks developed a hierarchy based upon holiness, which they identified with asceticism and therefore with monasticism. Monastic accounts of the endtime in which monks and nuns enter heaven before other saints were common.

The greatest influence on early medieval spirituality was a Syrian monk writing around the year 500; because he was incorrectly believed to be the Athenian whom Paul had converted in the Areopagus, he is known as "Pseudo-Dionysius the Areopagite." The author of the term *theologia mystikē*, "mystical theology," Dionysius distinguished between positive and negative theology. Positive, kataphatic theology emphasizes what the intellect can know about God; negative, apophatic theology emphasizes what the intellect is unable to know about God. Dionysius showed how the negative way not only undermines the positive but is itself undermined: we can know neither what God is nor what he is not. "Now we should not conclude that the negations are simply the opposites of the affirmations, but rather that the cause of all is considerably prior to this, beyond privations, beyond both every denial and every assertion."[20] He

[20] *Mystical Theology*, trans. Colm Luibheid, in *Pseudo-Dionysius* (Mahwah, N.J.: 1987), 136.

used the Greek word *hyper*, "above" or "beyond," attempting to transcend both negative and positive discourse with a hyper-discourse surpassing both.

Dionysius combined the idea of our kinship with God with the understanding that God is wholly other. God is completely beyond anything that we might understand about him, partly because our own reason is tiny and restricted, but more because he is himself beyond all reason. In order to be taken up in union with the divine reality that underlies appearances, we must strip all predicates away from God; we must renounce knowledge in order to understand; we must give ourselves over to longing. Whatever we say about God is metaphorical, and Dionysius preferred metaphors of distance and otherness in order to lessen the danger of confusing substance with shadow. It is safer to call God a stone than fire or fire than Perfect Beauty, for the reason that the closer we get to the truth, the more we forget we are using metaphor. Only God could give us a credible account of what he is, so that all we know certainly about him is what he has revealed through the Bible.

Dionysius' views, firmly rooted in both Old and New Testaments, developed from the Cappadocian emphasis on theosis and from Clement and Origen's emphasis on metaphor. God is what is. God chooses to pour himself forth, thus creating the cosmos, which is God's own stuff and yearns to be reunited with him, and which he yearningly draws back to himself. Since there is nothing but God, the cosmos exists immersed in God. Dionysius subsumed agape under eros. Human minds, misshapen by sin, are unable to understand the secret at the heart of the world, which is simple: it is the mutual longing between God and cosmos.

Dionysius developed and extended Origen's conception of eros. Eros produces uplifting and then return. God is Eros, Love itself, and the response of the cosmos to God is eros. Physical attraction is eros, and Dionysius quotes the Song of Songs, the Wisdom of Solomon, and the Second Book of Samuel to press the point: "Your love to me was wonderful, passing the love of women" (2 Sm 1.26). Dionysius, like other mystics, neither ignored sex nor dramatized it. Physical love is a vibrant shadow of the real Eros (*ho ontos eros*), the true Eros (*ho alēthēs eros*). "This Divine Yearning brings ecstasy so that the lover belongs not to self but to the beloved."[21]

Everything in the cosmos has been poured out from God, and every creature's vital instinct and yearning is to reunite with God, who is Beauty, Love, and Truth. God draws all things toward him, and with that motion he also draws them together with one another in a state of mutual wholeness. Humans have the great privilege of being free to accept or to reject God. Animals and plants are closer to God in that they are not alienated from him, but humans are more divine, because of our place in the ontological scale and, especially, because of the Incarnation. Through divine grace, which Dionysius calls Light, Christ transforms our souls and unites us in one true, pure, coherent knowledge.

This knowledge is an understanding entirely beyond normal human knowledge; Dionysius, like other monks and like Dante later, speaks of it in terms of "seeing." In heaven the blest will be "filled with the light of God shining gloriously around us as once it shone for the disciples at the divine transfiguration. And there we shall be, our minds away from passion and from earth, and we shall have a conceptual gift of light from [God], and somehow, in a way we cannot know, we shall be united with him and, our understanding carried away, blessedly happy, we shall be struck by his blazing light."[22]

The return to God is directional and hierarchical. God is above, and the cosmos is ranged beneath him, with each thing striving upward toward him. As animals are above stones, so humans are above animals and angels above humans. All creatures yearn to commune with their equals; higher creatures yearn for the things below so as to deepen their communion

[21] *The Divine Names*, trans. Colm Luibheid, in *Pseudo-Dionysius* (Mahwah, N.J., 1987), 82.
[22] *Divine Names*, 52–53.

with them. Thus the higher draw up the lower with love just as God draws the cosmos as a whole up with love. God's longing fills the creatures of the universe that he has made with an impulse toward "mutual harmony and communion . . . in accordance with the natural laws and qualities of each and without any confusion or intermingling of their characteristics."[23] All things are drawn to God; all creatures merge with God and with other creatures, yet in that merging do not cease to be what they essentially are. All creatures will be joyfully content with each other and with God.

The Greek monk Maximus Confessor (580–662) modified Dionysius' thought to make it more Christocentric. God is the heart of the cosmos, and the cosmos is a window through which we catch a glimpse of God. Our reason for being is theosis, which God's grace will complete for us in heaven. If our free will responds to grace with love, the Holy Spirit brings us into union with God. Through Christ's mediation we become divine on the model of the union of God and man in Christ himself, since we merge with God without losing our own character.

The Ladder, a book by another monk, John Climacus (570–649), makes a distinctively monastic argument for the combination of asceticism and eros. Physical love is a sign of our longing for God: our spirits long for God as the lover for the body of his beloved. The inherent goodness of earthly eros can be directed toward God through the practice of an ascetic life. The point of asceticism is to detach us from earthly desires, even those that are good in themselves, in order to open ourselves to the great eros of God, which embraces and transcends all other loves. Climacus urged the cultivation of *apatheia*, dispassion about and withdrawal from worldly matters. This dispassion is true eros, for it is our longing for personal relationship with Eros itself. Climacus' ascetic program, far from being hostile to the body, was designed for the fulfillment of the body. Body and eros are integrated in their yearning for God.

[23] *Divine Names*, 111.

Gregory the Great, monk and pope, had the authority to teach Christian society at large through his numerous pastoral books, letters, and sermons. He distinguished between *amor* (love) and *desiderium* (desire). Desire is unfulfilled longing and thus entails frustration, anxiety, and pain; love is the state of being fulfilled by the beloved. Mortals on earth desire God, but only in heaven will their desire be fulfilled in love. Angels have a desire that lacks the qualities of frustration, anxiety, and pain, because they are already fulfilled in the presence of God.

The soul is naturally immortal, because it can never cease to live; it is supernaturally mortal, because it can die to God through sin and alienation. The body is naturally mortal, because it perishes; it is supernaturally immortal when resurrected to salvation. There are two kinds of death, the natural (what we ordinarily call death) and the supernatural. At natural death, the soul is separated from the body. At that moment, the soul undergoes a particular, personal judgment. Soul and body remain separated in the interim before the Second Coming, and during the interim the souls of the blest enjoy the beatific vision. After the Second Coming of Christ, the body is resurrected, and the soul is reunited with it. Christ will judge the living and the dead in the Last Judgment, which will confirm the particular judgment. Then the souls of those who are saved will enjoy greater perfection through the restoration of their bodies. The reunited body and soul live forever with God.

The body we rise in is our present body. The resurrected body cannot be aerial or ethereal: "how can there be a true resurrection if there cannot be true flesh?" (*Moralia*, 14.56). Gregory did not hesitate to use the metaphor of erotic marriage: the elect are united with God in the bridal chamber. Our bodies will be the same as our present bodies in nature but different in their glory. This glorified body will shine with clarity while retaining its distinctive characteristics.

Some had argued that at out natural death we must wait for heavenly bliss until the resurrection. But Gregory confirmed the view that the soul enjoys the beatific vision after natural death and before the resurrection of the body. We await our bodies in bliss. Souls enjoy immediate bliss, which is continually enhanced, especially by the resurrection. Gregory differentiated between those who died before the coming of Christ and those who died after. No soul could enter heaven in the time before the Incarnation (except for Enoch and Elijah). The souls of the righteous who had died before Christ were not saved until Holy Saturday. Christ died on Good Friday; on the day before his Easter Sunday resurrection, he descended into hell and raised them up to eternal life.

A soul, once judged, is fixed in that judgment for eternity. This is not because God is inflexible but because the person had built an essential and unchanging character by the choices made in life. Those who are free from serious sin ascend immediately into bliss; others must undergo a moment, or perhaps a brief period, of purgation.

Immediately at death, the blessed see God clearly in both his essence and nature. This authoritative confirmation of earlier Western views banished from most subsequent Western thought the Eastern distinction between ousia and energeia. In God, essence and act, nature and glory, are one. Still, Gregory did make a distinction. He knew that the mind, even when supernaturally aided, is not capable of comprehending God fully. Neither we nor the angels are able to see God in the manner in which he sees himself. The blessed can never "exhaust the richness of this vision" (*Moralia*, 4.25). Joy is eternal, and complete and whole and perfect, yet it is incremental in that it keeps on deepening and opening. "Our thirsting will be satisfied, yet having been satisfied, we shall thirst" (*Moralia*, 18.54). The dynamic, inexhaustible, progressive joy of heaven, ever greater, is a recurrent theme in the Christian imagination, culminating in the vision of Dante.

The vision of God is full delight, but it brings with it other joys. As intellectual creatures, we shall have our intellects satisfied, and we shall know, not in a temporal sequence, but in the eternal moment. In eternity we shall know what, in time, we call the past, present, and future. We shall understand the cosmos in a manner and to a degree we have not imagined, and we shall see everything that is possible for our natures to understand. Faith and hope are no longer needed, and only love endures. Our souls, now purged, will remember our sins but will place them in the context of our redemption and with the freedom from pain brought by knowledge of their forgiveness. Pain is transformed by joy into mirth.

Socially, heaven is both horizontal and vertical. The saved fill the places vacated by the fallen angels and become the peers of the holy angels (though remaining generically separate from them). Yet although each is as happy as his or her potential allows, some have more capacity for love and joy than others. Gregory sometimes held that we are rewarded according to the works that we have performed through grace, but at other times he argued for what seem to be inherent differences: between monks and laity, for example, or between men and women. At any rate no one will feel any lack or any inferiority.

Heaven is the perfected community of Christ's body, in which the joy of each adds to the joy of each and so constantly expands. The joy of each spreads out its ripples of light to an uncountable number of points of intersection, ripples of fire meeting and sparking. As we love all, so shall we recognize all; we shall recognize not only friends and family but those we knew only by reputation, and those of whom we knew nothing at all. The good shall know the good in heaven, as the evil shall know the evil in hell.

But here Gregory, following Augustine, drew a harsh corollary. The good shall also know the evil; they shall know that the evil suffer eternally from the lack of the presence of love. "No mercy affects the minds of the elect" in heaven, because "they see the justice of the punishment of the damned and cannot regret it. Further, if they desired something that was not, they would desire something against God's will, and their beatitude would be lessened" (*Moralia*, 6.30).

Gregory saw the communion of saints as the heavenly assembly of joy, a joy reflected on earth in the liturgy and in the sacraments. Each Holy Communion, each Eucharistic feast, is a shadow of the feast to come. Heaven is our homeland (*patria*), the land of our Father (*Pater*), and the city of God (*superna civitas*).

Gregory's popular *Dialogues* reported visions of heaven experienced by people while still in this life. A soldier in Rome smitten by the plague eventually revived and recounted what he had seen of judgment, hell, and heaven.

> Across the bridge there were green and pleasant meadows carpeted with sweet flowers and herbs. In the fields groups of white-clothed people were seen. Such a sweet scent filled the air that it fed those who dwelt and walked there. The dwellings of the blessed were full of a great light. A house of amazing capacity was being constructed there, apparently out of golden bricks, but he could not find out for whom it might be.[24]

Gregory specified that the vision should be understood in the symbolic sense: for example, the house of gold indicates that people generous in almsgiving are building themselves "golden houses," that is, glorious abodes, in heaven. Still, the frequent confirmation and repetition of such imagery by theologians, poets, and artists lent it such strength that it was often taken in the overt sense.

Other authoritative writers of the period reported similar visions. Gregory of Tours (540–94) told of Saint Salvius, an abbot who after being revived from death in 584 recounted to his monks what he had seen. He had risen into the skies, where he looked down upon the earth, which appeared sad and dark, and also upon the clouds, sun, moon, and stars. Two angelic guides led him through a shining door into a room whose ceiling

---

[24] My modification of the translation by Carol Zaleski, *Otherworld Journeys: Accounts of Near Death Experience in Medieval and Modern Times* (New York, 1987), 29.

gleamed in gold and silver; the room was endless in size, the light within it pure. Countless people of both sexes were walking about in it. The angels placed Salvius upon a cloud shining with a brilliant white light; here dwelt the martyrs and confessors. Salvius now heard a voice speaking as the sound of great waters and telling him that for the sake of the Christian community he had to return to life and tell what he had seen. The voice, as well as the vision, of God, a dominant theme in the Old Testament (Hebrew Bible), now became a powerful theme in Christian literature.

Bede (673–735) reported a vision of Drythelm, a Northumbrian layman who upon being revived from death told his wife what he had experienced in the otherworld. Drythelm met an angel who showed him hell. Afterward, Drythelm and his angelic guide traveled east into a land of clear light, where they saw a wall of immeasurable length and height, without door, window, stairs, or ladder. Drythelm found himself atop the wall, from which he saw a vast and magnificent meadow full of flowers and perfumes, where the light was greater than that of the sun. A happy throng clothed in white was walking in this garden. The angel explained that this garden was not heaven. Whether deliberately or not, Drythelm—or Bede—firmly set aside the old model of heaven as Eden, the earthly paradise. The garden is where, according to Drythelm's account, souls who are basically good but need purification before entering heaven await the final resurrection. Approaching the kingdom of heaven itself, Drythelm heard sweet singing and enjoyed a fragrance and light even more glorious than before.[25] Such images were repeated and embellished by the prolific vision literature that followed in later centuries, culminating in Dante's *Divine Comedy*.

John Scottus Eriugena (810–77), a great philosopher at the court of the West Frankish king, translated into Latin works by the Greek theologians Gregory of Nyssa and Maximus Con-

---

[25] Summary from Zaleski, *Otherworld Journeys*, 32.

fessor; especially important was his translation of Dionysius. Later, Eriugena wrote a powerful work of his own, *On the Division of Nature*, under Dionysius' influence. Through Eriugena's translation and adaptation of Dionysius, the apophatic mystical tradition was absorbed and digested in the West and never again lost, even during the rationalist rule of scholasticism. Eriugena's strong apophatic sense had important corollaries. We can know nothing of God himself; his essence is totally beyond our understanding. Indeed, we can understand nothing at all on our own. To understand is not to analyze or to "know about" but rather to be embraced by, and thus illumined by, God. We do not understand the poppy by plucking and dissecting it, but by being embraced by it, by its poppiness, and through it by God, who has brought it forth from himself. Though we cannot know the divine essence, God shows us his energeia, his manifested nature in the cosmos, through all that comes from him. Every creature is a theophany, a manifestation of God. Our minds cannot clamber up to God, but God condescends, accommodates to us, catches us up to him in his love for us. Love, not intellect, raises us. Human love ascends to meet God's mercy descending, and mercy and love embrace.

The whole cosmos is a theophany. Owing to our divine image and likeness, God shines forth through humans more and differently than through other creatures. Most of all he shines forth through those who accept and love him and open their ears and minds to him. This is how Eriugena interpreted the Eastern idea of theosis. We become divine by opening ourselves up to God's love, which expands within us throughout this life and then on and on forever.

The apophatic theology that we can know nothing about God and that the loving will is the truest way to approach God was now imbedded in Christian thought. Affective love was always alive in the monastic tradition and would bloom again lavishly later in the Middle Ages among the Cistercians and Franciscans.

❖ 7 ❖

Journeys to Heaven

IN THE eighth and ninth centuries the cultural power of the monasteries, and some of their creative genius, declined, and the urban culture that in the twelfth century would replace monastic culture was still in embryo. Impressions of heaven came both from "above" (the clergy and theologians) and from "below" (popular culture). Though popular impressions were mainly derived from theology, notions originating in Celtic and Germanic sources also exerted an influence. The increasing power and prestige of the bishops as compared with that of the monasteries advanced the identification of heaven with the hierarchical church. Jerusalem was still the heavenly dwelling of angels and the saved, but some theorists, especially bishops, preferred to take it as the model of the pilgrim church, the church on earth, which could easily be molded to mean the structured institution that the bishops dominated.

In these centuries when missionaries, popes, and Frankish rulers cooperated in the effort to create a viable Christian society based on episcopal, royal, or imperial authority, the metaphorical equation of heaven with the earthly church grew. By the church on earth, most writers still meant the invisible church rather than the institutional church. The invisible church consists of true Christians, those in this life whose characters are turned toward God, who are part of the body of Christ, and who, upon death, will see God. Many on earth who claim to be Christians, including ecclesiastical authorities, are hypocrites and are not members of this true, invisible church. But the elision from the invisible church to the "visible church," the institutional church of bishops and kings, was an easy conceptual slide, encouraged by zeal for structure and order. A hierarchy of bishops and lay rulers gradually displaced the ascetic hierarchy of the monks. Against this trend some monastic reformers, such as Peter Damian (1007–72), explicitly called for the reestablishment of the hierarchy of holiness. Their eventual success would appear in the later growth of mystical, apophatic theology and in Dante's preference in the *Paradiso* for the contemplatives.

Affective theology still thrived in the monasteries. Paschasius Radbert of Corbie (790–865) wrote that his soul was so filled with love for God that it melted him. Paschasius and Peter Damian both understood that the eschatological kingdom dissolved space and time and that what is true at the end is true in eternity and therefore also true in the beginning. In Damian's *Poem on the Glory of Paradise*, the Sabbath, which is the Kingdom, is God's Day, the first Day, the end Day, and the eternal Day, when time is timeless and place placeless.

Though most poets and theologians were still to be found in monasteries, and monastic metaphor was still dominant, monastic influence was being challenged both by growing episcopal authority and by the deliberate revival of Roman forms and images by Alcuin (735–804) and Theodulf (750–821) at the court of Charlemagne. There were three periods of pronounced Greco-Roman influence in the Christian West before the Renaissance: that of the original Roman culture, that of the Carolingian revival, and that of the twelfth-century revival. Theodulf, for example, carefully recombined heavenly and "pagan" images, writing of the happy countryside of heaven, its rich and fruitful fields, the Tree of Life in the middle of the shady, flowered Elysian meadow. It was not his intent to repaganize heaven but rather to recapture for it the rich metaphors of the classics.

Later, classical motifs became far more self-conscious. When Andrew the Chaplain, writing at the end of the twelfth century, described the Garden, he explicitly intended the classical Garden of Venus rather than Eden. But even in that period, such was the authority of monastic affective and erotic metaphor that the poetry of love returned to the Christian heaven by way of Francis of Assisi (1182–1226), the mystical theologians, and Dante. Andrew feigned a visionary journey to the Garden of Venus along the lines of traditional visionary voyages to heaven. We came, he wrote,

> to a most delightful spot, where the meadows were very beautiful and more finely laid out than mortal had ever seen. The place was closed in on all sides by every kind of fruitful and fragrant trees, each bearing marvelous fruits according to its kind. Now in the middle of the first and innermost part stood a marvelously tall tree, bearing abundantly all sorts of fruits, and its branches extended as far as the edge of the interior part. At the roots of the tree gushed forth a wonderful spring of the clearest water, which to those who drank of it tasted of the sweetest nectar, and in this spring one saw all sorts of little fishes. Beside the spring, on a throne made of gold and every sort of precious stones, sat the Queen of Love, wearing a gorgeous crown on her head, dressed in very costly robes, and holding a golden scepter in her hand. At her right hand was prepared a seat that glowed with everything costly and bright, but no one was sitting on it. This section, the inner one, was called "Delightfulness," because in it every sort of pleasant and delightful thing was to be found. And in this inner part were prepared a great many couches, marvelously decorated and completely covered with silken coverlets and purple decorations. From the spring I have mentioned many brooks and rivulets flowed out in all directions, watering the whole of Delightfulness, and every couch had a rivulet by it.[26]

The earliest important vernacular literature was in Old English and Old Irish. The Celtic and Germanic languages were original and rich in their own vocabularies and metaphors for heaven. A large trove of English terms related to heaven,

---

[26] Andreas Capellanus, *The Art of Courtly Love*, transl. John Jay Parry (New York, 1941), 78–79.

including *uplyft* (upper air or sky), *ceaster* (fort, city), *heofon-ham* (heaven-house), *heofonheall* (great hall or court of heaven), *heofonsetl* (residence or throne), *upeard* (land above), *wyn-land* (wineland), *heofonrice* (heaven-kingdom) *heofonwuldor* (heavenglory), *wuldorthrymm* (glory-majesty), *wuldorfaest* (glorious cloister), *wuldordream* (glory-delight). Words such as *wlite* (brightness, beauty), *wynsum* (pleasant) and *wuldor* (glory) were used of God, of the original paradise, and of eternal heaven. Heaven is *wlitig* and *wynsum* or *wuldres wlite*.[27]

Vision literature appeared in increasing profusion. Both before and after the twelfth century, hell was more in evidence than heaven in the visions, yet the positive and encouraging was almost always present and was seldom overwhelmed. The heavenly Jerusalem was still a favorite model, but others persisted, and owing to the revival of physical cosmology and astronomy, the model of the celestial spheres came to dominate the twelfth century and beyond.

The most influential vision of the ninth century was that of Wetti, a German monk who died in 824; it was recorded by one Heito soon after Wetti's death. In Heito's version, Wetti has an angel guide who shows him hell and purgatory. And though such places are to be understood chiefly metaphorically, the immediacy of the visions lent vigor, color, and a sense of reality to hell, purgatory, and heaven. Wetti passes most of his vision time in places of pain, though eventually he is shown a place with chests of silver and gold and beautiful sculptures. There Wetti sees a great procession of the blessed, led by the Lord. The Lord shines with such majesty and glory that the human eye cannot see, the mind grasp, or the tongue report it. Thirteen years later

---

[27] Jane Roberts, "A Preliminary 'Heaven' Index for Old English." In *Sources and Relations: Studies in Honour of J. E. Cross*, Leeds Studies in English Series 16 (Leeds, 1985), 208–19; Catherine B. Tkacz, "More Christian Formulas in Old English: *Wlite, Wuldor, Wynn*, and Descriptions of Heaven," in Alberto Ferreiro, ed., *The Devil, Heresy, and Witchcraft in the Middle Ages: Essays in Honor of Jeffrey B. Russell* (Leiden, forthcoming from Brill).

the famous poet Walafrid Strabo (808–49) turned Wetti's story into an influential poem. Here for the first time purgatory was portrayed as a mountain, and here for the first time a series of historical and recent figures, such as Charlemagne, appeared.

Tenth-century Irish visions incorporated motifs from Celtic myth. One influential account described the vision of a seventh-century Irish abbot, Adamnan. The abbot and his angelic guide come to the Land of Saints, a bright country of good weather and gentle fragrance whose inhabitants wear white linen cassocks with radiant hoods. Through nine vaults resound the songs of angels and saints praising God. To the southeast is the city of heaven proper, the dwelling of God, separated from the Land of Saints by crystal veils or walls, or a circle of fire, or a golden portico. The floor of the city is crystal, "shot with blue, and purple, and green" (9–10). There, face to face, the angels and the blest contemplate the Lord seated upon his throne in shining splendor. Beneath the canopied throne are four columns made of singing stones (an Irish motif) or jewels. Three noble birds (possibly representing seraphim) perch on the throne, praising the Lord in sweet adoration. Over the throne, which burns with unconsuming fire world without end, is a great arch like a helmet or crown. Gems, jeweled chairs, singing stones, and fragrant candles decorate the throne room. The author introduced a striking image: even though all the angels and humans who love God are facing and contemplating God, no one turns back or side to another person. All face and love one another as all face and love God.

A popular Irish story, more voyage than vision, is the *Voyage of Brendan*. The historical Brendan was an Irish abbot who died about 580; the story was written in the tenth century. The Irish motif of the journey to blessed isles in the West reinforced the classical myths of a western otherworld. The ancient metaphor is rooted in the fact that the sun sets in the west; in the Christian tradition, the western heaven competed with the hint in Genesis that paradise lies in the east. When Brendan, after seven years, finally arrives at the Isle of the Blessed in the farthest West, he encounters only a youth and an angel, and beyond them a river that Brendan is unable to cross because he is still living.

Visions of heaven proliferated in the twelfth century. In 1110 a nine-year-old Italian boy in Campania named Alberic had a vision in which he visited hell, purgatory, and an earthly paradise. Then he mounted through the seven planetary spheres to heaven, about which he was forbidden to speak upon his return. Gottschalk, a German peasant, had a vision in 1188 of hell, paradise, and heaven. On his journey he encountered people that he knew who had died. In 1196 an English monk of Eynsham in Oxfordshire was guided by Saint Nicholas through hell and purgatory. Nicholas, like Dante's Vergil later, left the monk, who then proceeded into paradise by himself. In paradise the monk sees souls mounting to heaven, where he is himself unable to go. As with Dante, the monk's vision lasted from Maundy Thursday to Easter Monday.

In the *Vision of Gunthelm*, an English Cistercian of the twelfth century, Gunthelm, is shown two paradises. One is a place of great beauty; in its midst is a chapel, in which Mary sits on a throne with the elect surrounding her. Wearing a golden robe, she shines among them as the sun shines among the stars. Gunthelm then visits a second paradise, with a beautiful door and golden walls set with jewels. Inside the walls of the city is the garden, containing many kinds of plants and trees. Birds sing amidst fragrant flowers and plenteous fruits. The imaging of paradise as city when seen from outside and as garden when seen from inside appeared in poetry, art, liturgy, and public festival. Townspeople in the twelfth century sometimes decorated their city on the feast of its patron saint with fronds, greenery, and incense, to represent the sweet-smelling heavenly garden within the walled heavenly city.

Saint Patrick's Purgatory is the story of a knight named Owen who about 1150 descended into a cave that by tradition had been shown to Saint Patrick centuries before as the entrance to the otherworld. The story, written in Latin about 1180, enjoyed considerable popularity and was translated several times into the vernacular, once by the famous poet Marie de France. Owen's experience, like Brendan's, is presented not as a vision but as an actual physical journey. Without a guide he passes by the gate of hell and then crosses a bridge and enters through a jeweled gate into the earthly paradise, where the light is brighter than the sun. He meets a procession of clergy bound for heaven, bearing crosses, banners, candles, and golden palm fronds, and singing in a mode unknown on earth. In monastic literature, monks, Saint Peter, or angels led the voyager, but here two archbishops lead Owen through lush and flowered meadows on which trees were bearing fruit whose scent nourished him. It is a land where no discomfort of any kind can exist. The archbishops take Owen to a mountain from whose peak he sees a golden sky. A flame "descended on the head of the knight and entered him just as it entered the others. Then he felt such a sweet sense of delight in his body and his heart that he could scarcely tell, for the delight of the sweetness, whether he was living or dead; but time passed in an instant."[28] Owen wants to stay, but the archbishops send him back to this world, promising him that if he converts and leads a good life he will return to heaven at his death.

The trend toward the institutional imagery of the visible church on earth is clear in the figures of the two guiding archbishops and the preference shown the clergy in general. The earthly paradise has become a prequel to the celestial one. With the growth of the idea of purgatory, this meant two varieties of interim state, one for the already blessed souls awaiting the resurrection in peace; the other for those who need greater cleansing before they can enjoy beatitude. Implied is the idea that souls are released from purgatory once they are sufficiently purified and then repair to the earthly paradise, there to await the resurrection happily. A narrative sequence has developed: death; separation of soul from body; particular judgment; purgatory or

[28] Zaleski, *Otherworld Journeys*, 37.

else earthly paradise; resurrection; final judgment; final bliss in heaven. This sequence, which may be taken in both the overt and symbolic senses, describes the process of "going to heaven."

About 1150 an Irish Benedictine monastery in Regensburg produced the story of an Irish knight, Tondal, an account of vast influence in both the literary and artistic tradition. Tondal's guardian angel undertakes to dissuade him from sin by leading his soul through the torments of hell. The punishments are corporeal, detailed, sometimes gross, for souls deprived of their bodies before resurrection still preserve their senses, their ability to feel. Tondal experiences in his own disembodied soul the reality of the corporeal pain of damnation.

The soul is capable of experiencing sensual delight as well as pain, and after visiting hell Tondal is allowed to enter an enclosed earthly paradise. He comes to a dazzling wall of silver, through which he passes into a beautiful land where he sees men and women wearing white clothing and shining like sunlight. Scent fills the flowery meadow like music. Here is no darkness, no pain, no fear. The inhabitants are virtuous laypeople burning with love for one another and for the Lord, whose Second Coming they await laughing and praising God in song. They all run to meet Tondal, souls recognizing a soul (even though they have not known him on earth), and greet him with his own name.

Now the angel leads him through a shining golden wall to a room where men and women dressed in white silken robes are seated in golden chairs, their jeweled crowns golden above faces as bright as the noonday sun. These are people who in life had sexual experience but were later purified through martyrdom or through ascetic lives; together they sing "alleluia" in melody so sweet that Tondal forgets his own sinful past.

On a field within a wall yet deeper in the same golden land, Tondal sees pavilions of gold, silver, and silk. He hears instruments playing charming music. The institutional hierarchy reveals itself again, for here in glory rejoice the best monks and nuns—defined as those who on earth were obedient to their superiors. This place of refreshment is for contemplatives who speak no evil, indeed seldom speak at all, reserving their voices for ecstatic songs of praise to Christ. Tondal cannot enter, because the Holy Trinity is present and also because once a person has gone inside, he can no longer be separated from the communion of saints. Tondal is not dead and so must return to life and die in sanctity before he can enjoy the beatific vision. But the angel gives him a second reason: he cannot enter because he is not a virgin. Here in the inner monastic precincts of the golden land only perpetual virgins are allowed.

Tondal cannot enter, but looking in he sees holy men and women like angels, hears their voices more exquisite than any instruments, smells their delightful scent. The firmament above is shining intensely. From it hang golden chains through which were woven silver boughs, and from these hang chalices and cruets, cymbals and bells, lilies and golden orbs. A throng of golden-winged angels flying among these ornaments make sweet music.

Now Tondal turns and sees a great tree in a green meadow flocked with lilies and herbs; the tree bears sweet fruit, and birds sing in its branches. Here are the cloistered virgins of both sexes who have never ceased praising and blessing the Lord. Each wears a golden crown and bears a golden scepter. The angel explains that the tree is the church and that the men and women under its branches are builders and defenders of churches.

The writer increasingly magnifies the glory of monastic virgins, for now Tondal will find them among the very angels. He approaches a third and greater wall built of precious stones, with mortar as of gold. The stones include crystal, chrysolite, beryl, jasper, emerald, sapphire, onyx, topaz, chrysoprase, and amethyst, all derived from the Apocalypse of John, Ezekiel, and Exodus. Climbing the wall, Tondal and his guide see the nine orders of angels, and they hear words that human beings cannot and must not repeat. Tondal wakes up at last, wiser and converted from sin, and keeping silence until he can receive the Eucharist.

In this vision of the ascetic hierarchy, virgin monastic superiors are at the summit. The monastic enthusiasm for virginity had reached the point, however, where it may have provoked a counterresponse, contributing to the affect and eros characteristic of the later mystics. Later accounts include Giacomino da Verona's *On the Heavenly Jerusalem* (1260), which describes the celestial city ruled by Christ and Mary, and the Parisian poet Rutebeuf's *Way to Paradise* (1265), an allegory of redemption. Both works are characterized by deliberate, sophisticated literary invention. The figures Rutebeuf sees in his dream vision are highly allegorized. More traditional was the vision of Thurkill of Essex in 1206. Thurkill is guided by a saint through vistas of hell and purgatory to the mountain of joy, where he finds a great temple, inhabited by the saved, and the earthly paradise, with its four rivers and Tree of Life. Here Adam weeps for all the lost souls of his descendants. Passing through a gate of jewels, Thurkill meets his father and others that he recognizes; he then returns to this world.

Such Christian otherworldly journeys had Jewish counterparts. In the ninth and tenth centuries collections were made of legends about Joshua ben Levi, a third-century Palestinian rabbi. Two separate and quite different stories feature Rabbi Joshua's visit to heaven, with an angel as guide. In the first, the angel takes the rabbi to a wall and lifts him to the top, from which they see paradise. Rabbi Joshua jumps down into paradise; the angel orders him to leave, but he refuses. He finds "seven compartments, each of twelve myriads of miles in width, and twelve myriads of miles in length" (comparable to the twelve cubits of Solomon's Temple).[29] "The first compartment corresponds to the first door of paradise. Here dwell the proselytes, who had embraced Judaism of their own free will." This compartment is furnished with walls of glass and cedar. In the

[29] Quotations from M. Gaster, "Hebrew Visions of Hell and Paradise," *Journal of the Royal Asiatic Society of Great Britain and Ireland* 25 (1893): 591–98.

second compartment, also made of silver and cedar, are the repentant; in the third, made of silver and gold, are patriarchs, kings of Israel, and all the people of the Exodus. The fourth, of olive wood, holds the faithful and just. The fifth is of silver, gold, and crystal, and "through its midst flows the river Gihon. . . . Here dwell the Messiah and Elijah." In the sixth are "those who died through performing a pious act"; the seventh contains those who died of illnesses "caused by the sins of Israel."

In the second vision, Rabbi Joshua sees paradise with "two gates of carbuncle, and sixty myriads" of angels, the angels shining

> with the lustre of the heavens. . . . When the just man approaches them they divest him of the clothes in which he had been buried and clothe him with eight cloths woven out of clouds of glory, and place upon his head two crowns, one of precious stones and pearls and the other of gold, and they place eight myrtles in his hand. . . . Each has a canopy according to his merits. . . . And through it (paradise) flow four rivers, one of olive oil, the other of balsam, the third of wine, and the fourth of honey. . . . In paradise there are eighty myriads of trees, sixty myriads of angels, and in the midst the Tree of Life overshadowing all of paradise.

Journeys to heaven appear in both Jewish and Christian folklore. Souls are borne by birds, by angels, by a chariot of light, by boat, or by rope, ladder, arrow, chain, tree, or plant, or on horseback. Souls ascend pillars of smoke and light, climb a mountain, or pass through a window. Souls on the way to heaven pass through Eden, the earthly paradise. Often they must traverse barriers: doors, gates, veils of fire and ice, rivers of fire, cloud and mist, storm, hail, snow, high seas, fords, woods, glens, mountains, caves, walls of fire, gold, or silver, walls with locks and doors of iron. Tenantless houses with empty windows stand at the border, or a weird inn, or a witch's hut. The entrance to the otherworld is frequently a rainbow or bridge, sometimes of gold, glass, sunbeams—or else of knives, to repel the unworthy. Often it is a cave, leading first through hell and purgatory, then on to heaven. The entrance to the otherworld can be guarded by monsters, wild animals, giants, or fierce champions. The entrance may suddenly snap shut.

The traveler is guided, if not actually carried, by an angel or saint, and an angel or saint welcomes him to heaven or tests him at the entrance. Saint Peter, to whom Christ had delegated the keys of heaven, is usually the doorkeeper. Heaven lies toward the east, west, or south (east, the direction of Eden, is especially good), but north is the direction of evil, for it is there that Satan raised the standard of rebellion against the Lord. Choirs, instruments, birds, or the very stones themselves make joyful song to the Lord.

The saved dwell with the angels or even become angels themselves. Heaven contains gleaming cities, temples, chapels, houses, castles, or halls of gold, crystal, or silver. Both city and garden, it is refreshed by rivers of water, wine, honey, mead, olive oil, and milk. Jewels lie like pebbles under the clear ripples. There are wells of water or wine; springs of pleasing temperatures, musical fountains, trees. Heaven is always bright with light coming from God's throne or from its inhabitants themselves; it is as the light of dawn reflecting the heavenly rose.

Serious concerns and highminded feelings about heaven perhaps inevitably provoked reactions of levity in popular literature and folklore. A drunken man is fooled by his friends into thinking that he has made a journey to heaven and hell. In a French story, a student from *Paris* tricks a woman into thinking that he comes from *Paradise*. In Boccaccio's *Decameron* (4.2), Brother Alberto poses as the archangel Gabriel in order to advance his suit with his beloved Lisetta. In another story from folklore, a wife agrees to do her husband's penance for him, but when he discovers that now she will go to heaven instead of him, he breaks their bargain. Letters from heaven are frequent. People refuse to go to heaven: a Spanish knight refuses to go without hunting dogs; an Irish hero refuses heaven because his heathen fellow-warriors were not admitted. Once there, one can be expelled: a German tailor is thrown out for self-righteously hurling a stool down at a woman thief on earth.

The concreteness of the images in vision literature and in folklore stand in contrast to the abstract heaven of the theologians and the ascetic heaven of the earlier monastics. The diversity of the images reveal that popular imagination was not limited by the boundaries drawn by the theoreticians of heaven. Vision literature, folklore, and artworks presented heaven in conformity with the basic pattern that Gregory the Great had set for the West but added a wealth of concrete imagery. Dante's heaven, theologically complete, is also rich in material details of sight, sound, and the other senses. Nineteenth- and twentieth-century images of heaven also would build upon, sometimes even center on, specific details: clouds, harps, angels, gates, and Peter the gatekeeper still shape modern popular imagery both serious and comic.

❖ 8 ❖

Wooing the Bridegroom

In THE twelfth and thirteenth centuries both scholastic and mystical theologians would structure and rationalize the traditional consensus. The shift away from monastic toward scholastic thought accelerated in the twelfth century, as the schools (*scholae*) that would develop into universities emerged in the growing cities of Western Europe. The epistemological question of how we can know about heaven was caught up in intellectual and political struggles for influence in the church, provoking debate over who spoke with most authority about heaven—the seer, the ascetic, or the scholastic.

Scholasticism, represented by such diverse figures as Anselm of Bec (1033–1109) and Peter Abelard (1079–1142), was characterized by the desire to find as much knowledge as possible through natural theology (philosophy unaided by revelation). One first learns all that one can through the use of unaided reason; then one adds the revelation of Scripture; then one goes on to use the processes of reason to explicate revelation; the result is a body of knowledge known as revealed theology. For example, unaided reason shows that God exists, but only revelation tells us anything else about God. Revelation shows that there is a Father, Son, and Holy Spirit, but only revealed theology can define the nature of the Trinity. The fathers as far back as Justin Martyr had assumed these principles implicitly; now, in the cathedral schools of the twelfth century, they became explicit, structured, and systematized, particularly by the use of dialectical reasoning. In dialectic, twelfth-century theologians presented differing views on a range of philosophical, theological, and legal topics, and then resolved the differences through the use of logic. This scholastic method dominated the intellectual discourse of the thirteenth century, drawing support from the revival of Aristotle's lost works. Scholasticism was accompanied by a shift from Platonic to Aristotelian philosophy, although through most of the twelfth century Platonic and Augustinian thought remained more prominent. The *Book of Sentences* by Peter Lombard (1100–60) summarized and structured traditional Augustinian theology and became the standard theology textbook for more than a century.

Two other modes of thought remained influential rivals of scholasticism. One mode was the increasingly contemplative or "mystical" monastic theology, brilliantly represented by Bernard of Clairvaux (1090–1153) and the school of Saint Victor (the Victorines). The scholastics dismissed monastic exegesis and theology as too intuitive and as insufficiently logical, but Bernard and the Victorines used both scholastic logic and contemplation. Another mode was through art and literature, whose dependence upon formal theology declined as their expressions became more original.

Anselm was a transitional monastic theologian who stressed natural reason to the point of offering a logical proof of the existence of God entirely independent of revelation. Anselm understood that it was less true to say that the joy of heaven enters us than that we enter it. In heaven is whatever we love and whatever we desire. We shall wholly fulfill our own wills there, because our wills will be in harmony with God's. Our resurrected, spiritual bodies will transcend our present, natural bodies in beauty, strength, health, delight, "agility" (the ability to move from one point to another immediately, since everything is in one place in God), "penetrability" (the ability to pass through matter), and "perpetuity" (better, "eternity," for Anselm meant that all times are one in God). The community of the blessed resurrected love themselves, one another, and God. The heavenly life is the fulfillment of Christian life (especially monastic life) on earth; it is participation in the life of angels; its name is the City of God, the heavenly City, the heavenly Jerusalem.

Bernard of Clairvaux, himself versed in scholastic reasoning, preferred the will, which yields love, over the intellect, which yields knowledge. Bernard was an intensely affective homilist, theologian, and poet, whose character has been misunderstood owing to modern writers' fixation on his quarrel with Abelard, who (Bernard judged) missed the point of Christianity by over-emphasizing the intellect. Nor was Abelard the cold rationalist he seemed to his enemies, as his hymns such as *O quanta qualia* prove:

> O quanta qualia sunt illa sabbata
> quae semper celebrat superna curia,
> quae fessis requies, quae merces fortibus,
> cum erit omnia Deus in omnibus.
>
> .   .   .   .
>
> Nostrum est interim mentem erigere
> et totis patriam votis appetere,
> et ad Jerusalem a Babylonia
> post longa regredi tandem exsilia:

How great and beautiful are the sabbaths that the heavenly court celebrates eternally. When God is all in all things, these sabbaths give rest to the weary and reward to those who persevere. . . . Meanwhile it is ours to be attentive, to seek in prayer our native land, and after long exile to come back at last from Babylon to Jerusalem.

But it was Bernard, not Abelard or any other Christian theologian, thinker, mystic, or poet, who in the *Divine Comedy* would accompany Dante past the point where even Beatrice could no longer lead, into the beatific vision itself. The powerfully affective nature of monastic theology had been in evidence for centuries, but Bernard gave it new life and vigor in his poetry. The sensuous imagery of his writing derives from the

Song of Songs. Bernard devoted eighteen years to composing eighty-six sermons on the Song. He took its passionately erotic dialogue between the lovers allegorically (as Philo and Origen had done centuries before him) but without any diminution of passion. The Song is a jubilee of the heart, a tumult of internal joys, a harmony of wills. The soul's love for Christ, the community's love for Christ, and Christ's love for us are no abstractions. Love is intuitive, not discursive. Logic without love is dead. Love can be emotional, spiritual, and at its truest both emotional and spiritual. It is characterized by passionate desire and by the fulfillment of that passion in a union of spirit. Christ the Bridegroom will rejoice in the Bride, and the Bride (the blessed individual or the community of the blessed) will rejoice in him.

The erotic language and imagery drawn by Bernard from the Song was the basis of the so-called marriage mysticism that began in the twelfth century and continued through the sixteenth. Erotic imagery seizes the emotions; more, it means that in merging with God the Bridegroom we lovingly abandon ourselves to him while retaining as Bride our individuality and our own personal characters. In perfect union with God we do not vanish; we are fulfilled. More, we are deified (*deificari*), "as a little drop of water, mixed with much wine, seems to vanish completely as it takes on the taste and color of the wine; and as fiery, glowing iron becomes indistinguishable from the fire, putting off its own former appearance; and as air flooded with sunlight is transformed into the same brilliant light, so that it seems to be no longer lighted but rather light itself."[30] *Seems to be*, but is not. Air flooded with light remains air, though transfigured by the light; nor is it the source of light, Light itself. The Trinity is one substance, and humans and God absolutely cannot become the same substance or essence. But they can become one spirit by entering into each other in love.

[30] Bernard of Clairvaux, *The Steps of Humility*, trans. George Bosworth Burch (Notre Dame, Ind., 1963), 89.

Love is an act of will, and Bernard was a passionate advocate of freedom of will. In creating the cosmos, God allows a little place where his complete and unmediated ordering of things is suspended so as to allow freedom to humans and angels. God knows in eternity what our choices are; he permits those choices, and he eternally adjusts for them. One sort of freedom, which we had from the moment of creation and never lost, is the freedom of our will from external coercion: no one can force us to do evil. Before the Fall, we also had freedom from sin. We have lost this freedom, but Christ restores it to us, preparing us for the third freedom, freedom from sorrow, which we shall enjoy at the resurrection. After physical death, the soul longs for the body, even this weak and wretched body that we now have, because without the body we are not complete persons. Only with the reunion of soul and body can we see Christ in his divinity as well as in his humanity.

The leaders of the monastic school of Saint Victor, Hugh (d. 1142) and Richard (d. 1173), had similar views on heaven, derived in part from their revival of Eriugena's work. Spiritual and contemplative, the Victorines also sought definitional clarity for a number of ideas. Terms for the soul such as *mens, intellectus, intelligentia, anima,* and *animus* were in wide use but still ill-defined, owing to the underlying and never resolved psyche/pneuma tension going back to Paul and beyond. The Victorines attempted to clarify them. For Richard, *mens* is the same as *animus.* The mens/animus is divided into a higher mens/animus and a lower mens/animus. The higher is called *spiritus* or *anima,* meaning either that which gives us life or that part of us which is directed toward the transcendent. The lower mens/anima includes sensation, imagination, and reason. Intelligentia is an activity of anima, while spiritus is a faculty of anima. In scholastic terms a "faculty" is a power, such as sight or memory; spiritus is the faculty or power by which the whole soul can comprehend not only sense knowledge but also spiritual knowledge. The anima/spiritus can be caught up by God in contemplation, and in the beatific vision it will be caught up so deeply that it will see him face to face.

The Victorines queried how limited creatures such as we will be able, either overtly or symbolically, to see our Creator face to face. This was called the problem of the *medium* of the beatific vision: the *means* by which we will be able to see him. The Victorines rejected the view that we see only God's theophanies or energeia. If the beatific vision is seeing only an image of God, it cannot really be the beatific vision. In short, there can be no medium other than God himself. Hugh used the metaphor of sealing wax: we are the wax, the seal is the Trinity, and the medium is the likeness of the seal imprinted on the wax. We remain essentially different from God (we are wax; he is seal), but he has directly imprinted himself on us. The medium is the Trinity itself. The Victorines' understanding of the beatific vision sprang from their contemplative experience. In contemplation, we progress from seeing the things of this world with our bodily eyes, through seeing the spiritual meaning in the things of this world, through contemplating divine reality with the aid of images drawn from the things of this world, to contemplating divine reality without any mediate images, figures, or signs.

Time limits those who are in it, but in the beatific vision we see in the eternal moment all things that occur in the cosmos from its beginning to its end, and we shall see this, not with our bodily eyes (which would be impossible), but with the spiritual understanding of our transformed anima. On this earth time is transcended for a moment during the celebration of the Eucharist, for the mystery of Christ's sacrifice is eternal. It is not repeated at every Eucharist, for it happens only once, and each Eucharist is a manifestation on earth of the unique sacrifice. The community of lovers is partly in heaven, partly on earth, and in eternity it is simply and completely present.

The resurrected body will be identical with our earthly body, but transfigured; it will be immune from death and sorrow; it will be at the height of its powers, free from disease and deformity, and around thirty years old, the age at which Christ began his ministry. It will surpass anything we can imagine, even from the accounts of Christ's appearances on earth after his own resurrection. For Christ, knowing that earthly eyes had not the strength to see him as he really was in the true glory of his resurrected body, accommodated his disciples by showing them, not the full reality, but only what they were capable of understanding.

Grace gives us the option of choosing to love God of our own free will, and of our own free will we can reject grace. Grace yields faith, which yields virtues, which merit heaven. Faith, hope, and love inhere in us while on earth, but in heaven faith and hope, having been fulfilled, are replaced by contemplation. Good works also are unnecessary in heaven, so preaching and teaching will cease. Love remains, being the essence of God, and with it praise of God, expressed in the dynamic joy and harmony of music and dance.

Peter Lombard gave scholastic structure to the traditional Christian view. Heaven is the empyrean (*caelum empyreum*), the heaven beyond all the celestial spheres; thus it is overtly in a place that is not a place, that has no boundaries, that simply opens out to infinity. The particular or personal judgment is confirmed at the Last Judgment. We do not lose free will in heaven; rather, if on earth we freely choose with our whole will and with the force of our whole character to cleave to God, in heaven that choice continues to be free. Our will is free in heaven, but we do not change our minds, which are steadfast in God. We continue to grow in love and knowledge, and hence in merit and reward, and we receive more than we can possibly hope or imagine. We shall have the enjoyment not only of the *signa*, God's appearances or theophanies, but also of the *res*, God in his very self. We shall no longer need metaphors, for we shall know by pure ontology: direct intuition of absolute reality itself.

Peter recapitulated the distinctions being made at his time between subjective beatitude (having God in us) and objective beatitude (knowing God in himself). One of Peter's students worked out a scheme for distinguishing senses of beatitude. Beatitude by causation (*secundum causam*) is the blessing of good works that make the saint, the lover of God, worthy of bliss; beatitude by experience (*secundum usum*) is the blessed sight (understanding) of God by the saints; beatitude *secundum essentiam*, eternal life in its essence, is God himself. Peter himself viewed beatitude as the enjoyment (*fruitio*) of God, which included understanding, joy, and love.

Adam and Eve before the Fall saw God "face to face," without any medium. Since the Fall, we can no longer see directly, a medium of some kind is needed, either an external medium, or something proper to our bodies, or something in the soul itself. Some argued that the medium was the physical eye of the resurrected body, others that the eye is a metaphor for the intellect. Peter wished to narrow the vast natural gap between God and creation and said that the only medium is a power (*virtus*) of truth and love innate in the soul, a power similar to the Truth and Love inherent in God himself. Through this similarity God shows us himself in a way that we will be able to understand. Although God shows us his essence and not just a sign of his essence, we are unable to understand the divine essence in its infinite depth and fullness. This inability, though intensified by original sin, is proper to our human nature; it is itself no sin but part of the cosmos as God creates it. We shall understand God's essence as fully as our nature permits when body and soul are reunited, so that the state of the saved after the resurrection will be better or greater than their state during the interim.

Peter Lombard exemplified the scholastic effort to structure theology, to answer questions logically, to exclude inconsistencies. The arts, on the other hand, reveled in opening up and extending meaning through metaphor. They were less concerned with establishing defined truth than with experiencing reality in itself. What is real is the experience and the expression of the Godness of the cosmos. We see a willow tree. We do not measure it, analyze it, attempt to define it. We enter into it, merge with it, sense that we and it are one in the pattern of the cosmos. We understand not by narrowing down but by opening up, eternally. Writers often made a distinction between poetical allegory, which is words (*in verbis*) only, something that the writer uses for beauty or for effect, and the divine allegory found in the Bible, which is not only in words but in reality (*in facto*). God is the architect ("first builder") of the cosmos, but most of all God is a poet. Unlike the work of a human author, what God makes (*agit*) is eternally real. This idea of God as author of the cosmos appears in many languages (e.g., Greek *poiētēs*, Latin *auctor*, Old English *makar*).

The belief, later, that Dante wrote in facto as well as in verbis placed the *Divine Comedy* on almost the same basis of truth as the Bible itself. Dante's claim grew out of a tradition going back to the twelfth and thirteenth centuries that a poet of high purpose is quite different from poets of the ephemeral. The idea of poet-theologians, hinted at already by Augustine, now reappeared enhanced.

Visionary poetry began to elide the persona or "actor" in the poem with the author (*auctor*) of the poem. Raoul de Houdenc (d. 1225) wrote in his *Road to Paradise* of a pilgrim who ascends Jacob's ladder to God. Raoul wanted to be certain that his poem was read as a true vision or dream (*songe*), which he distinguished from poetry of fiction or falsehood (*mensonge*) that did not intend the truth. Poetry, like music, could intend eternal truth, not just enjoyment; like music it could be a metaphor for cosmic order, beauty, and harmony.

Poets, theologians, and philosophers now preferred the model of the celestial spheres to that of Jerusalem or the earthly paradise. Heaven was the highest celestial sphere or, more cosmologically correct, out and beyond the spheres. The early twelfth-century vision of Alberic of Montecassino, for example, distinguished between the garden paradise and the celestial home of God. The problem of representing space or the occupants of space in a "place" beyond space stimulated twelfth-century poets, theologians, mapmakers, and graphic artists. No

one could portray in the overt sense the point that is both everywhere and nowhere, both timeless and eternal. All were obliged
to construct metaphors drawn from time and space, and this is
as true of maps of the earth as of maps of heaven, and as true of
pictures and poems as of maps. All had to order chaotic spacetime so that celestial and terrestrial coalesced in word or image,
and to do it within the framework of tradition. This task was so
enormous that it often escaped the control of the artists; some
controlled it by joking descriptions of fanciful lands such as the
kingdom of Prester John or the land of Cockaigne. Satire, by no
means unknown in the earlier Middle Ages, became more common in the twelfth century, particularly satires of theology and
liturgy, revealing an increasingly plastic and fluid society.

Both rural and urban life were changing rapidly, and uncertainty encouraged efforts to fix a stable society in the other
world. Some arrangements placed Christians and Jews in different parts of heaven; some arranged souls by geographical origin.
Other arrangements were by types of sin or virtue, by social
classes, or, rarely, by family. Monks, of course, continued to put
monks first (on the grounds that monks devoted themselves
more completely to the spiritual life than did those who lived in
the world), and with the new monastic orders of the late eleventh through thirteenth centuries, members of each order tended
to rank their own brethren above those of the others. Monastics
who failed their high calling, on the other hand, occupy special
places in hell, on the principle of *corruptio optimi pessima*: the
worst corruption is the corruption of the best.

Male clergy usually constructed the rankings, placing themselves higher in heaven—that is, nearer to God—than women
and the laity. In the thirteenth and fourteenth centuries worldly
status, whether ecclesiastical or secular, found its counterpart in
the otherworld—for better or for worse. For example, Mechtild
of Magdeburg (d. 1297) would see hell as populated by powerful temporal and spiritual figures, mostly male. Earlier, a monk
of Arras saw a carefully structured heaven in which Peter and
Paul were first; then John the Baptist; then the other apostles;

then hermits; then monks; then bishops; then priests; then laymen; finally laywomen. The vocabulary of heaven was influenced by feudal titles such as *Herr, Lord, seigneur, señor, signore*. The Biblical image of God's court was reinforced by the images of medieval royal or episcopal courts. The literature and music of romantic love became metaphors for divine love. At the other end of the social scale, popular satirists observed that there was no room in heaven for peasants, since it was filled up by the rich and noble.

The thirteenth-century scholastics would now press the rationalizing of heaven even further into the service of order, for in the schools and universities theology became a discipline with strict rules as to what authorities could be cited and how arguments were to proceed. This punctilious search for definitions now reduced the breadth or area of speculation, pushing the spiritual, contemplative, apophatic tradition further toward the fringes while the kataphatic tradition prevailed in the schools.

❖ 9 ❖

The Desire of the Intellect

SCHOLASTICISM dominated thirteenth-century thought, its logical, almost geometrical structure reinforced by the growing influence of Aristotle, whom Thomas Aquinas (1225–74) called simply "The Philosopher," just as he referred to Paul as "The Apostle." The Aristotelian scholastics were concerned with refining the rational system established by Peter Lombard and his contemporaries, with adding Aristotle's physics, politics, and metaphysics to the structure, and with harmonizing this new philosophical system with Christian tradition and revelation. Scholasticism had few parallels in the East; Western theology, not to mention Western political aggression, alienated Eastern from Western thought. Of Greek writers, only Dionysius, John Damascene (675–749), and John Chrysostom were still well known in the West. Islam, however, produced a number of philosophers who attempted to construct, under the influence of Aristotle, a system combining revelation and reason.

Using Aristotle and the Muslim philosophers, Western Christian theologians filled out the sketchier cosmology of earlier Christian thought. They constructed a cosmological schema based on Aristotelian physics and Ptolemaic geography. Their arrangement of the cosmos fit the exact calculations of astronomers operating in a geocentric universe. The precision and coherence of this schema is so pleasing to the mind that it endured into the seventeenth century. The cosmos is arranged in a nest of concentric spheres; the earth is the innermost sphere and centers on the cosmos's lowest point; above the outermost sphere, the primum mobile, is the Empyrean, the dwelling place of God.

This system was so coherent as to create the impression of describing the real world in the overt as well as the allegorical sense. Human reason could read and understand what God has written in the great book of the cosmos; what God wrote in the cosmos as well as in Scripture is true both overtly and symbolically. Although this idea went back to Augustine and beyond, earlier writers sensed that an almost unbridgeable gap exists between reality and our ability to understand it. When Aquinas described the cosmos, he intended to convey what it is overtly, physically, as well as allegorically. Still, Aquinas and his contemporaries did not have as their primary intention the description of the physical cosmos but rather of the moral cosmos, the cosmos as inherently meaningful, the Word uttered by God. The physical cosmos is the allegory of the truly real cosmos, which is God's utterance or song. Physics is an inferior truth pointing to the greater truth, which is theological, moral, and even divine. This view is contrary to the basic assumptions—even biases—of Western society at the turn of the twenty-first century; indeed the modern material worldview is almost a total inversion of the moral worldview of the thirteenth and fourteenth centuries. In order to accommodate modern readers one must write as if the physical were more real than the moral, but this is the exact reverse of Aquinas's understanding that the physical is the allegory of the moral. The concern of these medieval writers was ultimate reality, which is the expression by God of a perfect harmony of matter and spirit, past and present, in a whole that is completely meaningful.

One concern of thirteenth-century scholastics was how, in the light of Aristotelian physics, heaven could be considered a place. A place implies "corporeality," especially if it is to be occupied by bodies, resurrected or not. It also implies boundaries. Traditionally heaven had been regarded as incorporeal, but Albert the Great (1200–80), philosopher, theologian, and natural scientist, believed that it is a body, meaning that it is composed of matter.

It is the noblest of simple bodies, a body composed of the highest element, fire. Or it is an essence beyond the four essences or elements: earth, air, fire, and water. The idea of a fifth, nobler state of being came from Aristotle through Dionysius. The scholastics called it "quintessence" (*quinta essentia*, "fifth essence") and used it as a device to make heaven either material or not material, according to the needs of the argument. Making heaven a quintessence placed it beyond both the starry sky and the crystalline and dimensionless primum mobile. That seemed to make it incorporeal. But the fact that the primum mobile can be conceived as being "within" it and that it can be called an essence or element, even though of a fifth and special sort, suggests some kind of corporeality, as does the fact that it contains resurrected bodies. It is a pure body, with the qualities of splendor, immobility, and freedom from the natural laws governing the four-essence cosmos.

Humans as well as cosmic bodies needed a place in which to exist. Arab philosophers such as Avicenna had suggested that the soul exists in God's mind, and therefore in creation, before the body does. This dualistic idea of the preexistence of souls was foreign to the dominant Christian tradition, which affirmed the simultaneous creation of body and soul as one integrated being. Yet the scholastics were unwilling to embrace wholeheartedly the ancient Judeo-Christian doctrine of the integrity of body and soul because they were impressed by the dominant, unbiblical theory that the soul existed by itself (at least for a while) after human death. Albert took a middle ground in arguing that the soul is a complete and independent substance in itself. Though it does not preexist the body, it can persist after the body's demise. Yet the connection between soul and body is not accidental but essential. The soul is the *forma corporis*, the essence or form of the body. A soul may be in a "temporary" state of being without the body, but essentially and eternally the body and soul are one.

The purpose of life is to live out one's moral potential in a process that will be completed at the end, in heaven. Peter

Lombard had taken the view that conscience, which contains elements of intellect and will, was not wholly extinguished by original sin. The intuitive knowledge of the basic principles of morality is available to every human as part of our nature, allowing us to choose good or evil. Abelard had shifted the ground, arguing that natural reason can, unaided, choose limited good but cannot direct itself toward perfect goodness until converted by grace into what the scholastics called right reason.

These discussions revived the question of who might be saved. Faith could be explicit, open participation in Christ's community, or it could be implicit, a yearning for God known only to God. Theologians considered the implications for unbaptized children, for contemporaries who had never heard of Christ, and for those who had lived on earth before Christ. Old Testament patriarchs, prophets, and indeed all obedient to the Law, Torah, were saved by Christ, though they were generally supposed to have had to wait for rescue until Christ's descent into the underworld after his crucifixion. At any rate, since God in his grace had revealed his Law to the Jews, faithful Jews number among the saved. Virtuous pagans presented a greater problem, since their virtues seemed to spring from natural conscience only and therefore could not lead them to heaven. Three general positions could be argued. The first, which had little support, was that, absent knowledge of Christ, natural virtue is sufficient for heaven. The second was that natural virtue was a sign that grace had produced an implicit faith in Christ. Alexander of Hales (1186–1245) argued that it would be inconsistent with God's justice to bar from heaven the philosophers and other virtuous pagans who had had no access to Christ's teaching. God grants them a special revelation, which may occur at any time up to the moment of death. All who are saved are saved by Christ, even if they do not know it: every saved person dies a Christian.

The third position, stronger in tradition and poetry than in theology, was that a virtuous pagan could be saved by a miracle. A persistent legend had it that the emperor Trajan was saved by Pope Gregory the Great, who in one version wept over a depiction of the good emperor and thus baptized him with his tears, or, in another version, raised him from the dead so that Trajan could consciously accept Christ. The underlying theological difference in the two stories is between the generally rejected idea of natural virtue engendering grace on the one hand and, on the other, the widely accepted principle that grace generates faith, which generates virtue, which generates the extra grace of salvation.

In trying to understand the beatific vision, the scholastics, like their predecessors, had to cope with the Scriptural tension between 1 John 3.2, "When he is revealed, we will be like him, for we will see him as he is," and 1 Timothy 6.16, which characterizes God as he "whom no one has ever seen or can see." Some argued that John did not mean the impossible act of seeing God's own essence, but rather seeing indirectly as if through a mirror, as Paul had said. The mirror shows us God's glory, goodness, and truth, but not his essence. The basic problem was how a finite intellect such as ours could understand the infinite, how a human eye could see the intrinsically invisible. The degree of perfection in the vision pertains to the degree to which we retain our own personality in heaven, for if we were to see entirely as God sees, we would all see alike, our vision completely obliterated in God's.

The center of the discussion of the beatific vision at this time was the "medium." We "see" God when we are in heaven. Either we see only his theophany (as the Eastern tradition preferred), or we see his essence. But if we see his essence, do we see through some kind of medium? The earlier, Augustinian tradition, dominant through the twelfth century, asserted that we shall see God "face to face" without a medium, but this seemed impossible to many on the basis of the passage from Timothy and on that of Aristotelian philosophy. We could not, Aristotelians argued, see God face to face without some kind of medium between our limitations and his infinity. This medium could be something between us and God, that is, something different from both us and God. Or it could be something within us or within God. Many theologians strove to preserve the spirit of the earlier tradition by affirming an internal medium. No thing could possibly stand between us and God, so the medium must not be a thing but rather a similarity between us and God. This similarity is inherent in the nature of both Creator and creature, rather than something independent of them. Throughout the century about equal numbers of theologians argued for or against the existence of a medium, and even those denying a medium had to admit that some extra strength needed to be given the soul to permit it to see God, even in heaven.

The question sharpened in the early years of the thirteenth century. About 1230, William of Auvergne (1180–1249) rejected any medium at all for fear that philosophical speculation would undermine the beatific vision. An anonymous disputation in the 1230s proposed that the medium by which we understand God is the likeness (*similitudo*) between God and humans. Our likeness to God is real and perfect, however infinitesimal. It lies partly in our having been created in God's image and likeness, so that we possess intellect and will. This natural light of the intellect gives us ideas about God, but God remains far beyond any of our ideas. So in order to see God without a medium, a supernatural gift must be infused into the soul. This is the light of glory (*lumen gloriae*) or light of grace (*lux gratiae*). This glory, whose essence is perfect love between us and God, is what can assimilate us to God. The phrase "light of glory," though found earlier in Jerome, Ambrose, and Peter Damian, lacked this technical meaning before the thirteenth century. For Bonaventure (1217–74), truth is absolutely unattainable without this light. Albert, drawing on Dionysius, said that the light is God's theophany or appearance to us, strengthening and elevating our intellect. The light of glory can itself be seen as a medium—or else as God himself and therefore no medium at all. Christ is not the medium by which we see God, although it is through Christ's mediation that we are able to enter heaven.

Alexander of Hales took another approach. Peter Lombard had written that we shall enjoy God fully in heaven, where we shall see him *per speciem*. Alexander and some others saw that by using the term *species*, a broad and vague word, one could finesse the question: we see God completely and without medium in his *species*, which can be taken as "essence," "substance," "face," or "image." God's essence might be seen in three ways: in itself, or *per speciem*, or *per similitudinem*. Only God can see his essence in itself. Glory infused into our souls enables us to see him in his *species*. And we can even see him in the natural similitude of our intellect and will to his.

From the 1230s, other theologians found such solutions unsatisfactory and increasingly reasserted the older Western view that in heaven we do see God's essence and without any medium. Robert Grosseteste (1175–1253) argued that "we see him face to face, and he is truly understood, and his essence is understood." Grosseteste also, however, confirmed that though we will understand God's essence we can in no way understand it as God himself does; therefore the "totality of his essence is not penetrated" (*Commentary on the Celestial Hierarchy*, 9.27–31, 48–50). William of Auvergne, explicitly attacking Aristotelian objections, insisted on "the most clear and immediate vision without any medium," God being "understandable" (*apprehensibilis*) in his nature and essence (*De anima*, 7). William feared that the Aristotelians were removing from the intellect the very reason for its creation, namely the ability to know the Creator. In 1241 the prestigious University of Paris settled the question for the remainder of the Middle Ages, formally asserting that God is seen in his essence and substance by the angels and by all the blessed in heaven.

Thomas Aquinas combined traditional, mystical, and philosophical thought in creating his great systematic theology. For Aquinas, God, unlike any created thing, is Being itself. His essence is Being. Creatures, on the other hand, are composed of matter and essence. God creates the cosmos, which proceeds

(Thomas eschewed the philosophically dangerous term "emanates") from him and will return to him. The Son proceeds from the Father, which is an eternal process in which the Son and the Father are one being, one essence. The proceeding (*processus*) of the Son from the Father takes place within the eternal moment and does not overflow it. In a completely distinct, yet analogous manner, the cosmos proceeds from God. The analogy is in the "proceeding" from the eternal One. But unlike Christ, the cosmos does not have God's essence. It overflows the eternal moment and becomes the world of matter and energy, time and space.

Every creature proceeds from God, and every creature seeks to return. Creatures lacking intellect fulfill their natures in a natural and inevitable return to God. Humans could have been fulfilled but for original sin, which blocked and twisted our natural course back to the Creator, so that we prefer wealth, sex, power, and other limited goods to the greatest Good. The path of return is therefore more complicated for humans. Our intellect has some natural love for the Good, since it can perceive and feed upon the traces or likenesses of God in the things he has made, but the natural intellect usually limits itself to the goods of this world. Aristotle had taught that we seek first fulfillment of our personal potential and then our fulfillment in society. Thomas postulated a further stage necessary for wholeness: fulfillment in God. Natural intellect is too stunted to be able to wish for that fully and clearly, and it easily fixes upon lesser goods, transforming them into idols. Our intellect needs the supernatural light of grace to be able to order itself toward the Good.

The illuminated intellect uses right reason to present the right choices to the will. Unlike Bonaventure, for whom the light of desire in the will enables us to understand with the intellect, Thomas placed the intellect first. The will has to have a goal toward which to direct its love, and it cannot love the goal or even perceive it until the intellect presents it. The will then can make right choices as presented to it by the intellect, but since natural will, like natural intellect, is stunted by sin, we need a supernatural rectitude of will infused by the Holy Spirit. We are unable to move toward God through our own natural virtues or powers.

The good of the intellect and the good of the will work together. Virtue requires both the intellect's right reason and the will's choice of what the intellect presents to it as good. Choices made for good on the purely natural level (unaided by grace) produce the natural or "cardinal" virtues of temperance, prudence, fortitude, and justice. The will needs supernatural grace infusing the necessary love (*caritas*), in order to transform the cardinal virtues into supernatural virtues and to add the theological virtues of faith, hope, and love. Only infused virtues bring us to heavenly glory. We need grace to do good; we need to choose to accept grace; this acceptance yields the theological virtues, which produce good works, which produce merit, for which heaven is the reward.

Those having superior potential, and therefore superior merits, are higher in heaven. All in heaven have the beatific vision. The vision itself is not subject to degrees, yet some have a greater intrinsic ability to enjoy that beatitude. Enjoyment is an act of the will that follows an act of the intellect.

Only one true heaven exists or can ever exist, Thomas argued, and Paul must have intended, in speaking of a third heaven, both the one true heaven and other entities loosely called "heavens." The air may be called the first heaven and the stars the second heaven, but these are figures of speech. Paul was taken up to the empyrean, the true heaven. The third heaven is not the sky, for Genesis reveals that the empyrean heaven was created on the first day, and the starry skies not till the second. Further, whereas the starry sky is essentially made of the highest of the elements, fire, the empyrean heaven is composed of none of the four elements but is a separate element, the quintessence. Although the name "empyrean" derives from *pyr*, fire, it is called that not because it burns but because it shines (*non ab ardore, sed a splendore*), terms that later delighted Dante. It is a body, although a divine rather than a natural one, a quintessential one, a fifth body differing from every other body in that there is nothing outside or beyond it that limits or defines it. Unmoved, it moves the cosmos. Since no physical body can move without being moved, it follows that the empyrean must be, not a physical, but a divine body. It is the most noble, glorious, and luminous of all bodies. It is no trick of the tongue to call it a body, for this outermost body defines, moves, and influences the spheres within it. The influence of the empyrean is felt most in the primum mobile, that dimensionless shell that nests within it, and then with decreasing power and decreasing directness down to the lowest sphere, which is earth.

Since heaven is a place (although unlike any material place), God cannot be said to be within it. Yet the Lord's Prayer begins, "Our Father in heaven." Here Thomas abandons the overt sense altogether. The phrase "Father in heaven" is meant, he says, to denote God's preeminence as a divine being above nature, not a body inhabiting a "place" called heaven; he is in no sense contained by anything, even the quintessence. Even the angels and the blessed, when said to be in heaven or to dwell in it, are not contained in it, for it has no boundaries. It is the place or state where the saved, like the angels, will enjoy forever the celestial glory that is the vision of God.

Thomas devoted two substantial sections of his *Summa theologiae* to the beatific vision, one concerning its relation to God, the other concerning its relation to humans (Ia.12; IIaIIae 1–5). Since everything is knowable through its acts, God is knowable. Moreover, as pure act, he is more knowable than anything. He is knowable because of the likeness between his intellect and ours. Our intellect can know him, but since he is beyond nature, our natural intellect cannot. Our intellect knows him only when it is strengthened by the light of glory (*lumen gloriae confortans intellectum ad videndum Deum*; Aquinas uses *lux* and *lumen* interchangeably). The light of glory enables our intellect to understand what cannot be understood; our eyes to see what cannot be seen. This is how we can see the invisible.

God is seen in and through his divine essence itself, not through any medium. We shall see God by the help of the light of glory, by which we are rendered similar to God (*deiformes*). All the saved will see God, but those in whom charity is stronger will see him more perfectly. We see and understand God's essence but can never fully comprehend it (grasp it entirely). The light of glory, itself infinite, is limited in any human mind to the capacity of that mind. No creature, even with divine help, can comprehend the essence of the Creator. Still, though no one can comprehend God, the more one understands, the more perfectly one sees.

Our blessedness or beatitude—our complete fulfillment—cannot consist of any created good. Our intellects and wills can be satisfied only by the universal Good, which is God. Our beatitude is uncreated in the sense that it is what we desire, that is, God; it is created in the sense that our desire for God is part of our created nature. The essence of beatitude is an act of intellect, but the joy is of the will. The will moves us toward the goal set by the intellect and then delights in the attainment of the goal.

We shall see things all simultaneously, not successively. In this life no one can see God's essence. In this life we are in space-time; in the other life we are in eternity.

> Eternity is simultaneously present to every instant of time. Each part of time coexists with the whole of eternity, although this part may be past or future in relation to other parts of time. Hence, every event in time is present to eternity; God sees each event actually occurring. . . . The copresence to eternity of events past, present, and future assures God an infallible and necessary knowledge of future contingents, including free acts. A contingent event is one actively or passively indeterminate in its causes; its indetermination lies in reference to the future. But once caused, it obviously occurs as this determinate event rather than some other. Socrates need not sit down while lecturing today, but if he is seen sitting down, he is necessarily sitting down. Just as it is evident to any observer that Socrates is now sitting down, so

every event in the whole history of the universe is infallibly known by eternal vision, since the whole of time is copresent to the whole of eternity.[31]

The scholastics did not mean that the particular judgment at an individual's death occurs at the same time (in the normal sense) as the Last Judgment, but rather in the same eternal moment. Seen from within spacetime, these events are separated by time, but seen in eternity they occur simultaneously. The end-time is the moment where we leave historical time and enter eternity.

Aquinas and the other scholastics, however, did not embrace the implications of this, as some modern theologians do. According to the latter, we participate in eternity immediately at death, so that we enter heaven directly, experiencing the particular judgment, purgation, the Last Judgment, and resurrection all at once. Our bodies rot in the earth; time proceeds; but while they do, we are simultaneously in eternity, so our whole life is one with God. For us within spacetime, the resurrection is in the future, but for God, the angels, and the blessed, who are not in spacetime but in eternity, the resurrection is now. Theologians who take this view are trying to assert the Biblical indivisibility of soul and body and the observation of scientific biology that human thought is impossible without a brain, as well as attempting to avoid the awkward interim period.

Aquinas did not take this view but rather held to the dominant belief of his time that souls must wait for reembodiment until the general resurrection and the Last Judgment. He might have objected to the modern view on the following ground. In eternity, the particular judgment and the resurrection are both "now." But then it is also true that the creation, the end of the world, and all events occurring between, are also eternally "now." From that point of view the resurrection and the Battle of Hastings are both "now," as are every snail and every atom that in time has been or will be. But the Christian heaven is

[31] *New Catholic Encyclopedia* (New York, 1967), s.v. "Eternity."

not static, for it promises not only eternity but also fulfillment and joy.

Aquinas, attempting to fit death into the pattern, argued that every person is mortal but also imperishable. No created being can be absolutely perishable, for nothing created is able "to not be." All works of God exist in eternity. But Thomas never blunted the reality of the experience of death. It is horrible when body and soul, which are created together and will be reunited at the endtime, are wrenched apart. Death is terrifying, unnatural, the worst of human evils, for the soul is the form of the body and belongs with it, and death is a violent separation of the two. A human being consists of body and soul, and when these are separated, he or she ceases to exist as a human being. Aquinas explicitly said that the soul separated from the body is not a person.

This represents a firm move away from Platonic dualism toward Aristotelianism. Aristotle had rejected Plato's dichotomy between soul and body. The body cannot exist without the soul, nor the soul without the body; together they are one human entity. The soul is not, as Plato taught, like a driver separate and distinct from the vehicle he is steering, but rather the form of the body itself. Soul and body are essentially inseparable. Aquinas went beyond Aristotle: where Aristotle said that a generic human soul is the form of humanity making the human race human, Aquinas's soul (anima) is not only a generic soul but an individual soul proper to Mary or John. The anima is the form of the body, by which the body exists. Since the soul is the form of the body, the soul and body are formally united. Therefore the separation of the soul from the body cannot last forever. Even when temporarily detached from one another in the interim period, body and soul remain one united human being. Not only is the soul more human with its body than without it, it is actually more like God, because with the body its nature is more perfected.

Still, Aquinas was haunted by the problem of the interim. It would seem that the body is necessary to human beatitude. And certainly a body is necessary in this life. This life is an imperfect blessedness, but in the interim between death and resurrection, the souls of the blest see God and enjoy a true and perfect blessedness. The state of the blest after the resurrection will be even more perfect. This difference of degree in perfection is consistent with Aquinas's ontological scale, in which things may be perfect according to their status but less perfect than something above them. The beatitude of the soul separated from the body is perfect for the status of separated souls but less perfect than the perfection of soul and body rejoined. The perfection of the human being requires the perfection of the body, for human beings remain composite even during the time when soul and body are rent apart and the body destroyed. The separated soul longs for its body, without which it is not complete, and its happiness will grow when its body is restored. In general the blest will not be embodied in heaven until the resurrection, but there are two exceptions: Jesus and Mary, who are already corporeally with the angels and in the state of final perfection. Enoch, Elijah, and Moses, previously believed to be in the empyrean, are really in the earthly paradise or else in a lesser "heaven" in the air, not in the empyrean (Dante would adopt this view). Christ's body is the earthly body of Jesus, the glorified body of Jesus, the church, and the consecrated Eucharist.

The problem of the interim continued to vex the theologians on into the fourteenth century. Either we have complete beatitude at the moment of death, or we do not have it before the Last Judgment. If we have to wait to the endtime, where and in what form are we waiting? But if we have it right away, do we have it without our bodies? The dispute racked the church of the early fourteenth century, as theologians ransacked the fathers to support one or another position. Most of the earlier fathers had assumed that souls had to wait until the endtime for the beatific vision. But others took the view that the blessed see God right away at death, and this latter view had become dominant in the West during the scholastic period and was asserted again at the

Council of Vienne in 1311. The East on the whole continued to accept the earlier view.

The question was reopened in 1331 by Pope John XXII (1316–34), who inclined to the position that we must wait till the end for the consummation of our bliss. John thought that beatitude might be granted to the elect at the moment of their death, but not the full vision of God, which they could have only at the end. John, unsure himself, never made an official statement; he let his opinion be known, but he asked Cardinal Jacques Fournier to study the question and report to him. Fournier declared that the pope's views on the subject were false and affirmed that we enter into full beatitude immediately on death. The question was discussed throughout Europe and soon became part of the complex political struggles of the day. For different political reasons, the University of Paris, King Charles VI, Emperor Lewis IV, and the Spiritual Franciscans all attacked John vigorously.

Fournier's views prevailed, and John, subdued, issued a retraction of his own opinion shortly before his death in December 1334. The question was then settled by Fournier, now Pope Benedict XII, in his constitution *Benedictus Dei* of January 29, 1336, which further alienated the Eastern Church but was confirmed by the Roman Catholic Church in the Constitution *Benedictus Deus* 550 years later in 1886. Benedict declared it as perpetual truth that the blessed dead, even before the resumption of their bodies and the Last Judgment have been, are, and will be in heaven. They see the divine essence face to face with intuitive vision, with no medium other than the divine essence showing itself to them clearly and nakedly. When they see in this way, they have full enjoyment of the divine essence. Thus there is no intermediate state for the blest (as opposed to those needing purgation). They enjoy the beatific vision in heaven immediately. But this decree did not resolve the question of how to perceive the so-called "time" that the soul passes waiting for its reunion with its body.

The efforts of the scholastics to define heaven along with other realities above nature were from the outset questioned by theologians arguing that such entities as heaven and God were beyond human reason. Thomas Aquinas, the greatest of the rationalists, understood this. Though the kataphatic way of reason dominated, other, more apophatic trains of thought, mystical and poetic, about heaven continued. The greatest Latin Christian hymns, the *Dies irae*, the *Stabat mater*, the *Pange lingua*, and the *Veni Sancte Spiritus*, are deeply affective and metaphorical, yet they are products of the thirteenth-century scholastic milieu. The contemplatives or "mystics" of the twelfth through fourteenth centuries offered other ways of seeing.

✣ 10 ✣

The Fire of Love

THE Christian view of the "mystical experience" is that it is the experience of the presence of God. The direct experience of the silence of God is ineffable, beyond words, and therefore notoriously difficult to discuss. Even the name for the phenomenon is unsatisfactory. The term "mysticism" was not invented before the eighteenth century, and though the word is rooted in Dionysius' *via mystica* (mystical path), it slumps today under burdensome connotations of superstition, credulity, and cult. At the end of the twentieth century the term "spirituality" is in use, though it too is a modern, eighteenth-century word and implies the life of prayer in general more than its culmination. In the Middle Ages the closest approximation was the "contemplative life," but this sounds almost exclusively monastic and also connotes a life of prayer that is much broader than, though it may culminate in, the direct experience of God. The best course is to use the term "spirituality," despite its difficulties. The essence of Christian spirituality in the Middle Ages was the intense, perfect communion of the individual, with the Christian community. This kind of spirituality characterized the monastic tradition; in the later medieval and modern periods spirituality transcended cloister walls, often becoming less communitarian and more individualistic.

Spirituality is loving prayer, above all a choice to live a life of love, to fulfill one's humanity by seeking one's natural state of being in love with God and the cosmos, open, flowing, free.

The spiritual life puts one in touch with something inaccessible that fills the cosmos but is beyond it, inexhaustible and incomprehensible. The spiritual tradition takes the apophatic view that we can receive God through love more than through the intellect.

Receptivity to God draws upon, transcends, and transforms both the intellectual and the affective; it is intuitive and unmediated. It is a connection of mutual interpenetration, as a fire leaps up from below and from above in one movement, merging the lover with the beloved in passionate union while preserving the identity of each. This is the fire of love. It may flash from contemplation of natural beauty, or of the beauty of art, or of the beauty that is within us. Isaac the Syrian (seventh century) called it a kindling of the heart for all creation. Most often it glows from attentive prayer. It often comes unwilled, and in the brief but eternal moment in which it embraces us, it is overwhelming. It shakes us, rearranges us, sorts us out. In it we know the tree, the music, the human most fully in themselves; each creature, by being most fully itself, is most fully in God. So a tree is a tree (an individual pine or olive), but it is also Tree, a theophany. For the contemplative, every thing is what it is in its particular individuality and at the same time something more. This is the heart of metaphorical ontology: to accept the overt sense while affirming the fuller truth of the metaphorical sense. Many of the key metaphors for the mutual opening to one another of God and a human soul are identical to the metaphors for heaven. Peace, quiet, freedom from worldly concern, and the wonderfully paradoxical metaphor, *negotissimum otium*, a complete leisure that is intense activity: these describe both the spiritual life and the life of heaven.

The Christian spiritual tradition was early exemplified by Augustine and Dionysius. In the twelfth and thirteenth centuries its outstanding examples in the West were Bernard and Francis of Assisi. Bernard, and the Cistercian monastic tradition after him, melded intellect and will, discipline and joy, love of soul and love of body. The Cistercians were often able to remove themselves from the experience of mutual opening enough to be able to write about it, even though they knew that conceptualizing or verbalizing stepped back from the mutual opening itself, which cannot be described except in metaphor. Francis himself seems to have been so often fully immersed in the connection that he did not discuss it, though Franciscans who followed him, such as Bonaventure, did.

The activity of contemplation is prayer. Not desultory prayer, but a devotion of one's life to living in God. Eating, reading, sleeping, writing, making love, running, singing—all activities good in themselves—are prayers when lifted lovingly to God. Contemplative prayer is above all the attitude of loving attention. Even the negative feelings that we naturally experience, such as envy, greed, anger, or contempt, are part of prayer when we hold them out to God with the intent that he transform them. Prayer entails complete honesty with oneself; we pray from where we are and who we are and what we feel, not from what we think we ought to be or feel.

Contemplative prayer is what we are born for. It is, were it not for the Fall, as natural and uninterrupted as breathing. It is our deepest human nature to be in a state of loving attention, but we deform that nature through both intellect and will. So we need the grace of Christ's creative love to open us up and to renew our original form. When one learns to do this, everything is rearranged. We are no longer the center of our own lives; God is the center. God prays through us, so that we pray "in from" God as much as we pray "out to" him; indeed, we pray "out from God" as well. Prayer is to all directions and from all directions, and the distinction between our selves and God shrinks and is concentrated in a tension of fiery proximity.

False spirituality shows itself in a longing to "have a mystical experience," to gain and possess it, instead of pouring out the self to God, even if he never favors one with such an experience. False spirituality shows itself in boasting of one's spiritual achievements or in withdrawing from others and attempting to love God without loving one's fellow creatures. For whoever says that he loves God, but does not love his neighbor, is a liar (1 Jn 4.20). The true life of prayer is both quiet and active: quiet in its security, active in works of love. In this too the life of prayer is analogous to the life of heaven. And also in this: all prayers are eternally present with God—prayers from the past, the present, the future, from all believers who are bound together in him. So close is the analogy between prayer and heaven that spiritual theologians speculated whether one might in this life flow so completely into God that one could have the beatific vision in this world. The consensus was no. As a great gift from God one might, like Paul, receive a startling intimation of ultimate reality, but that reality itself would be seen only in heaven.

The spiritual vision of contemplatives in this life, therefore, raised questions similar to that of the vision of the resurrected. Do we see with our physical eye, or with our spiritual eye? Do we experience reality with our whole being, body and soul, or primarily or exclusively with the soul? The spiritual writers used "soul" to mean either the active, thinking, willing principle in the mind, or a metaphorical "place" deep within us, the "place" where God dwells and where we meet him.

The idea of a union with God comparable in intensity to that of spouses in loving intercourse was reinforced by Bernard's commentary on the Song of Songs. The Song glorifies the body; bride and groom worship one another with their bodies. Human physical love is wondrously good in the sight of God, so much so that it is the best metaphor of the union of God with the human soul. With such assumptions, the spirituals often used sensuous, even sensual, imagery to describe this connection, and also that of the soul with God in heaven. Eros and agape become one. The idea of the mystical marriage between Christ and the soul, an image permeating theology, literature, and art, expressed the eternal union of two in one. Sometimes this union was expressed with an ethereal distance from the physical, more often in a sensual blend of the ethereal with the corporeal similar to that typifing the love poetry of these centuries. And sometimes it was expressed as sensual passion. German spirituals spoke of the *Minnesturm*, the storm of love that overcomes and transforms the lover in mystical as in sexual union. Ælfric (955–1020) represents Saint Agnes as saying of Christ, "When he enters me, he makes me whole."[32]

The description of sensual spirituality by Angela of Foligno (1248–1309) is well known:

> And he began to speak the following words, to challenge me to love of him. "My daughter sweet to me, my daughter my temple, my daughter my delight, love me, for you are much beloved by me, much more than you love me." And very often he called me, "Daughter and my sweet bride. . . . Therefore, since I have entered you and rested in you, you may now enter me and rest in me. . . . My beloved, my bride, love me, for your whole life, your eating and drinking and your sleeping and all your loving pleases me, if you will love me."[33]

Hildegard of Bingen (1098–1179) was an artist, poet, musician, theologian, and visionary. Her greatest visionary work is *Know the Ways of the Lord (Scivias)*, written between 1141 and 1150 and consisting of twenty-six visions, of which six are of the otherworld. Hildegard speaks of a "beautiful light in which was a human form which shone with a most loving and gentle fire, and that beautiful light permeated the gentle fire, and the fire permeated the lovely light, and both fire and light permeated the human form."[34]

The visions, letters, and poems of Hadewijch (early thirteenth century) are diverse, most of them intensely ascetic, filled with the unitive experience. "I saw his greatness oppressed under all. I saw his littleness exalted above all. I saw his hiddenness embracing and flowing through all things: I saw his breadth

---

[32] Aelfric, *Life of Saint Agnes*, in Walter W. Skeat, ed., *Lives of Saints* (London, 1881–1900), 1:170–74.

[33] *Vita Beatae Angelae*, 49–50, in Elizabeth Alvilda Petroff, ed. and trans., *Medieval Women's Visionary Literature* (New York, 1986), 17.

[34] Hildegarde, *Scivias*, trans. Valerie Lagorio, in Paul Szarmach, ed., *An Introduction to the Medieval Mystics of Europe* (Albany, N.Y., 1984), 165.

enclosed in all."[35] Here Hadewijch was speaking like Dionysius or like the later author of the *Cloud of Unknowing*. But she also recorded an intense spirituality of love. Hadewijch, like Francis of Assisi and Dante, used the poetry of romantic love to express the emotional tensions of the longing for God: the Beloved is passionate and understands passion in love.

> With what wondrous sweetness the loved one and the Beloved dwell one in the other, and how they penetrate each other in such a way that neither of the two distinguishes himself from the other. But they abide in one another in fruition, mouth in mouth, heart in heart, body in body, and soul in soul, while one sweet divine Nature flows through them both (2 Pt 1.4), and they are both one thing through each other, but at the same time remain two different selves—yes, and remain so forever.[36]

She had an ecstatic vision of Christ in the Eucharist:

> He came in the form and clothing of a Man . . . looking like a Human Being and a Man, wonderful, and beautiful, and with glorious face. . . . [After communion] he came himself to me, took me entirely in his arms, and pressed me to him; and all my members felt his in full felicity, in accordance with the desire of my heart and my humanity. So I was outwardly satisfied and fully transported.

And

> On a certain Pentecost Sunday I had a vision at dawn. . . . My heart and my veins and all my limbs trembled and quivered with eager desire and, as often occurred with me, such madness and fear beset my mind that it seemed to me that if I did not content my Beloved, and my Beloved did not fulfill my desire, dying I must go mad, and going mad I must die.[37]

---

[35] Hadewijch, Vision 6, translated by Mother Columba Hart, O.S.B., *Hadewijch* (Ramsey, N.J., 1980), 279.

[36] Translated by Lagorio, in Szarmach, *Introduction to the Medieval Mystics*, 176.

[37] Vision 7, in Hart, *Hadewijch*, 280–81.

Eastern Christian spirituality followed a distinct but similar path. The East was less influenced than the West by Greek philosophy, having been cut off from the ancient intellectual tradition since the emperor Justinian closed the schools of Athens in the sixth century. The monks, especially the hesychasts (Greek contemplatives of the fourteenth century whose intellectual roots went back to the Cappadocian fathers), insisted on the gulf between philosophy and Christianity.

The apophatic sense of God's utter unknowability had always been stronger in the East. In the East the gap was wide between that unknowability and theosis, the union of the soul with God. The hesychasts tried to bridge the gulf between God and the soul through the traditional distinction between ousia (essence; God-in-himself) and energeia (God's manifestation of himself in the world). God's essence is forever completely beyond us, but through his energeia he reveals himself to us, enters into us, and deifies us. Deification means membership in the body of Christ and is granted by free divine grace. It shows itself in apatheia, lack of passion, the idea being that any disturbance of the soul blocks us from Christ. Apatheia is not achieved by repressing the passions but rather by presenting them to God to be transformed.

The most important hesychast was Gregory Palamas (1296–1359), author of *For the Defense of Those Who Practice Sacred Quietude*. For Palamas, God would be merely a philosophical abstraction if he were not a personality that knows, creates, and loves. An impersonal God lacking these capacities would be less than God. It is God's energeia that we can know. "Human beings see and recognize the energies of God, as power, as light, as majesty, and in countless other ways. Therefore, the vision of God . . . does not have as its object the divine essence, but the divine energies. These appear sometimes without mediation, sometimes through the medium of creation."[38] Even in the unmediated vision we have only the experience of his glory, as the

[38] George Mantzardis, "Spiritual Life in Palamism," in Jill Raitt, ed., *Christian Spirituality: High Middle Ages and Reformation* (New York, 1987), 212.

apostles saw Christ in the transfiguration. For Palamas the most important metaphor for the medium was light. The light that we perceive on earth is an action (energeia) of God's own Light in the cosmos that he creates and loves. The light of the sun or stars is a creature; Light is God himself.

In the later medieval West, spiritual writers such as Meister Eckhart (1260–1327), Richard Rolle (1300–49), the anonymous author of *The Cloud of Unknowing* (about 1345), John Ruysbroeck (1293–1381), and Julian of Norwich (1342–1413) were often more personal and less communitarian in their spirituality. God produces the cosmos, dwells in it, and draws it to him. Individual objects do not and cannot exist independently but only so far as they are in God. Creatures are absolutely nothing without God; if God withdrew from a creature for a moment, it would cease to be.

Eckhart wrote that secretly all nature seeks God and works toward him. This inner force draws every created thing back to its divine source. God does not dwell more in one place or in one creature than in another; God is present everywhere and always and is equally ready to give himself to all. God is close to each human and to every other creature. God is present in a stick or a stone, though they do not know it. If the stick knew God and recognized how near he is, the stick would be as blessed as the angels. A person may be more blessed than a stick only because he or she has the power to recognize God and to know his presence. However, humans are also *worse* off than a stick, for a stick has no power to block God by putting something between itself and him, whereas humans construct shells to shield themselves from the divine reality. "As long as the soul's shells are intact—be they ever so slight—the soul cannot see God."[39] When the human opens himself or herself fully to God, they are united, and the person's "truest I" is God.

Eckhart's closeness to the Eastern idea of theosis or divinization was not much liked by contemporary theologians. He was

[39] Raymond Blakney, trans., *Meister Eckhart* (New York, 1941), 129–30.

accused of heresy for claiming that humanity was identical with God, although he intended merely that the soul is both in some way united/identified with God and in some way distinct from him. He speaks of a oneness in ground of being between God and the soul, a oneness that sin has blotted from our eyes. We can allow God to remove the alienation by detaching ourselves from the concerns of this world and by breaking through illusion to the reality of love.

Ruysbroeck understood the dynamism of the Trinity. The Persons of the Godhead perpetually renew their contentment in a new gushing forth of love, in an ever new embrace within the Unity. In this embrace, all things are consummated, and in the gushing forth of love all things are wrought, and in the life-giving and fruitful nature of God lie the power and possibilities of all things, the beginning of all life and all becoming. And so all creatures are therein, beyond themselves, one being and one life with God, as in their eternal origin.

Julian received a number of visions or "showings," which taught her too that our yearning for God will be met by God's yearning for us in absolute union. The human person and the whole cosmos are one with God, a concept for which Julian created a new word, "oneing." Her images of union are varied. Her vision of the cosmos as a hazelnut held in her hand expressed roundness, enclosure, containment; other of her images are indwelling; eating and nursing and drinking; Jesus as life-giving, nourishing, and fostering mother.

Heaven is more an eternal opening up than a static perfection. "However much the theologians of the thirteenth century might define blessedness as the stilling of desire, spiritual writers came increasingly to treat love as a longing that cannot be satiated or filled, magnifying itself forever as each increase of joy further stimulates need."[40]

These writers' affirmation of the divine nature of the cosmos, of the fact that creatures and creation have meaning only as part

[40] Bynum, *Resurrection of the Body*, 329.

of the divine, of the intense yearning of the cosmos and humanity for God, of God's use of his energeia, especially light, as means to draw us back to him, of the ecstasy of our union with God, of God as lover and spouse, and of the beatific vision surpassing all language and imagination—these insights of spirituality informed Dante's view of the celestial paradise in the *Divine Comedy*.

✥ 11 ✥

Approaching Paradise

THE *Paradiso* of Dante Alighieri (1265–1321) is the most sublime portrait of heaven from the Book of Revelation to the present. I conclude this history of the concept of heaven with Dante, because beyond Dante no merely human word has gone. The meaning of the *Paradiso* opens out infinitely, and Dante's heaven seems to pierce through the cosmos to the truth encompassing it. Dante was born in Florence in 1265, into an important, politically active family, and he expressed his political views in action and writing. It is extraordinary for his time that the pen of a politician, a layman rather than a priest, a poet rather than a theologian, produced a view of heaven that none has equaled.

In 1274, when he was almost nine, he met the eight-year-old Beatrice Portinari. He did not see her again for another nine years; they both married other spouses; but Beatrice was his first and greatest love on earth, and in 1290 she died. Dante needed to reconcile her death with the benevolent order of the universe, and he did so by imagining a "new life," *vita nuova*, in heaven, where he would be reunited with his beloved. For the young Dante, Beatrice was the unattainable lady of romantic love; for the older Dante she became much more. In 1292–93, several years after Beatrice's death, Dante composed his *Vita Nuova*, in which he wove his poetry together within a coherent prose commentary in Tuscan, which has become, largely owing to Dante, standard Italian.

In the *Vita Nuova* Beatrice is already more than a woman, more even than a romantic ideal. Dante claims to have had a dream or vision of Beatrice in heaven; such is the glory of her countenance that it wounds the eyes of one looking upon her, and no one can fix his gaze on her face. This is a stunning metaphor, for in the Bible and tradition it is the Lord's countenance upon which none can gaze and live. Beatrice's eyes, and the light of love emanating from them, would become one of the central metaphors of the *Paradiso*. The name Beatrice derives from "blessed" (*beata*), and Dante thought her name a sign of her ontological reality. Beatrice is a metaphor for the restoration of human nature in a state even more perfect than its beginning. Had Dante made the Beatrice of the *Vita Nuova* an end in herself, she would have been an idol, but he saw her as a medium drawing him and the whole world toward God. Beatrice, in her power to save, became a metaphor of faith, hope, and love, for grace, for Mary, even for Christ, but the power came not from herself but from God through her.

By 1308 Dante had finished his *Convivio* (*The Banquet*). The old notion that the *Convivio* was a philosophical detour in the progress of Dante's mystical and poetic vision is now rejected. The *Convivio* contains his first deep discussions of the meaning (as distinct from the form) of language. In the *Convivio* Dante followed tradition in asserting that Scripture has four senses (overt, allegorical, moral, and anagogical), but that other literature can have only two, the literal and the allegorical. Only God, the ultimate Author of the Bible, can speak words that correspond to ultimate reality. Dante wished his writing to be taken primarily allegorically and secondarily in the literal or overt sense.

The "Letter to Can Grande della Scala" presents a different view. Since 1819 scholars have disputed whether Dante himself wrote the "Letter." Several contemporary scholars are skeptical, but the letter's authenticity is accepted by most Dantists. The problem touches the central question of what Dante intended by writing the *Paradiso*, but it may be insoluble. The author of the "Letter," which is in effect an introduction to the *Paradiso*, indicated that Dante believed that the *Paradiso*, like the Bible, uttered all four senses, expressing reality as God knows it. This claim was taken seriously by commentators, who immediately after the poet's death began to gloss the *Divine Comedy* line by line, a process hitherto reserved for the Bible or to other texts of ancient authority, such as the *Aeneid* or the works of Aristotle. These commentators and glossators read the *Divine Comedy* not *as* Scripture but in some way *like* Scripture, applying the four senses of interpretation.

Even this extraordinary view, however, stopped short of considering the *Paradiso* a true revelation. The canon of Scripture had been set by the fourth century and could not be augmented. Closest to Dante in intention were the great mystics such as Dionysius, Eckhart, and Bernard—Bernard, who at the end of the poem leads Dante toward God himself. Dante the poet wrote that Dante the persona is given a divine vision through Vergil, Beatrice, and Bernard, but exactly what he meant is uncertain. He knew that the Christian community recognizes only the Bible as guaranteed revelation. But this means only that no other work can be *guaranteed* to be revealed, not that no other work is in fact revealed. Christian tradition also allowed that some works, though falling short of revelation, could be inspired by God. Dante may have viewed the *Paradiso* as less than revealed but more than merely inspired.

The main question can be simply stated: did Dante intend that the *Paradiso* be taken as divinely inspired in the fullest sense, that is, as a description of ultimate reality? Such an intent has been called a theological reading, or an allegory of the theologians (as opposed to profane allegory), or the prophetic mode, or metaphorical ontology, or what Marcia Colish calls redeemed rhetoric. In any event, the *Paradiso* expresses meaning in the symbolic, far more than the overt, sense. Dante was confident that although no human language can manifest God's ontological reality, the Divine Word could dwell in human words. Dante sought "to reverse the ancient exile of our language from its source, to bring our fallen words through hell and purgation so that in the context of heaven they may rejoin the divine syntax."[41] "For as the derived multiplicity of the creation returns to its common and original source, what the poet gives us is nothing less than the resurrection of every mortal word . . . edited at last into a single divine volume and bound together by love."[42]

The *Divine Comedy* is about language, not only Dante's language about heaven, but God's own language. In the *Comedy* one cannot separate the medium from the message. The narrative, and every word, phrase, turn of rhyme, even verse numbers, have meaning. To stretch human language further beyond its normal bounds, Dante invented neologisms, as had the Greek and Latin translators of the Bible. These new word creations were efforts to capture the eternal metaphysical realities that normal language cannot express.

Even with the doubt about the letter to Can Grande, the *Paradiso* itself indicates that Dante intended to write things-in-themselves, things that are eternally true in the mind of God. No one can judge the validity of such a claim, but in reading the *Paradiso* one encounters a living work of such lucid reality that one senses, as in the music of Mozart, the presence of a hand beyond the human.

The *Paradiso* is one of the three books (*cantiche*) of Dante's masterpiece, the *Divine Comedy*. Dante may have begun the *Comedy* as early as 1304; he finished the *Inferno* by 1314, the *Purgatorio* by 1319, and the *Paradiso* shortly before his death in 1321. His view of the *Comedy* developed between the *Inferno*, where he explicitly calls it a *comedìa* (16.128), and the *Paradiso*, where he calls it a "sacred poem" (cantos 23, 25). Dante the author grew spiritually as he approached the *Paradiso*; he seems to have had a powerful experience, perhaps a vision, before writing or while writing the *Paradiso*. In any event, conviction

[41] Peter S. Hawkins, "Trespassing on the Word," *Journal of the American Academy of Religion* 47 (1979): 47.

[42] Hawkins, "Resurrecting the Word," *Religion and Literature* 16 (1984): 69.

and feeling—as well as literary perfection—are at the core of the *Paradiso*. Still, the *Commedia* was not called the *Divina commedia*, *The Divine Comedy*, until two centuries after Dante wrote it.

The *Comedy* consists of three books of thirty-three cantos each, with the addition of the introductory canto of the *Inferno*, which brings the total to one hundred cantos. The poem is written in verse triplets, which Dante had never used before but now invented as suitable to a sacred text. The trinitarian symbol of three times thirty-three cantos written in triplets could scarcely be clearer.

Dante's purpose in undertaking the *Comedy* was intimately connected with his choice of language and form. He intended it as an expression of the deepest truth of the universe, its divine and moral purpose. He meant it to encompass the vastness of human experience edited and bound in a single volume written by God: God writes the cosmos, God writes the Bible, and God through Dante, writes the *Divine Comedy*.

Dante chose a traditional form of narrative, the vision expressed as voyage. Dante the poet presents Dante the narrator, who describes the voyage of Dante the persona. On the overt level it is the journey of the persona through hell and purgatory to heaven. The journey is a pilgrimage, and though Dante himself seldom called the persona "pilgrim," the term is at present employed to denote Dante as persona and so to distinguish him from Dante as narrator or poet. Dante the poet reports the experiences of Dante the pilgrim. Yet this can be misleading, for in the deeper sense what I have described as three aspects of Dante are identical: The journey is the journey of Dante himself, Dante the living poet. It is also the pilgrimage of everyman. The famous opening line situates the *Comedy* in the middle of the journey of *our* life (*nostra vita*). The journey, expressed in space and time, is a spiritual pilgrimage we all may undertake.

It is vision as well as voyage. Dante's model was the experience of Saint Paul; he goes to heaven even before his death as Paul did, and, as Paul did, returns. But unlike Paul, who said that he was not permitted to relate what he experienced in his vision, Dante tells us what he saw. And where Paul was ambiguous about his state of existence during his ascent—"whether in the body or out of the body I do not know" (2 Cor 12.2)— Dante's pilgrim journeys in his body. By choosing Paul as model, Dante chose a precursor who "went" as well as "saw." Debates as to whether Dante was poet or visionary are pointless. He was both: a master of language and the recorder of real spiritual experience.

The space and time through which the pilgrim passes are real, but not the same space and time that we experience in this life. As Dante's language surpasses normal human language, so his spacetime surpasses normal spacetime. Whenever he may have had his vision, the poet made the fictive date of the voyage 1300. In that year Dante was thirty-five, in the middle of his life, halfway through the allotted span of threescore and ten, and approximately the age of Christ at his Passion. On a lower level, it was the year of Dante's consulship and also of the Jubilee of 1300, an event planned by Pope Boniface VIII to have an anagogical, eschatological sense as well as a commemorative one. The poem is set in Holy Week of 1300, from Maundy Thursday through Easter Sunday, the period when Christ suffered, died, descended into the underworld, and rose again from the dead. The pilgrim's journey is similar, though not identical, to Christ's. He goes from earth through hell, purgatory, heaven, and back to earth. He is transformed by his journey, which he experiences psychologically as real time. The poet knows that in heaven time is different, but he has to report the pilgrim's journey in temporal terms because humans have no verbs or concepts to express the eternal moment.

The spatial arrangements of the *Divine Comedy* are fictive on one level; on another level, they are based upon current astronomical views, with theological additions; and on the deepest level, they express the divine, moral meaning of the cosmos. In the *Inferno*, the pilgrim descends downward through closed circles to the lightless, motionless center of the universe, which is

Satan's belly at the center of hell at the center of the earth. On the mountain of purgatory, the pilgrim moves upward in spirals; in heaven he rises through permeable spheres of light. Hell and purgatory gave Dante wide scope for invention; in heaven, however, he worked within the established physical cosmology of the spheres, mounting through those of the moon, Mercury, Venus, the sun, Mars, Jupiter, Saturn, and the fixed stars to the outermost sphere of astronomy, the primum mobile, the sphere that moves all the others. Beyond the primum mobile physical science did not and could not go; once again the poet turned to theology to describe that which is beyond all the spheres, the empyrean, heaven, the celestial paradise, the dwelling of God.

The nature of space in heaven had always been closely connected with its accommodation of resurrected bodies. Dante puts the pilgrim in what is present time on earth, that is, in the time between Christ's Passion and the general resurrection at the end of the world. As Caroline Bynum puts it, Dante gives "a body" to the human soul "at exactly that moment, theologically and ontologically speaking, at which it has none": the period between death and resurrection.[43] At the "time" of his journey, only the pilgrim, Christ, and Mary have true bodies in heaven, and the pilgrim only temporarily. What the pilgrim encounters are the blessed spirits awaiting the return of their bodies. But the poet, in assigning appearance, shape, speech, and motion to the spirits, was obliged to use the language of embodiment. Dante was, like theologians before him, unable to describe pure spirit, so he resorted to the old notion of aerial bodies. He explained that the shades are made of form plus air, unlike earthly bodies, which are made of form plus blood. But this is metaphor and close to the purely imaginary. The poet knew that the bodies are not and cannot be made of air, but he needed the figure of speech to allow him to assign recognizable characteristics of appearance and voice to the individual spirits that the pilgrim meets.

---

[43] Caroline Bynum, "Imagining the Self," in Sang Hyun Lee et al., eds., *Faithful Imagining* (Atlanta, Ga., 1995), 85.

The resurrection body will be completely different from the aerial body; it will be form and blood, true flesh, ontologically real in the overt sense. Though the poet intended the corporeal characteristics of the spirits as allegory, they point to the deeper truth that, as Aquinas said, both body and soul are required for a human self. Thus the poet made the body a part of the process of redemption, not something extrinsic to it.

The *Comedy* unfolds as narrative, and I treat it as such rather than imposing modern analytical categories upon it. Along with his overt journey through hell, purgatory, and heaven, the pilgrim goes on a spiritual journey, in the course of which he experiences three conversions. The first is at the beginning, when Beatrice causes Vergil to steer him out of the woods in the right direction; the second is his struggle in the earthly paradise at the summit of purgatory, where the waters of Lethe and Eunoë transform him; the third is at the end, when he is lofted into the celestial rose.

The first book (*cantica*) of the *Divine Comedy* is the *Inferno*, and the first canto of the *Inferno* is an introduction to the journey. The first triplet shows the pilgrim lost in a deep wood. Right at the outset the poet declares his primary intent to be moral allegory. But the allegory is intensely personal. When the poet describes the pilgrim as so lost that he is more or less dead (1.7), he is describing, without hyperbole, his poignant sense of his own moral state. Thus at the outset the poem announces that the pilgrim both is and is not the poet himself.

Dante also declares at the start the purpose of the entire poem: he wishes to write of the good that he found on his voyage, but in order to do so he must also speak of other things, pain and suffering (1.8–9). Still, those will come later. In cantos 1–2, the poet, before leading his readers down into hell, prepares them for future happiness. "The good that I found," he says, is love. The word *amor* appears already in the first canto, and it is "God's love that in the beginning set all the beauty of the universe in motion": *quando l'amor divino mosse di prima quelle cose belle* (1.39–40). In the first canto appears the first use

of the word "shade," *ombra* (1.66), to describe the state of the
people he encounters in the *Inferno*, a term the poet will explain
in the *Purgatorio*. The first shade he encounters in the poem is
Vergil, who makes the first reference to Beatrice (though not by
name). By the end of the first canto Dante has already unveiled
the mode, the purpose, the goal, and the main personae of the
poem.

The second canto introduces three images that will figure
powerfully in the poem: eyes, star, and light. Both the stars and
eyes, especially Beatrice's eyes, are mediums through which
Light itself shines. Soon Beatrice's name is mentioned for the
first time, by Vergil, who reports that she had told him that Love
had moved her to come from the place (the empyrean heaven) to
which she longs to return (2.70–72). These lines link *amor* and
disio, "love" and "desire," the poet's usual words for love, and
he will make no distinction between them. Beatrice has descended from her proper seat, next to Rachel in the highest
heaven. At the same "time" that Beatrice is "really" in highest
heaven, she descends to limbo (the first circle of hell) in order to
speak with Vergil. She is at the same "time" in two "places."
The cause of her coming is Love. God's Love prompts Mary,
the mother of Christ, to send Saint Lucy to tell Beatrice to come
down and help rescue Dante (both poet and pilgrim) from his
moral wandering (2.97). By her love and warmth, Beatrice frees
him to seek his original and true purpose: union with God.

Now Vergil leads Dante into hell, for whose inhabitants all
hope is lost, and where the dark shadow sinks ever deeper over
the pilgrim (3.1–22). The darkness is alleviated for a while by
occasional references to God and to Beatrice, but the pilgrim's
prayer to the Highest Wisdom (19.10–12) is the last hopeful
reference, the last glimpse of heaven, in the *Inferno* until its very
end. The poet frequently points to the distinction between the
pilgrim and the shades, who wonder or complain that the pilgrim visits them in his body while they lack their own (8.84–85).

The pilgrim moves down through the circles of hell to the
center of the earth and of the universe, to the still point of the

turning world, the dead center where all weight and all sin converge. At that point there can be no more motion; the whole gravity of the cosmos and the sum of all sins have here sunk to their true level and adhere in a great mass, pressing on Satan with all the weight of the world (*Parad.* 29.57). This stalemate is the sign of the futility, meaninglessness, darkness, and non-being of this point that is infinitely distant from God. Satan is God's opposite: darkness to light, cold to warmth, hatred to love, heaviness to buoyancy. He is blind, deaf, speechless, dead, ignorant, hideous, closed down rather than opening up. He is trapped, a grotesque parody of a king, the emperor of the miserable kingdom, ruling the wretched in his anti-city (34.28) as opposed to God ruling the joyful in Jerusalem (*Parad.* 12.40). He is nothingness and meaninglessness as opposed to being and truth, a vacuum or black hole draining color and joy from the world. Satan's forced motionlessness is the opposite of God's serene and voluntary stillness. Satan's three faces are a distorted mirror of the Trinity, his immersion in ice the inversion of Christ's baptism in the living waters of Jordan, his hideous windmill shape a distortion of the saving shape of the Cross. As we close in upon ourselves when we turn away from God toward nothingness, so the center of hell is a dark mass turned infinitely in upon itself, cut completely and forever off from reality. The frozen lake in which Satan is fixed immobile is the inversion of the fiery mirror in which the pilgrim will see God's reflection. In innermost hell, as in innermost heaven, the poet sees what he cannot express in words. Words are too feeble (34.22–24) in hell, because of its infinitesimal nonbeing; in heaven, because of its infinite being.

Only after the pilgrim has experienced the ultimate horror of hell, having to turn himself on Satan's hairy flanks in order to move away from the dead center to the surface of the earth, can the poet again offer a presentiment of heaven: "we went up, Vergil first and I following, so that I saw through a round opening some of the firmament's beauty, and from there we went out to see the stars again," *E quindi uscimmo a riveder le stelle* (34.136–39).

The pilgrim and Vergil, his guide, regain the surface of the earth in the southern hemisphere. In the midst of the southern sea is the mountain of purgatory—exactly opposite Mount Zion. Frightening though purgatory is, it is theologically and morally much closer to heaven than to hell, because all the souls in purgatory will eventually be united with God. No one is in purgatory who is not saved, a member of the body of Christ. Purgatory burns away faults and fills up lacks, but the character of all its inhabitants is set firmly in God. The souls are located in purgatory according to the seven cardinal sins, and, as in hell, sinners receive condign punishment.

The *Purgatorio* begins on the shores of the island beneath the gates of purgatory, and much of the action occurs before Vergil and his charge enter purgatory proper. Again the poet emphasizes the uniqueness of the pilgrim's being truly corporeal in purgatory, where all others, awaiting the resurrection, are not bodies but only similitudes of bodies (3.32). These shades can speak, move, and feel; they can suffer heat and cold. Vergil explains to the shades that the pilgrim is a complete human being, soul and body, sojourning in the otherworld by divine dispensation.

Cantos 7 8 of the *Purgatorio* describe the Valley of Princes, where dwell rulers whose preoccupation with earthly matters impeded their salvation. The valley foreshadows the earthly paradise, which the pilgrim will later visit on the peak of the mountain of purgatory. The Valley has many elysian motifs such as trees, flowers, and grass, yet the poet describes it as being painted by Nature; in so doing he makes the point that all beauty is artifact, whether the artificer be human or divine. Here the spirits are called souls (*anime*) rather than shades (*ombre*). And they are singing. The dead silence of hell, without song and prayer, has been left behind, and the souls are singing a hymn, the "Hail, Holy Queen," *Salve Regina* (7.82). In purgatory the spirits say the Our Father (the Lord's Prayer), and there Vergil and Dante enter with song. Joy mounts as the pilgrim ascends the mount of purgatory, whetting our desire for heaven, which fulfills all joy.

Vergil and the pilgrim now enter purgatory proper (9.49). As purgatory purifies souls from their sins, so the poet, speaking through Vergil, uses it to purge the pilgrim, that is, himself, from false ideas, particularly false ideas of love. The poet introduces the topic of love in canto 10.2 and then devotes cantos 15–18 to it. Love is greater when shared, less if kept to oneself. Love always produces more love. Unlike money, love, when spent, increases. Love cannot be hoarded. Here the poet again uses *caritate* and *amor* synonymously, along with light and warmth, *luce*, and *ardore*.

Dante, mingling Dionysius and Aristotle, explains that all creatures have a natural desire for the good, and ultimately for the Good. Humans have a special desire for it in the form of intellect and will. A properly functioning intellect determines the good, and a properly functioning will chooses it (18.96). The poet uses the word *animo* for the rational soul or intellect/will, rather than the more general term for soul, *anima*. But humans can misunderstand the nature of the good; they may point themselves in the wrong direction, away from God; or else they may stop short, putting something in God's place as their ultimate good. Even among those who truly choose the Good, some can be slow to love, thus meriting less than those who respond more quickly. In heaven, the degree of love determines whether a person stands nearer to or farther from the burning center.

A peculiarly important movement occurs in canto 24. The poet places in the pilgrim's mouth words that must also be applied to the poet himself. In one of his breathtaking claims, Dante responds to Vergil's disquisition on love: "I am one who takes note of what love breathes into me, and I interpret in words its deep meaning" (24.52–54).

At last they reach the top of purgatory, and Vergil, in his last speech, warns the pilgrim that he is unable to accompany him farther. He tells him to await the happy, beautiful eyes of Beatrice (27.136). Now the pilgrim enters paradise for the first time, not heaven (*il paradiso celeste*) but the earthly paradise (*il paradiso terrestre*). Dante's earthly paradise is traditional: birds, foliage, soft breezes, fountains, four rivers, springtime without end. The earthly paradise makes us wish even more keenly than before for the celestial paradise. Now, by bathing in the river Lethe, which erases the memory of sins, and in Eunoë, which restores the memory of virtues, the pilgrim is cleansed and essentially prepared for the celestial paradise.

In the terrestrial paradise, Dante encounters a long and strange procession or parade, whose imagery derives from apocalyptic roots, and as the pilgrim watches it, the poet forges a breathtaking link between Beatrice and Christ. Beatrice addresses seven women in the procession employing the precise words of Christ to his disciples before his Passion, and she affirms its liturgical power by using Christ's own words in the Vulgate Latin translation: *modicum et vos videbitis me*, "yet a little while and you shall see me" (*Parad.* 33.12; Jn 16.16). Vergil has departed, and Beatrice returns to become Dante's guide. She appears like the rising sun on a chariot, her face veiled, wearing white, green, and red, for faith, hope, and charity. At first the pilgrim does not recognize her. But she calls out poignantly, "Look closely. I am, I really am, Beatrice": *Guardaci ben! Ben son, ben son Beatrice* (30.73). Then, to the pilgrim's and the reader's surprise, Beatrice begins a series of reproaches, rebuking Dante for his cowardice, faithlessness, misunderstanding of love, lust for false beauty and for fame. Dante the pilgrim receives the blame due to Dante the poet. This is one of the passages in the *Comedy* that sets Dante's modesty against his astonishing claims. Beatrice continues her reproach that Dante has substituted false love in place of love for her and, through her, for God. The pilgrim, having been plunged into Lethe, recognizes Beatrice more fully than he has before; she is the splendor of eternal living light, *o isplendor di viva luce etterna* (31.139).

The earthly paradise is preparing the pilgrim for the translation to heaven, and he soon espies the glorious company of the blessed, arrayed like a victorious army (32.17–22). Even now Beatrice does not cease admonishing him, telling him he is as far from heaven as the heavens are above the earth and upbraiding him for his failure of will (33.88–90). But in response Dante offers her the matching gift to his previous compliment; now he calls her "O light, O glory of the human race," *O luce, o gloria de la gente umana* (33.115). And now Dante and Beatrice leave the mountain of purgatory, purified and ready to "leap up to the stars," *puro e disposto a salire a le stelle* (33.142–45).

✤ 12 ✤

The Heavenly Paradise

In the *Paradiso* Dante presses theology, physics, and language through their limits. He intends a metaphorical ontology as close to absolute reality as humans can reach. Through revelation and inspiration God accommodates his silence to Dante's limited human will, intellect, and language. The *Comedy* moves in a stately dance between God's singing silence and Dante's speech that is song. The cosmos is what God sings, and Dante hears its harmony throughout the planets (except on Saturn, where God quiets it in mercy, for on Saturn the beauty of both sight and sound is so intense that they must be muted lest they destroy the pilgrim. Dante the poet, knowing that what he has seen is beyond human language, must accommodate his readers as God accommodates him, using language, and even pressing through it with neologisms, in order to describe what is beyond description. The first neologism of the *Paradiso* is *trasumanar*, "to go beyond the human" to that which cannot be put in human words (1.70–71).

Even as he accommodates us by singing God's silence, the poet invites us to penetrate the accommodations to a direct experience of spiritual reality. The *Paradiso*, unlike the rest of the *Divine Comedy*, is a special sort of metaphor, for its referent is unmediated, absolute reality, and Dante was obliged to report his vision in images that he could communicate to his contemporaries. The poet creates the persona (the pilgrim) as God creates the cosmos; ultimately, poet and pilgrim are one, as God and the cosmos are one.

Dante was able to imagine and arrange hell and purgatory largely as he chose, within the broad context of the tradition, but in the *Paradiso* he deliberately worked within current cosmology and astronomy in order not to contravene any cosmological truth understood in his time. The nesting spheres that surround the sphere of the earth are those of medieval astronomy. On each great sphere is set, like a jewel, the planet or stars appropriate to it. Naturally, the poet had no access to modern astronomical observations, so he did not place the pilgrim on the "surface" of a planet. When the pilgrim visits a planet, he visits a globe set upon a sphere. On Mercury, for example, as on the other planets, the pilgrim is supposed to be standing near or at or on or in the planet. Being in a planet is like being in a cloud that is bright, dense, firm, solid, and clean, like a diamond struck by the sun (2.32–33).

Theologically speaking, God, heaven, and the blest are not on the planets or in the spheres at all, but beyond them in the empyrean, beyond the cosmos itself in the highest heaven. Dante the poet pretends that to greet him the blest descend from the empyrean to spheres appropriate to their lives: warriors descend to Mars, contemplatives to the sun.

The first words of the *Paradiso* are *La gloria*, "glory," expressing the theme of the whole *Divine Comedy*. The first line also contains the verb "to move," which appears again in the last line of the *Comedy*, emphasizing the dynamism of God, heaven, the cosmos—and the poem. God moves everything; his glory penetrates through the entire cosmos, and the universe reflects it back (1.1–2). The Creator and his unique Creature, the cosmos, move in a contrapuntal dance whose consummation is union.

The cosmos reflects or refracts the ultimate Light that is God. It does so more in some places than in others (1.3). This statement at the outset of the *Paradiso* prepares for the later discussion between Beatrice and the pilgrim about the moon. Celestial bodies were believed to be perfect in their kind, but the only celestial body whose features we discern with the naked eye is the moon, which has dark spots upon a light background. The pilgrim assumes at first that some parts of the moon are denser and less translucent than others, so that the light that percolates downward from the primum mobile through sphere after sphere is less able to penetrate the dark spots. Beatrice refutes this error. Light is an expression of God's Being. All light, she says, originates in God, whose Being and Light are passed through the primum mobile down through the sphere of the fixed stars, which break it up into diverse essences (2.116). Each successive sphere diffuses the Light and Being, both in the sense of spreading it and in the sense of diluting it from level down to level, *di grado in grado* (2.122). This means that some heavenly bodies—and by extension other creatures as well—have more light and being, and therefore more virtue (power of goodness), than others. The light of God penetrates the whole universe, but according to the worth of its components (31.23). Such diffusion is needed in order to differentiate the cosmos; the original symmetry and homogeneity must be broken if a variety of creatures is to exist. This diversity does not logically require hierarchy, but hierarchy was assumed in Dante's time (as equality is assumed in ours, or at any rate, in contemporary Western rhetoric; no society can be sure that its assumptions are true). The cosmos is constructed on a descending moral and ontological scale, from God (Light, Being, Truth, and Love) all the way down to the lowest creature, that which is most lacking in light, being, truth, and love. In the midst of Beatrice's explanation, she makes the pilgrim the promise that the light she shows him will be so living that it will seem to him to tremble (2.110–11).

The word "light," *luce*, appears already in the second triplet of the *Paradiso*, the first of many instances (1.4). Dante uses *luce* and *lume* interchangeably, and he connects them both with Lucy, whom Mary sent to ask Beatrice to come down to help the sinful pilgrim. Saint Lucy is so called because in her martyrdom her tormentors crushed her eyes (*luci*). The poem is strewn brightly with synonyms for light.

At the outset of the *Paradiso* the poet announces that he writes as one who has been in the empyrean and is looking back and striving to recall what he saw and to express what he recalls.

He saw some things that he could not understand, others that he understood when he saw them but is unable to hold in memory, others that he can remember but cannot express in speech. This is one of the frequent elisions of poet and pilgrim, an explicit claim by the poet to have actually had the pilgrim's experiences and now to be recounting them. It also reminds the reader that Dante enters paradise on three levels, first the earthly paradise on the summit of purgatory, then the heavenly spheres beginning with the moon, and finally the empyrean, where dwells the Trinity itself.

Beatrice is still the pilgrim's guide, and as light percolates down through the cosmos from God, so the light of Beatrice's eyes will conduct him upward through the layered cosmos to the discovered God. She looks upward to gaze at the sun more intently than any living mortal could; the pilgrim imitates her for a moment and then turns so that his own eyes are fixed in hers as hers are fixed in the sun. Beatrice, like the sun itself, mediates God's light, and the pilgrim sees such an access of light that it is as if another sun has added its brightness to the first (1.63). The eye is both active and passive for Dante, receiving light and also sending out its own ray; thus Beatrice's eyes project God's light and so carry the pilgrim aloft. God's being and light are also love, and the love that rules the heavens draws Dante toward it (1.74–75).

As light is to the eye, so is harmony to the ear, and God draws the poet with music as he draws him with light (1.78–82). Harmony blends the melody of the angels, of the blessed, and of the spheres into one great polyphonic consonance, which signifies the perfect order of the cosmos, in which all things, apparently dissonant, are reconciled. Song and silence dance and merge.

Beatrice looks upon Dante and sees him, exactly as he is in truth: *vedea me sì com' io* (1.85). For Dante, as often for Aquinas, to see, *vedere*, is to understand, to grasp truth with the intellect. Beatrice explains to the pilgrim that he is rushing upward from the earth like lightning (1.92). This canto ends with Beatrice turning her gaze up again toward the heavens. As she looks up, Dante looks into the light of her eyes, which speeds them together upward like an arrow shot from the bow. They shoot up straight to the moon, and their bow-shot course will carry them in a straight line through the spheres, taking no account of the relative motion of the planets.

Arriving with Beatrice on the moon, which is fixed in the first sphere (counting upward from earth), the pilgrim begins his questions, each question appropriate to the sphere that he is visiting. The first soul he meets is Piccarda Donati. Looking at her, the pilgrim at first has difficulty understanding what he is seeing, for the shades, which appeared more clearly in the lower worlds, are now, in the light of the moon, as faint as a pearl on a white forehead. In the *Paradiso*, the shades become fainter as the pilgrim mounts to higher and higher spheres and are eventually entirely absorbed into light. As that process occurs, the poet gradually shifts from the term *ombra* to other terms such as *spirito, anima,* or *splendor.*

The pilgrim inquires as to the identity of Piccarda, the moon's first pale shade. Piccarda is a monastic whose lack of spiritual constancy caused her not to resist those who forced her out of the monastery. Though the least of all the monastics in heaven, Piccarda is the first blessed soul (other than Beatrice) whom Dante meets. The highest soul he will meet on his way to God will be Bernard, in Dante's view the greatest of monks and of contemplatives, and between Piccarda and Bernard the poet assigns high roles to other monastic contemplatives. The moral core of the *Paradiso* is the contemplative tradition.

The pilgrim now follows up the questions raised in the discussion of the spots on the moon. Dante is still troubled about the question of hierarchy. Why are different souls on different spheres? Why are all souls whom God saves not equally blest? But they are. All souls are really in the empyrean with God all the time, from Piccarda to the seraph that shines brightest, that most "endays itself," *s'india* (4.28). Only in a secondary sense do some spirits seem to descend through the spheres to converse with Dante. Everywhere in heaven is fully blest (*ogne dove in cielo è paradiso*), but some souls have the potential for greater love and joy than do others (3.88–90). Since each is completely and perfectly happy according to his or her potential, there is no envy, no striving; no one aspires to be higher than he or she is.

Most of the remaining time on the moon is devoted to the question of truth and intellect. God is the First Truth, *primo vero* (4.96), and Dante understands that God lifts our intellects up to him because we desire to know him (4.124). Will urges us to learn; we learn with the light of love illuminating our intellect; and our will then assents to the truth that the intellect presents. In the meanwhile the pilgrim exalts Beatrice above mortal women: *o amanza del primo amante, o diva*, "O divine beloved of the First Lover, what you speak both floods and burns me," *m'inonda e scalda* (4.118–20). Beatrice, whose own intellect and will are perfected, sees that the eternal light already blossoms in Dante's mind, and that this light in his mind kindles love, which is assent to truth and enjoyment of it (5.7–9).

Again Beatrice turns longingly upward where there is more light and love, and again the power of her gaze speeds them like arrows up to the next sphere, that of Mercury. Mercury, closer to the sun and to God than the moon is, shines brighter than the moon, and Beatrice's joyous presence makes it brighter still (5.94–96). More than a thousand shining spirits (*splendori*) approach and declare that the pilgrim increases their joy because every soul in heaven increases the joy of every other in the dynamic of love. Here the shades are so filled with the light of joy as to be transfigured (5.107–8). The first soul encountered on Mercury, Justinian, is already a light (*lumera*, the antonym of *ombra*), and he glows even more intensely as Dante addresses him (5.130–32). So brilliantly does he shine that his shape is invisible inside the brilliant ray of joy surrounding him (5.136–37).

In Mercury, Justinian and his righteous companions dance and sing hosanna to the Lord (7.1). Beatrice expresses her mounting joy in a bright smile and explains that the Incarnation of Christ is a unique, eternal act of divine love (7.17, 33). The pilgrim, when he sees Beatrice become even more beautiful, knows that he has ascended into the next sphere, that of Venus, which represents love, especially in the sense of community (8.15). The pilgrim can actually increase the joy of the blessed spirits; Charles of Naples grows brighter when he speaks to him. The poet calls Charles the "life of that holy light" (9.7), not only indicating the eternal life of heaven but also hinting that the whole life of the blest is a union of body and soul. Dante then encounters Fulk of Marseille, who appears as a shining "joy," *letizia* (9.67). The pilgrim asks Fulk to speak, since he is unable to enter into Fulk in the same way as Fulk, already a blessed spirit, can enter into him (9.81).

A great paean to love, harmony, and motion begins the canto in which the pilgrim ascends to the sun. The Trinity, breathing love dynamically within itself, transpires love out of itself, creating everything that moves in mind or space, and in such beautiful order that anyone contemplating it tastes God (10.1–6).

As they ascend, Beatrice's actions become swifter: she raises the pilgrim to the sun so quickly that he has no sense of movement. He sees within the sun lights brighter than the sun itself and distinguishable from the sun and from one another by degree of brilliance. Dante regrets not being able to help the reader imagine something brighter than the sun. The pilgrim sees approaching twelve lights brighter than the sun; "they form a crown around him, a crown even more beautiful to hear than to behold":

> Io vidi più folgór vivi e vincenti
> far di noi centro e di sé far corona,
> più dolci in voce che in vista lucente.
>
> (10.64–66)

Matching the beauty of movement to sight and sound, the twelve dance around the travelers in silence until one of the lights speaks.

From within the light, so bright that no figure is visible to the eye, comes the voice of Thomas Aquinas. Grace produces love, Thomas says, and love has grown within the pilgrim so much that it is given him to mount through the spheres. Thomas then introduces the other lights. They are the wise, including Solomon, who (the poet well knows from Bernard's commentaries) blended wisdom and love in his Song of Songs. Another light, Dionysius, was also renowned for a wisdom rooted in desire. The holy wheel of stars has not completed its first revolution when it is surrounded by another, outer circle, which harmonizes with it in a song that far surpasses any music on earth. Rainbows, garlands, dance, flame, and roses illustrate the harmony, which pauses while one of the new lights speaks. This is Bonaventure, another philosopher of love. Dionysius and Bonaventure prepare the reader for the appearance of the contemplatives later, in the highest planetary sphere. Throughout the *Paradiso*, it is not heaven itself that changes but the pilgrim, and, through him, the reader. Bonaventure, the great Franciscan, praises the founder of the Dominicans and in his praise utters the first triple rhymed *Cristo* in the *Comedy* (lines 12.71, 73, and 75 end in the word *Cristo*, strengthening the Trinitarian solemnity of the passage).

Aquinas speaks again, explaining that all things seen and unseen, mortal and immortal, constitute the splendor of the cosmos, to which God lovingly gives birth (the image of God the mother is strikingly appropriate to affective wisdom [13.52–54]). The souls in heaven, though perfectly blessed, still wish for their bodies and long to embrace those they loved on earth. In the three praises sung by the souls to the Trinity appears the historical dialectic of body/soul united, followed by body/soul separated, followed by body/soul reunited and glorified.

Dante now ascends to Mars. As the dancing circles on the sun, and later the eagle in Jupiter and the ladder in Saturn, the figure for Mars is the cross. On Mars the pilgrim sees Christ crucified, a sight too great for him to bear or remember. He can describe the cross, but not Christ upon it. Appropriately, it is here that the second rhymed triple *Cristo* of the *Comedy* appears (14.104–8).

Like the concentric circles on the sun, the cross is in constant dynamic motion around the still point of the turning world, which can be taken as Christ in his absoluteness. On Mars, in the middle cantos (15–18) of the *Paradiso*, Dante meets his ancestor Cacciaguida, who engages him in a discourse on intellect, will, and freedom. Those who know God, the pilgrim tells Cacciaguida, know that will and intellect are equal in God, who is like the sun in bringing both warmth and light (15.73). Dante asks his ancestor about the complex question of free will because he knows that Cacciaguida is with God, in the empyrean, in eternity, at the "point where all times are present at once," *il punto a cui tutti li tempi son presenti* (17.17–18). Near the end of his stay on Mars, he sees Beatrice smiling with such love that he is unable to recall the sight to his mind, but she warns him not to make her beauty or her eyes an idol, "for paradise is not only in my eyes" (18.21). The passion of earthly love is a valuable token of divine love, but a token merely.

The warning is timely, for on Jupiter the joy and purity of Beatrice's eyes increase again, and as they grow more joyful, the pilgrim learns that it is by increase of joy (not of guilt or worry) that one is aware of advancing in the kingdom of heaven. Eyes, light, understanding, and love permeate his description of Jupiter (18.70–72). Dante sees the souls or lights on Jupiter forming words in the sky, a reminder of the power of written as well as spoken language in a poem meant to be read visually as well as recited. The words are the beginning, in Latin, of the Book of Wisdom: "Love justice, you who judge the earth," *diligite iustitiam qui iudicatis terram* (18.91–93). No detail is accidental: near the middle of the quotation is the letter *M*, the Roman numeral for one thousand, the millennium.

All the lights join and settle on the *M*, which becomes the head and neck of a great eagle. The eagle is the symbol of Saint John the Evangelist, the "Eagle of Christ" (26.52) and the apostle who wrote the words "God is love" (1 Jn 4.8). The pilgrim sees and hears something never before known: the eagle, though composed of thousands of souls, speaks with one voice, or rather sings with one voice, for it is woven of hymns and songs. The excitement is accompanied by a quadruple *Cristo*, three rhymed and one unrhymed. The eagle sings, and as it sings, the lights become brighter. The poet gives the pilgrim a treasure of words to present to Beatrice: "O sweet love clothed in a smile, how you seemed to blaze in those torches whose every thought was holy. . . . After the dear, clear gems that jeweled the sixth planet ceased their angelic pealing, I seemed to hear a river's murmur (20.13–19).

The eagle speaks of the riddle of time and eternity. Our prayers are effective, not because they come to God unexpected or as a novelty, for God knows in eternity what we pray. Yet we pray because we choose to pray, and God knows in eternity what our choice is. We choose to pray because God desires that we pray and gives us the grace of prayer. The eagle gives an exegesis of Matthew 11.12 along similar lines. The kingdom of heaven is conquered by force, and the violent shall bear it away. The force it admits is the force of our hot love and living hope, which conquer the divine will (20.95–96). But the divine will yields only when it wants to yield (20.98). God gives us the grace and hope and love that we need to conquer him.

When Beatrice's countenance again intensifies, Dante knows he is in Saturn, the planet of the ladder. Here in Saturn, the highest of the planets, the spirits do not sing, nor does Beatrice smile, for if they did, the pilgrim would be consumed by the power of their beauty. The central figure of Saturn is the golden ladder through which the light shines from above and which stretches up farther than Dante can see into heaven (21.28–29). Like the dancing circles, the cross, and the eagle, the ladder is dynamic, for the pilgrim sees countless souls upon it, ascending and descending. But the ladder is even more dynamic, for it is a metonymy for the whole ascent of the pilgrim and prefigures his final mounting to the empyrean. The ladder is the ladder of

Jacob (Gn 28.12), which in contemplative literature signified the ascent of the soul to God.

Saturn is the planet of contemplative monastics, and the first soul that addresses the pilgrim is Peter Damian, the great monastic reformer, who in the midst of images of love and light says that he "enwombs himself," *m'inventro*, in light (21.84). *Inventro* could even be translated, perhaps not too fancifully, as "embelly," since the poet soon turns to images of food (21.115). The higher Dante ascends, the more he balances exalted with homely images. Next appears Benedict of Nursia, founder of Benedictine monasticism, and other contemplatives. Benedict, like the other souls hidden by blazing light from Dante's vision, tells him that he will be able to see his face later, when the pilgrim has ascended to the empyrean, for there each wish and longing is perfect, ripened, complete; every potential is realized. There every element of the cosmos is where it always "was," eternally, for the empyrean has no space, no movement, no time: *perché non è in loco e non s'impola* (22.67).

Having heard this presentiment of perfection, the pilgrim is moved up Jacob's Ladder from Saturn to the sphere of the fixed stars with a mere blink of Beatrice's eye (22.101). He looks back down from the sphere of the stars, down through all the concentric spheres, to the earth at the center, at the bottom, in the place of least honor. This vision reconfirms the view of the cosmos where up and out are better than down and in, because more open to the divine light.

From looking downward, the pilgrim turns his gaze to meet Beatrice's eyes, which have moved him toward God (22.154), and the brilliant light of Beatrice is transmuted into the brilliant light of Christ. On Mars the pilgrim had been able to see only the cross, not the figure of Christ upon it; here among the stars he sees the living light of Christ. He cannot endure such a manifestation of power and glory and must turn away. Dante's sight is weak because of his human limitations and because of sin. His sight strengthens marvelously as he ascends, but as the essence of Light shines more and more clearly through the light that he sees, his eyesight is as yet too weak to bear it (23.31–33). This vision of Christ prepares him and the reader for the final vision of the poem, when Trinity and Incarnation will at last be seen.

Christ and Mary descend to meet the pilgrim in the starry sphere. It is a breathtaking event. From now on the poet will make more and more a point of the failure of language to convey what he sees. "In order to represent or image the highest heavens, the sacred poem must leap a gap, like one who finds the road washed out before him":

> E così, figurando il paradiso,
> convien saltar lo sacrato poema,
> come chi trova suo cammin riciso.
>
> (23.61–63)

These words assert the divinely inspired nature of the *Paradiso*. They also confess its failure, and the failure of all language, to image God. The pilgrim has just left the planet of the contemplatives, who tend to follow the negative or apophatic theology that says that all we can know about God is that we can know nothing about him.

The poem now shifts to garden imagery and to Mary, the New Eve in a paradise reclaimed, reflowered, under the warm rays of Christ (23.71–72). Mary, mother of God, among humans less great only than her Son, is the "rose in which the divine Word made himself flesh," *quivi è la rosa che 'l verbo divino carne si fece* (23.73–74). Mary is attended by the archangel Gabriel, who announces: "I am angelic love; I wheel round the great joy that springs from Mary's womb, which was lodging for Christ, our Desire" (23.103–5). Gabriel praises Mary, and then she and Christ ascend beyond the pilgrim's gaze into the empyrean. The souls strain upward in longing toward Mary, as babies stretch their arms up to *mamma* (23.121). Subsiding, they sing the *Regina coeli*, the highest hymn to the Queen of Heaven.

The pilgrim will now undergo a personal examination on the theological virtues: faith, hope, and love. He will be examined by the three apostles who were present at the Transfiguration of Christ: Peter, James, and John. Though faith and hope are not needed in heaven, because all knowledge and desire are fulfilled, Dante must learn while he can, in order to report back to us, who still need all three virtues. The pilgrim says to Peter that though Peter once had faith, he no longer needs it, because now Peter actually sees what he used to believe (24.124–25). When Peter asks the pilgrim what he himself believes, Dante responds, rock-solid: "I believe in one eternal God, who though himself unmoved moves all the heavens with love and desire":

> E io rispondo: Io credo in uno Dio
> solo ed etterno, che tutto 'l ciel move,
> non moto, con amore e con disio.
>
> (24.130–32)

"I believe this through both philosophy and revelation, and I believe in three eternal Persons, the origin of the cosmos and the spark that burns like a star in it and in me" (24.145–47).

Approved by Peter in his faith and inspired by the Holy Spirit, the poet now makes the claim for the *Paradiso* that places it in the same category as the Bible, representing truth itself. He calls it the sacred poem to which both heaven and earth have set their hand: *'l poema sacro al quale ha posto mano e cielo e terra* (25.1–2). Such a statement, lacking the evidence that shines from the text itself, would be a blasphemous boast.

James quizzes Dante on hope, and then John appears in a light so bright that were it a star, winter on earth would be one long day. The pilgrim, his sharpening senses still unequal to the increasing splendor, is blinded, like Paul, by the glory of what he sees. He can no longer see even Beatrice. Up till now he has, like other mortals, been obliged to rely on faith and hope. Now, encountering love itself, he goes blind and thus is prepared to truly see. John begins to speak, whereupon motion and music stop. John's quiz reveals that God is first lover and true author of the cosmos. God is Love more essentially than he is faith or hope, for faith and hope are not part of God's eternal Being as love is. When John has illumined Dante on love, Beatrice restores his sight, and he is ready to ascend to the primum mobile, the outermost sphere and the very skin of the cosmos.

As Dante prepares for this, his last ascent, all paradise sings the *Gloria*: "Glory be to the Father and the Son and the Holy Spirit, so that the sweet singing poured through me. It seemed to me that what I saw was the whole universe smiling. . . . O joy, O unutterable gladness, O life perfected with love and peace, fulfilling all need and desire."

> "Al Padre, al Figlio, a lo Spirito Santo,"
> cominciò, "gloria!" tutto 'l paradiso,
> sì che m'inebriava il dolce canto.
> Ciò ch'io vedeva mi sembiava un riso
> de l'universo; per che mia ebbrezza
> intrava per l'udire e per lo viso.
> Oh gioia! oh ineffabile allegrezza!
> oh vita intègra d'amore e di pace!
> oh sanza brama sicura richezza!
>
> (27.1–9)

Before mounting higher, Dante takes a last look down through all the spheres to earth, the little threshing floor, at the bottom of the cosmos (27.86). Now that his sight is healed, the pilgrim can see Beatrice again. She will now "imparadise" his mind, *quella che 'mparadisa la mia mente* (28.3). Her gaze propels him immediately to the "swiftest heaven," the primum mobile (27.99). Each sphere is swifter than the one beneath it, in the sense that the rim of a wheel moves more swiftly (in linear velocity) than a point nearer the center, while the center itself is the still point.

The sphere of the primum mobile, though it moves all the spheres below it, is unlike them, for it has no depth; it is the dimensionless shell or skin of the entire cosmos. It is not a place, because it is enclosed by nothing physical, only by Light and Love. Despite their profound differences, medieval and modern cosmology must deal with the same problem: the universe is limited, finite, bounded, though bounded by nothing but itself. There is nothing, literally no thing, outside the universe. The Light and Love of God "outside" Dante's cosmos are not things; they cannot be situated in a place or a time, and are therefore "outside" only by metaphor. The primum mobile has no place except figuratively, in the divine mind, in which burns the love that turns it and the power that rains down from it (27.109–11).

The primum mobile, a dimensionless sphere, is the bound and measure of all the lower spheres but is not bounded or measured itself. Again language must leap, and in order to describe the pilgrim's experiences "in" the primum mobile, the poet feigns that it has depth. Here Dante encounters the nine choirs of angels, the heavenly host. From the dimensionless primum mobile, he can look through to the otherworld, the empyrean, which has no space, time, or physical being. The term "existence" is equivocal: if a spoon or a planet are said to "exist," then the empyrean does not "exist," and if *it* "exists," *they* do not. Dante followed Aquinas in preferring the word "subsist" (29.15), for God and his heaven are not physical creatures that physics can show to exist or not to exist. They are infinitely more real.

What the pilgrim sees, chiefly, is a blazing point emitting light so sharp that no one has the strength to gaze at it (28.16–18). Now, "where" is this Point? Nowhere; that is, it is not anywhere in time and space. It is beyond the cosmos. The pilgrim is looking into a "place" where there is no dimension, no time, no space. Physically it is not the universe at all, but morally it is the center of the universe. The poet again must use metaphor, invoking space and shape so as to accommodate his audience. No vision can hear, no hearing can see, God's heaven as it truly is.

For his unique purpose, Dante employs what may be the greatest metaphor in the history of language. To understand its point is to understand the point of the entire poem. Up until now, Dante and his readers have been progressing upward from the center of the universe, which is the earth, through a series of concentric spheres, to the outermost and highest sphere. But as soon as he puts his head through (as it were) the skin of the universe to look at God's heaven, a complete inversion occurs. From the "point" on the primum mobile from which he can look down and in toward the earth, he can, by looking in the "other direction," see "down" through another series of spheres that circle around the blazing Point, which is God. Thus the true center, the moral center, of the cosmos, is not the earth, nor Satan in the dark and narrow depths of the earth, but God the Source and the Light. Angelic hierarchies circle as a ring of light around the blazing Point (28.25).

When one has grasped that image, one must be ready for yet another breathtaking inversion, for the pilgrim is not "really" looking "down," but "up": the burning Point is not only the center, the innermost, but it is also the highest, in a sense the outermost, because literally endless, infinite, unbounded. Whereas a map of the cosmos below the primum mobile may be made, a map of the empyrean fails; Dante's ultimate cosmology, like that of quantum physics, cannot be drawn or imagined; it is beyond the experience of the human senses. Beatrice explains, with the simplicity of Christ affirming the Great Commandment, that from this Point hangs the whole cosmos: *da quel punto depende il cielo e tutta la natura* (28.41–42). When Beatrice has explained it, the pilgrim at last sees truth as clearly as a star in the sky (28.87). Beatrice continues to gaze at the point that is still beyond Dante's inmost vision, and she tells him that it both contains and exceeds all time and space, every "where" and every "when": *là 've appunta ogne ubi e ogne quando* (29.12). This is eternity, where there is no "before" or "after," *né prima né poscia* (29.20). It is everywhere and everywhen.

Arriving in the empyrean itself, Dante learns that it is not named from the fire known on earth but from the fire of love dear to the contemplatives. "This living light poured round and

through" him: *mi circunfulse luce viva* (30.49). As it had for
Paul on the road to Damascus, "suddenly a great light from
heaven overwhelmed him"; in the Latin Vulgate that Dante
used, the phrase is *subito circumfulsit eum lux de coelo* (Acts
22.6).

Again the light both blinds Dante and gives him a new sight
(30.58). This is the theologians' *lumen gloriae*, the "light of
glory" that bestows the beatific vision. Now Dante sees with
spiritual eyes prepared to see beyond sight. And what he sees is
both divine and homely, lofty and sweet: "I saw light as a river
flowing between banks bedecked in marvelous springtime.
From the river living sparks ascended and then settled everywhere on the green meadow upon the flowers. The red sparks
settling upon the flowers appeared like rubies set in gold. Each
spark, drunk with the flowers' scent, sank again into the waters
as another took flight" (30.61–69). Garden and gems and living
water from the throne of God, old images of paradise lent
new light.

Beatrice explains to Dante that all these beauties are shadows
prefacing the absolute Beauty that they refract (30.78). She explains too that it is not any lack in them that makes them shadows, for they are perfect bearers of the light; rather, Dante's
range of vision is as yet too narrow to see them as they truly are.
As in the earthly paradise Dante had to drink to see more
clearly, he now rushes to drink of the heavenly waters, like an
infant eager for its mother's breast. Hitherto he thought he saw;
now he truly sees, and, overwhelmed, he exclaims, "I saw, I saw,
I saw" (*vidi . . . vidi . . . vidi*) three times, a sign that what the
poet wrote he had really in some manner experienced (30.94–
99). Indeed poet and pilgrim in the last four cantos dissolve into
one another. Here for the first time Dante addresses God himself, praying for strength to be able somehow to convey what he
has seen.

And now he begins to describe it: a circular light of immense
circumference emanates from God. At the moment all he can see

of it is its reflection, for even now his sight must be prepared. The light shines down onto the plane on which Dante "stands," which is the plane at the "bottom" of the empyrean's "hemisphere." He does not yet have the fortitude to look up at the Light but must look down to its reflection on the plane. All he can see is the mirrored Light. The plane is circular, and "up from it" (though Dante still can see them only in reflection) rise, as in a theater or a stadium, circular rows of seats for all the souls of the saved. Even as this metaphor persists, another one, wholly original and more vital, enters it as a meta-metaphor: the Rose (30.117). The celestial Rose, alive, bright, opening always more and more to light and love, is the exact opposite of dead, cold hell, narrowing down into total darkness. The rose is yellow (30.124) and white (31.1), as angels are gold and the blessed souls white (Ez 1.13; Dn 7.9; Rv 10.1; Mt 28.3).

Dante again addresses God, the triune Light in a single "star" (31.28), and begs to see more of the heaven whose shape has just been revealed to him. He turns to Beatrice for help, but to his surprise finds in her place an old man dressed, like the other blessed souls, in shining white (31.59–60). This is Bernard of Clairvaux, who now succeeds Beatrice as Beatrice succeeded Vergil. Bernard is Dante's final guide on the path to God because he represents highest contemplation. Where Beatrice has been kataphatic, trying to explain reality to the pilgrim, Bernard the contemplative is apophatic, knowing that it cannot be shown. Bernard was also distinguished in the poet's mind for his Marian piety, his use of erotic metaphor, and his affective poetry. The pilgrim even at this high stage feels bereft at the loss of Beatrice and utters a question poignant in its brevity: "Where is she?" *Ov' è ella?* (31.64). She is, of course, where she has "really" always been, sitting "above" in the third rank of heaven, below only Mary, John, Peter, Adam, and Moses, and right next to Rachel, whom Israel loved first and best. Beatrice is no longer at hand for the pilgrim; he can no longer speak with her. But once aware of her above, he experiences the distance between them as no distance at all, and he prays to her directly.

She smiles at him before returning her gaze to the font of Light (31.93).

Bernard addresses him, telling him to prepare for deeper understanding by looking around the flowered garden, to ground himself in homely images before gazing up the divine ray, *lo raggio divino* (31.99). Then Bernard permits Dante to look up from the reflection, up to unreflected reality, up through the Rose, to Mary, Queen of Heaven (31.100). Mary, on her throne atop the ranks of heaven, is the center around which thousands of angels circle, singing in joyful praise. Bernard gazes at Mary with such love that it enkindles Dante's. The poet utters a triple unrhymed *Cristo* (32.20–27) followed by a triple rhymed *Cristo* (32.83–87), indicating how close he is approaching to the ultimate. Of all the saints, Mary's countenance is closest to that of God (32.93). Gabriel, who sang the "Hail Mary" at the Annunciation, sings it still, and all heaven replies in a song that makes it "more serene" (32.99).

Now—such a thing can hardly be said, let alone imagined—Bernard invites Dante to look directly upon God, the First Love, "so far as the divine glory permits," *quant' è possibil per lo suo fulgore* (32.142–44). Bernard addresses Mary in the first line of the last canto of the *Comedy* in an ancient formula: Virgin Mother, daughter of your Son, *Vergine Madre, figlia del tuo figlio* (33.1), and sings her a beautiful litany that includes words such as love, warmth, eternal peace, flower, hope, living fountain, kindness, and goodness (33.1–21).

The sight of Mary prepares Dante for that of God, and Bernard beseeches the Blessed Mother to help the pilgrim lift his eyes to God. Mary looks at Dante, then at God, and through her gaze (as below through Beatrice's) Dante approaches the goal of all his burning desire (33.46–48). Now another stunning claim: Dante's sight and understanding open up so that he enters deeper and deeper into the ray of the lofty Light that is itself Truth (33.52–54).

From now on Dante keeps his eyes fixed on God, and what follows is unique: "I do remember that my vision bore the intensity of the divine ray until it joined Infinite Being and Good it-self. Ah, overflowing grace through which I could presume to fix my gaze on the Eternal Light so fully that I used up all my sight":

> E' mi ricorda ch'io fui più ardito
> per questo a sostener, tanto ch'i giunsi
> l'aspetto mio col valore infinito.
> Oh abbondante grazia ond'io presunsi
> ficcar lo viso per la luce etterna
> tanto che la veduta vi consunsi!
>
> (33.79–84)

Even more than in the triple *vidi*, Dante's intellectual vision has become so infused by God that he now can see all that is given to any creature to see.

He sees all the scattered diversity of the universe as fallen leaves gathered and bound in a book (33.85–87), and memory and language fail the poet yet again, a topos to be sure, but hardly that alone, for "the clarity of his vision in the divine light sharpens until he can see within the depth and clarity of the Trinity itself three circles, of three colors but aspects of one sole Being" (33.115–17). Incredibly, he addresses the Trinity itself: "O Eternal Light, you who alone dwell within yourself, you alone understand yourself, and, loving, smile upon yourself":

> O luce etterna che sola in te sidi,
> sola t'intendi, e da te intelletta
> e intendente te ami e arridi!
>
> (33.124–26)

Dante sees farther, to the profoundest truth, the Incarnation, the union of the divine Trinity with humanity in Jesus Christ. He sees it in the shape of a human form set within the divine Light:

> dentro da sé, del suo colore stesso,
> mi parve pinta de la nostra effige.
>
> (33.130–31)

At the very end of the *Divine Comedy*, the poet again confesses the limitations of human mind, memory, and art: "but by now, the Love that moves the sun and the other stars was turning my desire and my will together as elements of one moving wheel."

> ma già volgeva il mio disio e 'l velle
> sì come rota ch'igualmente è mossa,
> l'amor che move il sole e l'altre stelle.
>
> (33.143–45)

God moves him: "God moves intellect and will, knowledge and love, equally and uniformly, and, like a wheel, he moves them ever forward on the axis of love."

We cannot bear ourselves aloft, but when the flash of God's lightning strikes us, our souls turn, like wheels, with desire and will to be turned by the Love that turns the sun and the other stars—*che move il sol e l'altre stelle.*

✣ 13 ✣

Hearing the Silence

Historically, heaven is what it has been thought to be, and the concept was firm by the time of Dante. What heaven is spiritually and psychologically is more difficult to discern.

Every human from the beginning has one fundamental question that underlies his or her whole nature. The question is: Do you love me? That question is soon transformed—by genetics, by nurture, by original sin, or by existential neurosis—into: "Am I worthy to be loved?" or "What can I do to be worthy to be loved?" The young pilgrim soon seizes on answers provided by parents or society: I will be famous, I will be rich, I will wield power, I will intimidate others, I will be elected—or even, I will be the greatest victim or failure. In the process, we convince ourselves that we really *will* be happy (meaning we will be loved) if we achieve one of these goals. Often we persist in these delusions after experience has repeatedly proved them false. We continue to make the same mistake of trying to find in the limited and temporal the response that is found only in what is the real object of our desire. So falsely convinced, we make idols of our strength, our money, our fame, our power, or even some misery we claim as uniquely ours. Idols block our view of, our path to, reality. To the question: Do you love me? God and the cosmos reply resoundingly and forever: Yes. And to the question, What can I do to be worthy of being loved, the answer is: Open yourself to love, and return it. Everything else is an idol. Everything else is a veil, even a dirty rag, before our eyes. To seek our true happiness, to seek our true selves, to find the true answer to the existential question we began with, we need to smash our idols, one by one. Then the illusion that "I" am the center of the cosmos ceases. It will absolutely and inevitably cease, whether death is finality or whether another life does exist. Either way, the self-flattery of self-importance will stop, dead.

(Meanwhile there is pain. Whatever we do, we will experience pain. Love meets us and embraces us, saying, I know your pain, beloved; I know and feel it in myself; and I fill it and you with my melting love. Heaven is acceptance of love, which burns through and shines through the pain, transforming it. Love would rather go through hell than go to heaven without us.)

The best answer to the spiritual question of heaven is to declare it a mystery, yet one that can be illuminated by a number of paradoxes. Heaven is supernatural *and* natural. Only humans are saved, *and* the whole cosmos is saved. Salvation is for all, *and* only for the chosen. A person is chosen by grace *and* by free will. The chosen are equal *and* not equal in heaven. Heaven is now *and* in the future. Heaven is an eternal now *and* has a mode of spacetime, either different from ours or emerging at the end of the world. Heaven is *both* in time and in eternity (as moderns assume that light is *both* wave and particle). Heaven is static *and* dynamic; it is motion *and* stillness; it is silence *and* song. Heaven begins at the moment of death *and* at the end of the world. The heavenly paradise is *and* is not the earthly paradise. Heaven is a return to paradise, *and* a renewal of paradise, *and* something entirely new. Heaven is a temple *and* a garden *and* a city *and* a pasture *and* the sky. It is Jerusalem on both the overt *and* the symbolic levels; it is the earthly *and* the heavenly Jerusalem.

The particular judgment is *and* is not the same as the Last Judgment. We enter heaven immediately at death *and* enter into an intermediate state as we await the end of the world. Body and soul are separated at death *and* not separated at death. The resurrected body is this earthly body *and* is radically changed. In heaven we retain our individuality *and* are absorbed by God.

We are saved as individuals *and* as the communion of saints. The body of Christ is the communion of saints *and* the church *and* the Eucharist *and* the historical Jesus—and more, always more.

In heaven, before and after the resurrection, we are aware of events on earth, and because we love those still in this world, we pray for them. Perhaps the most common modern concern about heaven is whether we associate there with those we love on earth.

Suppose that when we go to heaven, we first encounter those whom we have loved. We enter with each of them into the totality of the love between us that we had wished for on earth but had never fulfilled. Now suppose that a third person, perhaps one we did not know on earth, observes the absorption of our love for A and A's corresponding love for us. Then that third person is drawn into the perfect love between us and A. So that relationship is perfect love as was the first, and by extension the love of every lover touches the love of every other, spreading and growing in immeasurable multiplication of the power of love. This fabric of love is constantly woven outward from each of its centers, forming a tapestry of infinite richness. Heaven has no boundaries and its center everywhere. The joy and love are multiplied beyond all conception as the universe of love whirls ever outward, yet closer and closer to that Point that is itself fulfilled Love. So those whom we have never known, or with whom we have quarreled, even those whom we have hated or who have hated us, all these we love, for whatever is evil in them has been washed away, and all that remains is the pure goodness that God has made, which is perfect love loving. God's love for us is not reduced by his loving others equally, nor is the love of one human being for another reduced by his or her loving still others; rather, love increases love and continues increasing.

Another concern is justice. Are some not saved, not chosen, not elect? If so, do the blessed rejoice in God's justice, or weep out of pity for the damned? Can a Hitler or a Stalin be saved? But perhaps blessedness is not so very difficult. In medieval cosmology, the cosmology of Dante, an angle of even the tiniest degree opening up at the center of the earth (or of the inferno) eventually opens out infinitely wide. Moreover, though at any particular point some angles are wider than others, in infinity any angle of hope ultimately opens up as widely as any other. Every person, of any religion and of any degree of faith, whose heart leans to love and whose life leans to good will is in heaven. Perhaps the only way to avoid heaven is to stay "hard at work, to hear no music, never to look at earth or sky, and (above all) to love no one."[44]

Heaven is whatever and whenever God wants it to be. More deeply, heaven is where God is, in the rose of fire that keeps opening dynamically in one eternal moment. We have loved the stars too much to fear the night. So shall every love every love more enkindle, until the cosmos coruscates with loving light, living more and ever more.

[44] C. S. Lewis, *Till We Have Faces* (London, 1956), 80–81.

❖ *Bibliography* ❖

Amat, Jacqueline. "L'authenticité des songes de la Passion de Perpétue et de Félicité." *Augustinianum* 29 (1989): 177–91.

—————. *Songes et visions: l'au-delà dans la littérature latine tardive.* Paris, 1985.

Anderson, William. *Dante the Maker.* London, 1980.

Andriani, Beniamo. *La forma del Paradiso dantesco: Il sistema del mondo secondo gli antichi e secondo Dante.* Padua, 1961.

Ariès, Philippe. *The Hour of Our Death.* New York, 1981.

—————. "Le Purgatoire et la cosmologie de l'au-delà." *Annales* 38 (1983): 151–57.

—————. *Western Attitudes toward Death: From the Middle Ages to the Present.* Baltimore, Md., 1974.

Armstrong, John. *The Paradise Myth.* London, 1969.

Asín Palacios, Miguel. *La escatología musulmana en la Divina Comedia: Seguida de la historia y crítica de una polémica.* 2d ed. Madrid and Granada, 1943.

Assunto, Rosario. *Ipotesi e postille sull'estetica medioevale: Con alcuni rilievi su Dante teorizzatore della poesia.* Milan, 1975.

Aubrun, Michel. "Caractères et portée religieuse et sociale des 'Visiones' en Occident du VIe au XIe siècle." *Cahiers de civilisation médiévale* 23 (1980): 109–30.

Auerbach, Erich. *Studi su Dante.* Milan, 1963.

Baarlink, Heinrich. "Friede im Himmel: Die lukanische Redaktion von Lk 19:38 und ihre Deutung." *Zeitschrift für die neutestamentliche Wissenschaft* 76 (1985): 170–86.

Badham, Paul. *Christian Beliefs about Life after Death.* New York, 1976.

Bailey, Lloyd R. *Biblical Perspectives on Death.* Philadelphia, Pa., 1979.

Balthasar, Hans Urs von. "Apokatastasis." *Trierer Theologische Zeitschrift* 97 (1988): 169–82.

Barolini, Teodolinda. *Dante's Poets: Textuality and Truth in the Comedy*. Princeton, N.J., 1984.

———. *The Undivine Comedy: Detheologizing Dante*. Princeton, N.J., 1992.

Beasley-Murray, G. R. *The Book of Revelation*. London, 1974.

Beauvois, E. "L'Elysée transatlantique et l'Eden occidental." *Revue de l'histoire des religions* 8 (1883): 273–318, 673–727.

Beek, C.I.M.I. van. *Passio Sanctae Perpetuae et Felicitatis*. Bonn, 1938.

Begg, Christopher. "Josephus's Portrayal of the Disappearances of Enoch, Elijah, and Moses: Some Observations." *Journal of Biblical Literature* 109 (1990): 691–93.

Bergin, Thomas. *Dante*. New York, 1965.

Bernardo, Aldo. "Dante's Divine Comedy: The View from God's Eye." In William De Sua and G. Rizzo, eds., *A Dante Symposium* (Chapel Hill, N.C., 1965), 45–58.

Bernstein, Alan. *The Formation of Hell: Death and Retribution in the Ancient and Early Christian Worlds*. Ithaca, N.Y., 1993.

Bernstein, JoAnne Gitlin. "Science and Eschatology in the Portinari Chapel." *Arte Lombarda* 70 (1981): 33–40.

Bianchi, Ugo. *Prometeo, Orfeo, Adamo: Tematiche religiose sul destino, il male, la salvezza*. Rome, 1977.

Bietenhard, Hans. *Die himmlische Welt im Urchristentum und Spätjudentum*. Tübingen, 1951.

Black, Matthew, ed. *The Book of Enoch or I Enoch: A New English Edition*. Leiden, 1985.

Blamires, Harry. "Heaven: The Eternal Weight of Glory." *Christianity Today* 35 (1991): 30–33.

Bogdanos, Theodore. "'The Shepherd of Hermas' and the Development of Medieval Visionary Allegory." *Viator* 8 (1977): 33–46.

Boies, Jack Jay. *The Lost Domain: Avatars of the Earthly Paradise in Western Literature*. Lanham, Md., 1983.

Börresen, Kari E. "Augustin, interprète du dogme de la résurrection: Quelques aspects de son anthropologie dualiste." *Studia theologica* 23 (1969): 141–55.

Boswell, Charles Stuart. *An Irish Precursor of Dante: A Study of the Vision of Heaven and Hell*. London, 1908.

Bougerol, Jacques-Guy. *La théologie de l'espérance aux XIIe et XIIIe siècles*. 2 vols. Paris, 1985.

Bourke, Vernon J. "St. Augustine and the Cosmic Soul." *Giornale di metafisica* 9 (1954): 431–40.

Boyde, Patrick. *Dante Philomythes and Philosopher: Man in the Cosmos.* Cambridge, 1981.

Brandon, Samuel G. F. *The Judgment of the Dead.* New York, 1967.

Brown, David. "No Heaven without Purgatory." *Religious Studies* 21 (1985): 447–56.

Brownlee, Kevin. "Why the Angels Speak Italian: Dante as Vernacular *Poeta* in *Paradiso XXV.*" *Poetics Today* 5 (1984): 597–610.

Busnelli, Giovanni. *Il concetto e l'ordine del "Paradiso" dantesco: indagini e studi.* 2 vols. Città di Castello, 1911–12.

Bynum, Caroline Walker. "Imagining the Self: Somatomorphic Soul and Resurrection Body in Dante's *Divine Comedy.*" In Sang Hyun Lee et al., eds., *Faithful Imagining: Essays in Honor of Richard Niebuhr,* 83–106. Atlanta, Ga., 1995.

———. *The Resurrection of the Body in Western Christianity, 200–1336.* New York, 1995.

Camporesi, Piero. *The Fear of Hell: Images of Damnation and Salvation in Early Modern Europe.* Oxford, 1990.

———. *The Incorruptible Flesh: Bodily Mutation and Mortification in Folklore.* New York, 1988.

Cantarino, Vicente. "Dante and Islam: History and Analysis of a Controversy." In William De Suo and G. Rizzo, eds., *A Dante Symposium,* 175–98. Chapel Hill, N.C., 1965.

Carboni, C. *Tavole sinnotiche e critiche di studio alla "Divina Commedia."* 3 vols. Rome, 1963.

Carey, John. "The Location of the Otherworld in Irish Tradition." *EISGE: A Journal of Irish Studies* 19 (1982): 36–43.

Carr, Wesley. *Angels and Principalities: The Background, Meaning and Development of the Pauline Phrase hai archai kai hai exousiai.* Cambridge, 1981.

Carugati, Giuliana. *Dalla menzogna al silenzio: La scrittura mistica della Commedia di Dante.* Bologna, 1991.

Casey, R. P. "The Apocalypse of Paul." *Journal of Theological Studies* 34 (1933): 1–32.

Cassell, Anthony K. *Inferno I.* Lectura Dantis Americana. Philadelphia, Pa., 1989.

✓ Cavallin, Hans C. C. *Life after Death: Paul's Argument for the Resurrection of the Dead in I Cor. 15.* 2 vols. Lund, 1974.

✓ Cavendish, Richard. *Visions of Heaven and Hell*. New York, 1977.

Cerulli, Enrico. *Il "Libro della Scala" e la questione delle fonti arabo-spagnole della Divina Commedia*. Vatican City, 1949.

Chadwick, Henry. *Augustine*. Oxford, 1986.

Charity, A. C. *Events and Their Afterlife: The Dialectics of Christian Typology in the Bible and Dante*. Cambridge, 1966.

Charles, R. H., ed. and trans. *The Apocrypha and Pseudepigrapha of the Old Testament in English*. 2 vols. Oxford, 1913.

Charlesworth, James H. *The New Testament Apocrypha and Pseudepigrapha: A Guide to Publications, with Excursuses on Apocalypses*. New York, 1987.

————. *The Old Testament Pseudepigrapha and the New Testament: Prolegomena for the Study of Christian Origins*. Cambridge, 1985.

————, ed. and trans. *The Odes of Solomon*. Oxford, 1973.

————, ed. *The Old Testament Pseudepigrapha*. 2 vols. Garden City, N.Y., 1983–85.

Chiarenza, Marguerite Mills. "The Imageless Vision and Dante's *Paradiso*." *Dante Studies* 90 (1972): 77–91.

————. "Time and Eternity in the Myths of *Paradiso* XVII." In Aldo S. Bernardo and Anthony L. Pellegrini, eds., *Dante, Petrarch, Boccaccio: Studies in the Italian Trecento in Honor of Charles S. Singleton*, 133–50. Binghamton, N.Y., 1983.

Ciccarese, M. P. "Alle origini della letteratura delle visioni: Il contributo di Gregorio di Tours." *Studi storico-religiosi* 5, no. 2 (1981): 251–66.

Clifford, Richard J. *The Cosmic Mountain in Canaan and the Old Testament*. Cambridge, Mass., 1972.

Cohn-Sherbok, Dan. "Death and Immortality in the Jewish Tradition." *Theology* 90 (1987): 263–73.

Coli, Edoardo. *Il paradiso terrestre dantesco*. Florence, 1897.

Colish, Marcia. "Medieval Allegory: A Historiographical Consideration." *Clio* 4 (1975): 341–56.

————. *The Mirror of Language: A Study in Medieval Theory of Knowledge*. 2d ed. Lincoln, Neb., 1983.

————. *Peter Lombard*. Leiden and New York, 1994.

————. *The Stoic Tradition from Antiquity to the Early Middle Ages*. 2d ed. 2 vols. Leiden, 1990.

Colli, Agostino. "La Gerusalemme celeste nei cicli apocalittici altomedievali e l'affresco di San Pietro al Monte di Civate." *Cahiers archéologiques* 30 (1982): 107–24.

Collins, John J. *The Apocalyptic Imagination: An Introduction to the Jewish Matrix of Christianity.* New York, 1984.

———. *The Apocalyptic Vision of the Book of Daniel.* Missoula, Mont., 1977.

Colombo, Manuela. *Dai mistici a Dante: Il linguaggio dell'ineffabilità.* Firenze, 1987.

Colvin, Howard. *Architecture and the After-Life.* New Haven, Conn., 1991.

Constable, Giles. "The Vision of Gunthelm and Other 'Visiones' Attributed to Peter the Venerable." *Revue bénédictine* 66 (1956): 92–114.

Coppens, Joseph. "L'Elu et les élus dans les Ecritures Saintes et les écrits de Qumrân." *Ephemerides theologicae lovanienses* 57, no. 1 (1981): 120–24.

Cornish, Alison. "Planets and Angels in *Paradiso* XXIX: The First Moment." *Dante Studies* 108 (1990): 1–28.

Cousins, Ewert H. "Bonaventure and Dante: The Role of Christ in the Spiritual Journey." In Leonard Bowman, ed., *Itinerarium: The Idea of Journey,* 113–31. Salzburg, 1983.

Crocco, Antonio. *Simbologia gioachimita e simbologia dantesca: Nuove prospettive d'interpretazione della Divina Commedia.* 5th ed. Naples, 1965.

Croce, Benedetto. *La poesia di Dante.* 2d ed. Bari, 1958.

Crouzel, Henri. "L'Hadès et la Gehenne chez Origène." *Gregorianum* 59 (1978): 291–331.

———. *Origen: The Life and Thought of the First Great Theologian.* San Francisco, 1989.

Cullmann, Oscar. *Christ and Time.* Philadelphia, Pa., 1954.

———. *Immortality of the Soul or Resurrection of the Dead? The Witness of the New Testament.* London, 1958.

Cumont, Franz. *Afterlife in Roman Paganism.* New Haven, Conn., 1922.

———. *Lux Perpetua.* Paris, 1949.

Dales, Richard C. *Medieval Discussions of the Eternity of the World.* Leiden, 1990.

Daniélou, Jean. "Terre et paradis chez les pères de l'église." *Eranos Jahrbuch* 22 (1953): 433–72.

Dauphiné, James. *Le cosmos de Dante*. Paris, 1984.

Davenport, Gene L. *The Eschatology of the Book of Jubilees*. Leiden, 1971.

Davidson, Clifford, ed. *The Iconography of Heaven*. Kalamazoo, Mich., 1994.

Davies, J. G. *He Ascended into Heaven: A Study in the History of Doctrine*. London, 1958.

Davies, Malcolm. "Description by Negation: History of a Thought Pattern in Ancient Accounts of Blissful Life." *Prometheus* 13 (1987): 265–84.

Dean-Otting, Mary. *Heavenly Journeys: A Study of the Motif in Hellenistic Jewish Literature*. New York, 1984.

Delmay, Bernard. *I personaggi della "Divina Commedia": Classificazione e regesto*. Florence, 1986.

Delumeau, Jean. *Une histoire du paradis*. 2 vols. Paris, 1992.

Demaray, John G. *Cosmos and Epic Representation: Dante, Spenser, Milton and the Transformation of Renaissance Heroic Poetry*. Pittsburgh, Pa., 1991.

———. *Dante and the Book of the Cosmos*. Philadelphia, Pa., 1987.

———. *The Invention of Dante's Commedia*. New Haven, Conn., 1974.

Didier, J.-C. "'Angélisme' ou perspectives eschatologiques?" *Mélanges de science religieuse* 6 (1954): 31–48.

Diehls, Hermann. "Himmels- und Höllenfahrten von Homer bis Dante." *Neue Jahrbücher für das klassische Altertumsgeschichte und deutsche Literatur* 49 (1922): 239–53.

Diekamp, Franz. "Johannes von Damaskus Ueber die im Glauben Entschlafen." *Römische Quartalschrift* 17 (1903): 371–82.

Dinzelbacher, Peter. "Klassen und Hierarchien im Jenseits." *Miscellanea medievalia* 12 (1978): 20–40.

———. "Reflexionen irdischer Sozialstrukturen in mittelalterlichen Jenseitsschilderungen." *Archiv für Kulturgeschichte* 61 (1979): 16–34.

———. *Vision und Visionsliteratur im Mittelalters*. Stuttgart, 1981.

Dinzelbacher, Peter, and Harald Kleinschmidt. "Seelenbrücke und Brückenbau im mittelalterlichen England." *Numen* 31 (1984): 242–87.

Dods, Marcus. *Forerunners of Dante: An Account of Some of the*

More Important Visions of the Unseen World, from the Earliest Times. Edinburgh, 1903.

Dondaine, Henri F. "L'objet et le 'medium' de la vision béatifique chez les théologiens du XIIIe siècle." *Recherches de théologie ancienne et médiévale* 19 (1952): 60–130.

Douie, Decima. "John XXII and the Beatific Vision." *Dominican Studies* 3 (1950): 154–74.

Dronke, Peter. *Dante and Medieval Latin Traditions*. Cambridge, 1986.

———. *Women Writers of the Middle Ages: A Critical Study of Texts from Perpetua (+203) to Marguerite Porete (+1310)*. Cambridge, 1981.

Dupré, Louis. "The Christian Experience of Mystical Union." *Journal of Religion* 69 (1989): 1–13.

Dykmans, Marc. *Pour et contre Jean XXII en 1333: Deux traités avignonnais sur la vision béatifique*. Vatican City, 1975.

———. *Les sermons de Jean XXII sur la vision béatifique*. Rome, 1973.

Easting, Robert. "The Date and Dedication of the 'Tractatus de Purgatorio Sancti Patricii.'" *Speculum* 53 (1978): 778–83.

Ebel, Uda. "Die literarischen Formen der Jenseits- und Endzeitsvisionen." *Grundriss der romanischen Literaturen des Mittelalters* (Heidelberg) 6, no. 1 (1968): 181–215.

Eliade, Mircea. *A History of Religious Ideas*. 3 vols. Chicago, 1978–85.

Elliott, Alison Goddard. *Roads to Paradise· Reading the Lives of the Early Saints*. Hanover, N.H., 1987.

Emmerson, Richard, and Bernard McGinn, eds. *The Apocalypse in the Middle Ages*. Ithaca, N.Y., 1992.

Enciclopedia dantesca. Dir. Umberto Bosco; ed. Giorgio Petrocchi. 6 vols. Rome, 1970–79.

Fallani, Giovanni. *Dante e la cultura figurativa medievale*. Bergamo, 1971.

———. *Dante: Poeta teologo*. Milan, 1965.

———. *L'Esperienza teologica di Dante*. Lecce, 1976.

———. *Poesia e teologia nella Divina Commedia*. 3 vols. Milan, 1965.

Feuillet, A. "La demeure céleste et la destinée des chrétiens." *Recherches de science religieuse* 44 (1956): 360–402.

Field, Rosalind. "The Heavenly Jerusalem in *Pearl*." *Modern Language Review* 81 (1986): 7–17.

Filipponi, Osvaldo. *Le profezie di Dante e del Vangelo Eterno*. Padua, 1983.

Filoramo, Giovanni. *A History of Gnosticism*. Oxford, 1990. *L'attesa della storia della Gnosi*. Bari, 1983.

Finucane, R. C. *Appearances of the Dead: A Cultural History of Ghosts*. Buffalo, N.Y., 1984.

Foster, Kenelm. "Dante's Vision of God." *Italian Studies* 14 (1959): 21–39.

———. *The Two Dantes and Other Studies*. London, 1977.

Freccero, John. *Dante: A Collection of Critical Essays*. Englewood Cliffs, N.J., 1965.

———. *Dante: The Poetics of Conversion*. Cambridge, Mass., 1986.

———. "Dante's Pilgrim in a Gyre." *PMLA* 76 (1961): 168–81.

———. "The Final Image: *Paradiso* XXXIII.144." *Modern Language Notes* 79 (1964): 14–27.

———. "*Paradiso* X: The Dance of the Stars." *Dante Studies* 86 (1968): 85–111.

Frye, Northrop. *The Great Code: The Bible and Literature*. New York, 1982.

Gardiner, Eileen, ed. *Visions of Heaven and Hell before Dante*. New York, 1989.

Gardner, Edmund G. *Dante and the Mystics: A Study of the Mystical Aspect of the Divina Commedia and Its Relations with Some of Its Mediaeval Sources*. London, 1913.

———. *Dante's Ten Heavens*. 2d ed. London, 1900.

Gaster, Moses. "Hebrew Visions of Hell and Paradise." *Journal of the Royal Asiatic Society of Great Britain and Ireland* 25 (1893): 571–611.

Gatch, Milton M. *Death: Meaning and Mortality in Christian Thought and Contemporary Culture*. New York, 1969.

Gatto, Giuseppe. "Le voyage au paradis: La christianisation des traditions folkloriques au moyen âge." *Annales* 34 (1979): 929–42.

Giamatti, A. Bartlett. *The Earthly Paradise and the Renaissance Epic*. Princeton, N.J., 1966.

Gilson, Etienne. *Dante et la philosophie*. Paris, 1939.

———. "Dante's Notion of a Shade: *Purgatorio* 25." *Mediaeval Studies* 29 (1967): 124–42.

González-Alió, José-Luis. "La visión beatifica como realidad trinitaria." *Scripta Theologica* 19 (1987): 597–631.

Goodman, Leonard E. *The Book of Theodicy: Translation and Commentary on the Book of Job.* New Haven, Conn., 1988.

Goubert, Joseph, and L. Cristiani. *Les plus beaux textes sur l'au-delà.* Paris, 1950.

Gousset, Marie-Thérèse. "La réprésentation de la Jérusalem céleste à l'époque carolingienne." *Cahiers archéologiques* 23 (1974): 47–60.

Gowan, Donald E. *Eschatology in the Old Testament.* Philadelphia, Pa., 1986.

Grabar, André. "L'iconographie du Ciel dans l'art chrétien de l'Antiquité et du haut Moyen Age." *Cahiers archéologiques* 30 (1982): 5–24.

Gray, John. *The Biblical Doctrine of the Reign of God.* Edinburgh, 1979.

Grelot, Pierre. "Aujourd'hui tu seras avec moi dans le paradis (Luc, 23.43)." *Revue biblique* 74 (1967): 194–214.

Greshake, Gisbert, and Jacob Kremer. *Resurrectio mortuorum: Zum theologischen Verständnis der leiblichen Auferstehung.* Darmstadt, 1986.

Griffiths, J. Gwynn. *The Divine Verdict: A Study of Divine Judgement in the Ancient Religions.* Leiden, 1991.

Grimm, Reinhold. *Paradisus coelestis; Paradisus terrestris: Zur Auslegungsgeschichte des Paradieses im Abenland bis um 1200.* Munich, 1977.

Gurevic, Aaron J. "Au moyen âge: Conscience individuelle et image de l'au-delà." *Annales* 37 (1982): 255–75.

———. "Per un'antropologia delle visioni ultraterrene nella cultura occidentale del medioevo." In C. Prevignano, ed., *La semiotica nei paesi slavi: Programmi, problemi, analisi,* 443–62. Milan, 1977.

———. *Das Weltbild des mittelalterlichen Menschen.* Dresden, 1978.

Halperin, David. *The Faces of the Chariot: Early Jewish Responses to Ezekiel's Vision.* Tübingen, 1988.

Hanson, Paul D. *The Dawn of Apocalyptic.* Philadelphia, Pa., 1975.

———, ed. *Visionaries and Their Apocalypses.* Philadelphia, Pa., 1983.

Harris, Murray J. *From Grave to Glory: Resurrection in the New Testament.* Grand Rapids, Mich., 1990.

———. *Raised Immortal.* Grand Rapids, Mich., 1985.

Hawkins, Peter S. "By Gradual Scale Sublimed: Dante's Benedict and Contemplative Ascent." In Timothy G. Verdon, *Monasticism and the Arts*, 255–69. Syracuse, N.Y., 1984.

———. "Dante's Paradiso and the Dialectic of Ineffability." In Peter S. Hawkins and Anne Howland Schotter, eds., *Ineffability, Naming the Unnameable: From Dante to Beckett*, 5–22. New York, 1984.

———. "Resurrecting the Word: Dante and the Bible." *Religion and Literature* 16 (1984): 59–71.

———. "Trespassing on the Word: God's Book and Ours." *Journal of the American Academy of Religion* 47, no. 1 (March 1979): 47–54.

Hawkins, Peter S., and Anne Howland Schotter, eds. *Ineffability, Naming the Unnameable: From Dante to Beckett*. New York, 1984.

Hellholm, David, ed. *Apocalypticism in the Mediterranean World and the Near East*. 2d ed. Tübingen, 1989.

Hennecke, Edgar, and Wilhelm Schneemelcher, eds. *New Testament Apocrypha*. 2d ed. 2 vols. Westminster, Md., 1991.

Hick, John D. *Death and Eternal Life*. New York, 1976.

Hiers, Richard. *The Kingdom of God in the Synoptic Tradition*. Gainesville, Fla., 1970.

Hill, C. E. "Paul's Understanding of Christ's Kingdom in I Corinthians 15:20–28." *Novum testamentum* 30 (1988): 297–320.

Himmelfarb, Martha. "Apocalyptic Ascent and the Heavenly Temple." *Society of Biblical Literature Seminar Papers* 26 (1987): 210–17.

———. *Ascent to Heaven in Jewish and Christian Apocalypses*. New York, 1993.

Hinard, François, ed. *La Mort, les morts et l'au-delà dans le monde romain: Actes du Colloque de Caen 20–22 Novembre 1985*. Caen, 1987.

Hoekema, Anthony. "Heaven: Not Just an Eternal Day Off." *Christianity Today* 29, no. 13 (1985): 18–19.

Holdsworth, C. J. "Visions and Visionaries in the Middle Ages." *History* 48 (1963): 141–53.

Hollander, Robert. *Allegory in Dante's Commedia*. Princeton, N.J., 1969.

———. "Dante *Teologus-Poeta*." *Dante Studies* 94 (1976): 91–136.

———. *Dante's Epistle to Cangrande*. Ann Arbor, Mich., 1993.

Holmes, George. *Dante*. Oxford, 1980.

Holtz, Traugott. *Die Christologie der Apokalypse des Johannes*. 2d ed. Berlin, 1971.

Horsley, R. A. "Pneumatikos vs. Psychikos: Distinctions of Spiritual Status among the Corinthians." *Harvard Theological Review* 69 (1976): 269–88.

Hossain, Mary. "Women and Paradise." *Journal of European Studies* 19 (1989): 293–310.

Hoven, René. *Stoïcisme et stoïciens face au problème de l'au-delà*. Paris, 1971.

Hughes, Robert. *Heaven and Hell in Western Art*. New York, 1968.

Ingrisch, L. *Reiseführer ins Jenseits*. Vienna, 1990.

Jacoff, Rachel, ed. *Cambridge Companion to Dante*. Cambridge, 1993.

James, Montague Rhodes, ed. and trans. *The Apocryphal New Testament*. Oxford, 1924.

Kelly, Henry Ansgar. *Tragedy and Comedy from Dante to Pseudo-Dante*. Berkeley, Calif., 1989.

Kirkpatrick, Robin. *Dante: The Divine Comedy*. Cambridge, 1987.

——. *Dante's Paradiso and the Limitations of Modern Criticism*. Cambridge, 1978.

Kirschner, Robert S. "Maimonides' Fiction of Resurrection." *Hebrew Union College Annual* 52 (1981): 163–93.

Knibb, Michael A. *The Ethiopic Book of Enoch: A New Edition in the Light of the Aramaic Dead Sea Fragments*. 2 vols. Oxford, 1978.

Koch, Klaus. *The Rediscovery of Apocalyptic*. London, 1972.

Kovach, Francis J., and Robert W. Shahan. *Albert the Great: Commemorative Essays*. Norman, Okla., 1980.

Knight, W. F. Jackson. *Elysion: On Ancient Greek and Roman Beliefs Concerning Life after Death*. New York, 1970.

Kreitzer, Joseph. *Jesus and God in Paul's Eschatology*. Sheffield, 1987.

Kretzenbacher, Leopold. *Die Seelenwage*. Klagenfurt, 1958.

Kroll, Jerome, and Bernard Bachrach. "Visions and Psychopathology in the Middle Ages." *Journal of Nervous and Mental Disease* 170 (1982): 41–49.

Kruger, Stephen F. *Dreaming in the Middle Ages*. Cambridge, 1992.

Kung, Hans. *Eternal Life? Life after Death as a Medical, Philosophical, and Theological Problem*. Garden City, N.Y., 1984.

Ladner, Gerhart B. *The Idea of Reform.* Cambridge, Mass., 1959.

————. "Medieval and Modern Understandings of Symbolism: A Comparison." *Speculum* 54 (1979): 223–256.

Lang, Bernhard. "Afterlife: Ancient Israel's Changing Vision of the World Beyond." *Bible Review* 4 (1988): 12–23.

————. "The Sexual Life of the Saints: Towards an Anthropology of Christian Heaven." *Religion* 17 (1987): 149–71.

Leclercq, Jean. *The Love of Learning and the Desire for God: A Study of Monastic Culture.* New York, 1960.

LeGoff, Jacques. *The Birth of Purgatory.* Chicago, 1984.

————. "Dreams in the Culture and Collective Psychology of the Medieval West." In *Time, Work, and Culture in the Middle Ages* (Chicago, 1980), 201–4.

Lewis, C. S. *The Discarded Image.* Cambridge, 1964.

Lincoln, Andrew T. *Paradise Now and Not Yet: Studies in the Role of the Heavenly Dimension in Paul's Thought with Special Reference to His Eschatology.* Cambridge, 1981.

Lincoln, Bruce. "On the Imagery of Paradise." *Indogermanische Forschungen* 85 (1980): 151–64.

Lodolo, Gabriella. "Il tema simbolico del paradiso nella tradizione monastica dell'occidente latino (secoli VI–XII): Lo spazio del simbolo." *Aevum* 51 (1977): 252–88.

————. "Il tema simbolico del paradiso nella tradizione monastica dell 'occidente latino (secoli VI-XII): Lo svelamento del simbolo." *Aevum* 52 (1978): 177–94.

Lossky, Vladimir. *The Vision of God.* 3d ed. New York, 1983.

Lotz, David W. "Heaven and Hell in the Christian Tradition." *Religion in Life* 48 (1979): 77–92.

Luck, Georg. "The Doctrine of Salvation in the Hermetic Writings." *Second Century* 8 (1991): 31–41.

Mahn-Lot, Marianne. "Iles des bienheureux et Paradis terrestre." *Revue historique* 569 (1989): 47–50.

Mandonnet, Pierre. *Dante le théologien: Introduction à l'intelligence de la vie, des oeuvres et de l'art de Dante Alighieri.* Paris, 1935.

Markus, Robert A. *The End of Ancient Christianity.* Cambridge, 1990.

Marti, Kevin. "Dante's 'Baptism' and the Theology of the Body in *Purgatorio* 1–2." *Traditio* 45 (1989–90): 167–90.

Masseron, Alexandre. *Dante et Saint Bernard.* Paris, 1953.

Mathews, Thomas F. *The Clash of Gods: A Reinterpretation of Early Christian Art*. Princeton, N.J., 1993.

Mauser, Ulrich. " 'Heaven' in the World View of the New Testament." *Horizons in Biblical Theology* 9, no. 2 (1987): 31–52.

Mavrodes, George. "The Life Everlasting and the Bodily Criterion of Identity." *Nous* 11 (1977): 27–39.

Mazzeo, J. A. *Structure and Thought in the Paradiso*. Ithaca, N.Y., 1958.

Mazzotta, Giuseppe. *Dante, Poet of the Desert: History and Allegory in the Divine Comedy*. Princeton, N.J., 1979.

———. *Dante's Vision and the Circle of Knowledge*. Princeton, N.J., 1992.

———, ed. *Critical Essays on Dante*. Boston, 1991.

McClain, Joseph P. *The Doctrine of Heaven in the Writings of Gregory the Great*. Washington, 1956.

McClung, William Alexander. *The Architecture of Paradise: Survivals of Eden and Jerusalem*. Berkeley, Calif., 1983.

McLaughlin, Megan. *Consorting with Saints: Prayer for the Dead in Early Medieval France*. Ithaca, N.Y., 1994.

McDannell, Colleen, and Bernhard Lang. *Heaven: A History*. New York, 1988.

McGinn, Bernard. *The Foundations of Mysticism*. New York, 1991.

———. *Visions of the End: Apocalyptic Traditions in the Middle Ages*. New York, 1979.

Miles, Jack. *God: A Biography*. New York, 1995.

Milik, J. T., ed. *The Books of Enoch: Aramaic Fragments of Qumran Cave 4*. Oxford, 1976.

Mohrmann, Christine. "Locus refrigerii." In *Etudes*, 2:81–91. Rome, 1961.

Moltmann, Jurgen. *God in Creation: An Ecological Doctrine of Creation*. London, 1985.

Montano, Rocco. *Storia della poesia di Dante*. 2 vols. Napoli, 1962.

Montgomery, James A. "The Highest, Heaven, Aeon, Time, etc. in Semitic Religion." *Harvard Theological Review* 38 (1931): 143–50.

Morgan, Alison. *Dante and the Medieval Other World*. Cambridge, 1990.

La mort au moyen âge. Colloque de l'Association des historiens médiévistes français, Strasbourg, June 1975. Strasbourg, 1977.

Moschner, Franz M. *The Kingdom of Heaven in Parables*. London, 1960. *Das Himmelreich in Gleichnissen*. Stuttgart, 1953.

Mossay, J. *La mort et l'au-delà dans Saint Grégoire de Nazianze*. Louvain, 1966.

Motto, Anna Lydia. "Seneca on Death and Immortality." *Classical Journal* 50 (1955): 187–89.

Mourant, John A. *Augustine on Immortality*. Villanova, Pa., 1969.

Nardi, Bruno. *Dante e la cultura medievale: Nuovi saggi sulla filosofia dantesca*. 2d ed. Bari, 1983.

Nickelsburg, George W. E., Jr. *Resurrection, Immortality, and Eternal Life in Intertestamental Judaism*. Cambridge, Mass., 1972.

Neveux, Hugues. "Les lendemains de la mort dans les croyances occidentales (vers 1250–vers 1300)." *Annales* 34 (1979): 245–63.

Oesterley, W.O.E. *The Doctrine of the Last Things: Jewish and Christian*. London, 1908.

Okeke, G. E. "The After-Life in St. Matthew as an Aspect of Matthean Ethic." *Communio viatorum* 31 (1988): 159–68.

Olschki, Leonardo. "Mohammedan Eschatology and Dante's Other World." *Comparative Literature* 3 (1951): 1–17.

O'Meara, John J. "Eriugena's Use of Augustine in His Teaching of the Soul and the Vision of God." In R. Roques, ed., *Jean Scot Erigène et l'histoire de la philosophie*, 191–200. Paris, 1977.

Osei-Bonsu, Joseph. "Does 2 Cor. 5:1–10 Teach the Reception of the Resurrection Body at the Moment of Death?" *Journal for the Study of the New Testament* 28 (1986): 81–101.

Palgen, Rudolf. *Dantes Sternglaube: Beiträge zur Erklärung des Paradiso*. Heidelberg, 1940.

———. *Mittelalterliche Eschatologie in Dantes "Komödie."* Graz, 1975.

Pamment, Margaret. "The Kingdom of Heaven according to the First Gospel." *New Testament Studies* 27 (1981): 211–32.

Paparelli, Gioacchino. *Ideologia e poesia di Dante*. Florence, 1975.

———. "Il Paradiso". *Cultura e scuola* 4 (1965): 391–405.

Pasquazi, Silvio. *All'eterno dal tempo*. Florence, 1966.

Pasquini, Emilio. "Le metafore della visione nella 'Commedia.'" *Letture classensi* 16 (1987): 129–51.

Patch, Howard Rollin. *The Other World according to Descriptions in Medieval Literature*. Cambridge, Mass., 1950.

Paxton, Frederick S. *Christianizing Death: The Creation of a Ritual Process in Early Medieval Europe*. Ithaca, N.Y., 1990.

Pearson, Birger A. *The Pneumatikos-Psychikos Terminology in 1 Corinthians*. Missoula, Mont., 1973.

Pelikan, Jaroslav. *The Christian Tradition: The Emergence of the Catholic Tradition*. Chicago, 1971.

――――. *The Christian Tradition: The Growth of Medieval Theology (600–1300)*. Chicago, 1978.

――――. *The Christian Tradition: The Spirit of Eastern Christendom (600–1700)*. Chicago, 1974.

――――. *The Shape of Death: Life, Death and Immortality in the Early Fathers*. London, 1962.

Pellauer, Mary. "Is There a Gender Gap in Heaven?" *Christianity and Crisis* 47 (1987): 60–61.

Pépin, J. "Recherches sur le sens et les origines de l'expression *caelum caeli* dans le livre XII des *Confessions* de S. Augustin." *Archivum latinitatis medii aevi* 23 (1953): 185–274.

Perham, Michael. *The Communion of Saints: An Examination of the Place of the Christian Dead in the Belief, Worship, and Calendars of the Church*. London, 1980.

Perrin, Norman. *The New Testament: An Introduction*. New York, 1974.

Pestalozza, Luigi, ed. *La musica nel tempo di Dante*. Milan, 1988.

Petersen, Joan M. *The Dialogues of Gregory the Great in Their Late Antique Cultural Background*. Toronto, 1984.

Petraglio, R., et al., eds. *L'Apocalypse de Jean: Traditions exégétiques et iconographiques, IIIe-XIIIe siècles*. Geneva, 1979.

Petrocchi, Giorgio. "Dante e la mistica di San Bernardo." In *Letteratura e critica: Studi in onore di N. Sapegno*, 1:213–29. Rome, 1974.

――――. *Il Paradiso di Dante*. Milan, 1978.

――――. *Vita di Dante*. Rome and Bari, 1983.

Pieper, Josef. *Death and Immortality*. New York, 1969.

Pike, Nelson. *Mystic Union: An Essay in the Phenomenology of Mysticism*. Ithaca, N.Y., 1992.

Pilcher, Charles V. *The Hereafter in Jewish and Christian Thought*. London, 1940.

Pirrotta, Nino. "Dante musicus." In *Music and Culture in Italy from the Middle Ages to the Baroque: A Collection of Essays*, 13–25. Cambridge, Mass., 1984.

Prestige, Leonard. "Hades in the Greek Fathers." *Journal of Theological Studies* 24 (1923): 476–85.

Pritchard, James B. *Ancient Near Eastern Texts Relating to the Old Testament*. 3d ed. Princeton, N.J., 1969.

Rahner, Karl. "Beatific Vision." In Karl Rahner et al., eds., *Sacramentum Mundi*, 1:151–53. New York, 1968.

Rahner, Karl. "The Life of the Dead." In *Theological Investigations*, 4:347–54. London, 1961–66.

———. *On the Theology of Death*. New York, 1961.

———. "The Resurrection of the Body." In *Theological Investigations*, 2:203–16. London, 1961–66.

Ratzinger, Joseph. *Eschatology: Death and Eternal Life*. Washington, 1988.

Rizzo, Gino. "Dante and the Virtuous Pagans." In William De Sua and Gino Rizzo, eds., *A Dante Symposium*, 115–240. Chapel Hill, N.C., 1965.

Roberts, Jane. "A Preliminary 'Heaven' Index for Old English." In *Sources and Relations: Studies in Honour of J. E. Cross*, Leeds Studies in English Series 16, 208–19. Leeds, 1985.

Robinson, John T. "The 'Parable' of the Sheep and the Goats." *New Testament Studies* 2 (1956): 225–37.

Robinson, J. Armitage, ed. *The Passion of S. Perpetua*. Cambridge, 1891.

Rohde, Erwin. *Psyche: the Cult of Souls and Belief in Immortality among the Greeks*. 8th ed. London, 1925.

✓Rowland, Christopher. *The Open Heaven*. London, 1982.

Rüegg, August. *Die Jenseitsvorstellungen vor Dante und die übrigen literarischen Voraussetzungen der Divina Commedia*. Einsiedeln, 1945.

Russell, David Syme. *The Method and Message of Jewish Apocalyptic*. London, 1964.

Russell, Jeffrey B. *The Prince of Darkness: Evil and the Power of Good*. Ithaca, N.Y., 1988.

Satran, David. "Fingernails and Hair: Anatomy and Exegesis in Tertullian." *Journal of Theological Studies* 40 (1989): 116–20.

Sayers, Dorothy. *Further Papers on Dante*. London, 1957.

———. *Introductory Papers on Dante*. London, 1954.

————. *The Poetry of Search and the Poetry of Statement, and Other Posthumous Essays on Literature, Religion and Language*. London, 1963.

Schade, Herbert. "Das Paradies und die 'Imago Dei.'" In *Wandlungen des Paradiesischen und Utopischen: Studien zum Bild eines Ideals*, 2:79–182. Berlin, 1966.

Schafer, P. "Things Unutterable: Paul's Ascent to Paradise in Its Greco-Roman, Judaic, and Early Christian Contexts." *Numen* 36 (1989): 283–86.

Schildgen, Brenda. "Dante's Neologisms in the *Paradiso* and the Latin Rhetorical Tradition." *Dante Studies* 107 (1989): 101–19.

Schmidt, Paul Gerhard. "The Vision of Thurkill." *Journal of the Warburg and Courtauld Institutes* 41 (1978): 50–64.

Schmöle, Klaus. *Läuterung nach dem Tode und pneumatische Auferstehung bei Klemens von Alexandrien*. Münster, 1974.

Schnapp, Jeffrey T. *The Transfiguration of History at the Center of Dante's Paradise*. Princeton, N.J., 1986.

Scipio, Giuseppe di. *The Symbolic Rose in Dante's Paradiso*. Ravenna, 1984.

Segal, A. F. "Heavenly Ascent in Hellenistic Judaism, Early Christianity, and Their Environment." In Wolfgang Haase, ed., *Principat*, 1333–94. Berlin, 1980.

Segre, Cesare. "*L'itinerarium animae* nel Duecento e Dante." *Letture classensi* 13 (1984): 9–32.

Selmer, Carl, ed. *Navigato Sancti Brendani abbatis*. Notre Dame, Ind., 1959.

Le sentiment de la mort au moyen âge: Etudes présentées au cinquième colloque de l'Institut des études médiévales de l'Université de Montréal. Montreal, 1979.

Seymour, St. John D. *Irish Visions of the Other-World*. London, 1930.

Silverstein, Theodore. "Dante and the Legend of the Mir'aj: The Influence of Islamic Literature on the Christian Literature of the Otherworld." *Journal of Near Eastern Studies* 11 (1952): 89–110, 187–97.

————. "The Vision of Saint Paul: New Links and Patterns in the Western Tradition." *Archives d'histoire doctrinale et littéraire du moyen âge* 26 (1959): 199–248.

√ Simon, Ulrich. *Heaven in the Christian Tradition*. New York, 1958.

Singer, Irving. *The Nature of Love*. 2d ed. Vol. 1, *Plato to Luther*. Chicago, 1984.

Singleton, Charles S. *The Divine Comedy, Translated with a Commentary by C. S. Singleton*. 6 vols. London, 1971–75.

———. *Journey to Beatrice*. Cambridge, Mass., 1958. *Viaggio a Beatrice*. Bologna, 1958.

✓Smith, C. Ryder. *The Bible Doctrine of the Hereafter*. London, 1958.

Smith, Forrest S. *Secular and Sacred Visionaries in the Late Middle Ages*. New York, 1986.

Smith, Mark S. "'Seeing God' in the Psalms: The Background to the Beatific Vision in the Hebrew Bible." *Catholic Biblical Quarterly* 50 (1988): 171–83.

Soggin, J. Alberto. *Introduzione all'Antico Testamento*. 4th ed. Brescia, 1987.

Sparks, H.F.D., ed. *The Apocryphal Old Testament*. Oxford, 1984.

Spilling, Herrad. *Die Visio Tnugdali: Eigenart und Stellung in der mittelalterlichen Visionsliteratur bis zum Ende des 12. Jahrhunderts*. Munich, 1975.

Spronk, Klaas. *Beatific Afterlife in Ancient Israel and in the Ancient Near East*. Neukirchen-Vluyn, 1986.

Stevenson, Jane. "Ascent through the Heavens, from Egypt to Ireland." *Cambridge Medieval Celtic Studies* 5 (1983): 21–35.

Stone, Michael E. "The Metamorphoses of Ezra: Jewish Apocalypse and Medieval Vision." *Journal of Theological Studies* 33 (1982): 1–18.

Stuiber, Alfred. *Refrigerium interim: Die Vorstellungen vom Zwischenzustand und die frühchristliche Grabeskunst*. Bonn, 1957.

Strawson, William. *Jesus and the Future Life*. Philadelphia, Pa., 1959.

Sumption, Jonathan. *Pilgrimage: An Image of Mediaeval Religion*. London, 1975.

Swanston, H.F.G. "Liturgy as Paradise and as Parousia." *Scottish Journal of Theology* 36 (1983): 505–19.

Sweeney, Leo. *Divine Infinity in Greek and Medieval Thought*. New York, 1992.

Tabor, James D. "Returning to the Divinity: Josephus's Portrayal of the Disappearance of Enoch, Elijah, and Moses." *Journal of Biblical Literature* 1989 (108): 225–38.

———. *Things Unutterable: Paul's Ascent to Paradise in Its Greco-Roman, Judaic, and Early Christian Contexts*. New York, 1987.

Tambling, Jeremy. *Dante and Difference: Writing in the Commedia.* Cambridge, 1988.

Tardiola, Giuseppe, ed. *I viaggiatori del paradiso: Mistici, visionari, sognatori alla ricerca dell'aldilà prima di Dante.* Florence, 1993.

Thompson, Marianne Meye. "Eternal Life in the Gospel of John." *Ex auditu* 5 (1989): 35–55.

Tibiletti, Carlo. "Le anime dopo la morte, stato intermedio o visione di Dio?" *Augustinianum* 28 (1988): 631–59.

Tkacz, Catherine B. "More Christian Formulas in Old English: *Wlite, Wuldor, Wynn,* and Descriptions of Heaven. "In Alberto Ferreiro, ed., *The Devil, Heresy, and Witchcraft in the Middle Ages: Essays in Honor of Jeffrey B. Russell.* Leiden, forthcoming from Brill.

√Toon, Peter. *Heaven and Hell: A Biblical and Theological Overview.* Nashville, Tenn., 1986.

Travis, Stephen H. *Christ and the Judgment of God: Divine Retribution in the New Testament.* Basingstoke, U.K., 1986.

Tsirpanlis, Constantine M. "Origen on Free Will, Grace, Predestination, Apocatastasis, and Their Ecclesiological Implications." *The Patristic and Byzantine Review* 9 (1990): 95–121.

√Tugwell, Simon. *Human Immortality and the Redemption of Death.* London, 1990.

Turner, Victor. "The Center Out There: Pilgrim's Goal." *History of Religions* 12 (1973): 191–230.

Vallone, Aldo. "Il 'silenzio' in Dante." *Dante Studies* 110 (1992): 43–56.

Van den Brink, Antonie. "Non Posse Peccare: On the Inability to Sin in Eternal Life." *Religious Studies* 25 (1989): 521–35.

Van Inwagen, Peter. "The Possibility of Resurrection." *International Journal for Philosophy of Religion* 9 (1978): 114–21.

Van Os, Arnold B. *Religious Visions: The Development of the Eschatological Elements in Mediaeval English Religious Literature.* Amsterdam, 1932.

Verbeke, Werner, Daniel Verhelst, and Andries Welkenhuysen, eds. *The Use and Abuse of Eschatology in the Middle Ages.* Louvain, 1988.

Visio Tnugdali: The German and Dutch Translations and Their Circulation in the Later Middle Ages. Ed. Nigel F. Palmer. Munich, 1982.

Vitto, Cindy L. *The Virtuous Pagan in Middle English Literature.* Philadelphia, Pa., 1989.

Von Hügel, Friedrich. "What Do We Mean by Heaven? And What Do We Mean by Hell?" In *Essays and Addresses on the Philosophy of Religion*, 195–224. London, 1921.

Von Rad, Gerhard. *Old Testament Theology*. 2 vols. New York, 1962–65.

Vorgrimmler, Herbert. *Geschichte der Hölle*. Munich, 1993.

Wainwright, Geoffrey. *Doxology: The Praise of God in Worship, Doctrine and Life*. New York, 1980.

Weber, Hermann J. *Die Lehre von der Auferstehung der Toten in den Haupttraktaten der scholastischen Theologie von Alexander von Hales zu Duns Skotus*. Freiburg, 1973.

Wheelwright, Philip. *The Burning Fountain*. Bloomington, Ind., 1954.

Wicki, Nikolaus. *Die Lehre von der himmlischen Seligkeit in der mittelalterlichen Scholastik von Petrus Lombardus bis Thomas von Aquin*. Freiburg, 1954.

Wilkins, Ernest Hatch, and Thomas Goddard Begin. *A Concordance to the Divine Comedy of Dante Alighieri*. Cambridge, Mass., 1965.

Wilson, Peter Lamborn. *Angels*. London, 1980.

Winslow, Donald. *The Dynamics of Salvation: A Study in Gregory of Nazianzus*. Cambridge, Mass., 1979.

Wolfson, Harry A. "Immortality and Resurrection in the Philosophy of the Church Fathers." *Harvard Divinity School* 22 (1956–57): 5–40.

———. "Patristic Arguments against the Eternity of the World." *Harvard Theological Review* 59 (1966): 351–67.

Woodward, Kenneth. *Making Saints: How the Catholic Church Determines Who Becomes a Saint, Who Doesn't, and Why*. New York, 1990.

Young, N. H. "The Kingdom of Heaven according to the First Gospel." *New Testament Studies* 27 (1981): 211–32.

Zaleski, Carol. *Otherworld Journeys: Accounts of Near-Death Experience in Medieval and Modern Times*. New York, 1987.

Zorn, R. O. "II Corinthians 5:1–10: Individual Eschatology or Corporate Solidarity, Which?" *Reformed Theological Review* 48 (1989): 93–104.

✥ Index ✥

Abelard, Peter, 114, 116, 128
Abraham, 27, 34, 43; bosom of, 49, 69
Adam and Eve, 13, 43–45, 61, 71, 86, 110, 121, 182
Adamnan: vision of, 105
Aelfric, 145
Aeneid, 153
agape (love), 5, 71, 89, 92, 144
Agnes, St., 145
Alberic: vision of, 106, 122
Albert the Great (Albertus Magnus), 126–27, 130
Alcuin, 102
Alexander of Hales, 128, 131
Ambrose of Milan, 79–82, 89, 130
amor, amore, 85, 89–90, 95; in Dante, 158–59, 162, 177–78, 185
Andrew the Chaplain, 102–3
Angela of Foligno, 145
angels, 4; in Dante, 168, 174–76, 179–83; in early Christianity, 50-53, 57–62; in Judaism, 29–38; in late antique Christianity, 67, 75, 82, 85–86; in medieval thought, 93–99, 101, 104–13, 116–18, 131, 138, 148
anima, animo, animus, 67–68, 118–19, 137, 162
Anselm, 114–16
Antichrist, 78
Apocalypse of John (Revelation, Book of), 31, 34, 50–52, 67, 89, 109, 151, 182
apokatastasis, 74–76, 83
apophatic (negative) theology, 91–

94, 100–102, 124, 140–42, 127; in Dante, 176, 182
Aquinas, Thomas, 125–26, 131–40; in Dante, 158, 168, 172, 175, 179
Aristotle, 10, 19, 22, 115, 125–32, 137, 153, 162
Ark of the Covenant, 15, 31–32, 51
"Ascension of Isaiah," 57, 60–61
asceticism. *See* monasticism
Athanasius, 69, 72
Augustine, 6–7, 10, 19, 56, 69, 84–90; *City of God*, 78, 85–86; Commentary on Genesis, 7; *Confessions*, 10

Babylonian Captivity of the Jews, 26–27, 32
Bartholomew, apocryphal Gospel of, 54
Baruch, apocryphal Book of, 31
Basil of Caesarea, 83–84
beatific vision: in Dante, 180–85; definition of, 5, 33, 119; in early Christianity, 43, 49; in late antique Christianity, 69, 77, 84, 88–89; in medieval thought, 95–97, 107–9, 116, 119–21, 129–30, 133–39, 144, 147–48, 150; medium of, 119–121, 129-31, 135, 139, 147–48
Beatrice, 116, 151–53, 158–59, 163–83
Bede, 118
Being: absolute, 7–9, 11, 19, 33, 120, 131; in Dante, 167–68, 178, 184. *See also* ousia

211

Ephraim the Syrian, 13–14, 79
eros: Christian, 71, 83, 92–94, 110, 144; Greco-Roman, 20–21. *See also* amor
erotic imagery, 80, 90–95, 103, 117, 182, 144–46
eschatology, 18, 28, 35–36, 43, 69–71, 78, 84–85, 102, 156
essence, God's, 5; in Dante, 175; in Jewish thought, 33; in late antique Christian thought, 69–70, 73, 83–84; in medieval thought, 90, 96, 100, 117, 120–21, 129–32, 135, 139, 141, 147. *See also* Being; ousia
eternity, 5, 9–12, 187; in Dante, 173–74, 180; in early Christian thought, 48–49, 57, 60; in late antique Christian thought, 67, 76, 80, 85; in medieval thought, 96–97, 102, 115, 118–19, 135–37
ether, 22–23
Eucharist, 41, 47, 56, 63, 81–82, 98, 109, 119, 138, 146, 188
evil, and Devil, xiii, 4–6, 18, 27, 36, 40–42, 53–54, 69, 75–78, 85–86, 97, 112, 118, 128, 137, 188; in Dante, 157, 160, 180. *See also* hell
Exodus, Book of, 26, 32, 109, 111
eyes, image of, 8, 37, 88, 134, 149; in Dante, 152, 159, 163, 167–69, 173–76, 181–83
Eynsham: vision of monk of, 106
Ezekiel, 14, 31–34, 51, 109, 122, 182

Ferreiro, Alberto, 104
fire, image of, 5, 22–23, 35–38, 67, 92, 97, 105–7, 111, 141–42, 145, 189; in Dante, 172, 180
flowers, image of, 13–14, 21, 57–59, 62, 81, 84, 98–102, 106–8; in Dante, 161, 181, 183. *See also* rose

folklore, 16, 111–13
Fourth Lateran Council, 79
fragrance, odor, or scent, as metaphor, 7, 9, 35, 38, 57–58, 63, 81, 98–99, 103–9; in Dante, 181
Francis of Assisi, and Franciscans, 103, 139, 142–43, 146; in Dante, 172
Fulk of Marseille, 171

Gabriel, Archangel, 112, 176, 183
garden, image of, 13–14, 21–22, 31, 51–63, 99, 102–3, 106, 112, 122, 187; in Dante, 176, 181–83
Garden of Eden, 18, 31–32, 35, 43, 55, 99, 111–12
Gaster, M., 110
gate, image of, 15, 35, 37, 50–51, 59–60, 62, 107, 110–12
Gehenna, 27–31, 39
gems, image of, 18, 50–51, 57, 60, 81, 105–12; in Dante, 166, 174, 181
gender, 4, 63, 68, 77, 88, 97–99, 109, 123, 149. *See also* mother; sex
Genesis, Book of, 7, 13, 26, 35–36, 105, 133, 175
Giacomino da Verona, 110
gloria: as word, 144, 152, 164, 144, 178, 181
glory, image of, 4; in Dante, 175–77, 183; in early Christian thought, 41, 47- 48, 50–52, 55–58, 61; in Greco-Roman thought, 24; in Jewish thought, 29–38; in late antique Christian thought, 65, 76, 79, 83–84; in medieval thought, 95–96, 102–4, 108–9, 111, 120, 129–35, 147
gnosticism, 40–45, 52–55, 68–73, 79
gold, image of, 18, 21, 51, 59–61, 98–99, 103–12; in Dante, 174, 181–82
Golden Age, 18, 22

Jeffrey Burton Russell is Professor of History and Religious Studies at the University of California, Santa Barbara. He is the author of fifteen previous books, including most recently *Mephistopheles: The Devil in the Modern World*; *The Prince of Darkness*; *A History of Witchcraft: Sorcerers, Heretics, Pagans*; and *Inventing the Flat Earth: Columbus and Modern Historians*.